MW00995201

WARRIOR OF GOD

A Knyght ther was, and that a worthy man . . .
And ever honoured for his worthynesse . . .

Geoffrey Chaucer, *The Canterbury Tales*

WARRIOR OF GOD

JAN ŽIŽKA
AND THE
HUSSITE REVOLUTION

Victor Verney

Foreword by
David Muhlena

Frontline Books, London

Warrior of God
This edition published in 2009 by Frontline Books,
an imprint of Pen & Sword Books Ltd,
47 Church Street, Barnsley, S. Yorkshire, S70 2AS
www.frontline-books.com

Copyright © Victor Verney, 2009

ISBN: 978-1-84832-516-6

The right of Victor Verney to be identified as the author of this work
has been asserted by him in accordance with the Copyright,
Designs and Patents Act of 1988.

All rights reserved. No part of this publication may be reproduced,
stored in or introduced into a retrieval system, or transmitted, in any form,
or by any means (electronic, mechanical, photocopying, recording or otherwise)
without the prior written permission of the publisher. Any person who does
any unauthorized act in relation to this publication may be liable to criminal
prosecution and civil claims for damages.

CIP data records for this title are available from the British Library
and the Library of Congress

For more information on our books, please visit
www.frontline-books.com, email info@frontline-books.com
or write to us at the above address.

Maps produced by Paul Davis

Printed in the UK by the MPG Books Group

CONTENTS

Illustrations

Hussite veuglaire siege gun
Hussite battle flags
Žižka's ancestral family coat of arms
Fifteenth-century Czech pavises
Nineteenth-century engraving of Žižka planning a campaign
Mikoláš Aleš, *Husitský tábor*, 1877: Žižka's arrival at Tábor
Portrait of condottiere Pippo Spano, *c.* 1450.
George of Poděbrady and Kunštát, *c.* 1885
Jiri Liebscher, *Jan Žižka after the Battle of Kutná Hora*, 1890
The Jan Hus monument in Prague's Old Town Square
Bethlehem Chapel, Prague
Josef Strachovsky, statue of Jan Žižka in Žižka Square, Tábor
Statue of Jan Žižka in Belkovice-Lastany
Statue of Jan Žižka on Vítkov Hill, Prague
Jan Žižka Monument in Trocnova, 1956–60
Vojtech Kubasta, commemoration of Žižka memorial statue on
 Vítkov Hill, 1950
Adolf Liebscher, *Jan Žižka of Trocnova*, 1889

MAPS

FOREWORD

In my position as library director at the National Czech & Slovak Museum & Library, one of the most satisfying aspects of my job has been to assist students, scholars, and authors with their research projects. Vic Verney is one of those inquisitive souls to cross the threshold into our library seeking to learn more about Czech and Slovak history and culture. I don't recall specifically telling him about the need for a new English-language book about the medieval Czech general, Jan Žižka. The idea most likely came out of our conversations about his articles for *Military History* magazine about war veterans – Lord Byron, Leo Tolstoy and George Orwell – who were also great writers. So, why a book about Žižka and the Hussite revolution? I imagine Vic saw in Žižka and the Hussites the opportunity to tell a fascinating story, in the words of former British Prime Minister Neville Chamberlain, 'of a quarrel in a far-away country between people of whom we know nothing'.

The last full-length book about the subject written in English, *John Žižka and the Hussite Revolution* by Frederick Heymann, was published more than fifty years ago. Heymann's book, while quite thorough, was aimed at the scholarly community, so the book has had limited exposure to a broader audience. Vic's book introduces Žižka and the story of the Hussites to a new generation of readers who are serious students of history from within the context of war and struggle for freedom.

What makes the story of Žižka so compelling to a twenty-first-century audience? Modern readers will no doubt identify with and appreciate the adversities Žižka faced and overcame. Žižka was not from the elite aristocratic class; rather, he was born into a family of lower nobility, a relative outsider who proved that one did not need to be of high noble birth to be a leader. He was handicapped, blind in one eye since youth and totally blind near the end of his life. His visual impediment perhaps served to focus his mind's eye for visualising the placement of his troops in the most advantageous strategic positions, as evidenced in his success at the Battle of Vítkov Hill.

Žižka was truly a renaissance man. As a pragmatist, he presents a perfect example of how necessity breeds innovation. His peasant forces vastly outnumbered by Catholic and imperial armies, Žižka adapted the tools of agriculture into the tools of war, figuratively making ploughshares into swords. Among the military innovations credited to him and the Hussites was the *tabor*, heavily fortified wagons that were drawn into a defensive circle; the *houfnice* or howitzer, an early form of artillery; the *píšťala* or pistol; and the modified agricultural flail. As a charismatic leader, he understood the power of faith to motivate people to action. Jan Hus's speaking truth to powers both temporal and ecclesiastical served as an example for the Hussite community in general and Žižka in particular. Military innovations alone cannot fully explain the success the Hussites had over their vastly superior adversaries. The combination of a charismatic figure like Žižka and a religiously fervent people like the Hussites proved to be a force to be reckoned with, sometimes even for Žižka himself. After his troops defied his orders not to kill defeated combatants, Žižka ordered his army to pray for forgiveness of their sins. Afterwards, he wrote a code of military conduct that established rules of engagement and proscribed disciplinary measures in their breach.

But the story of Žižka and the Hussites is about more than just religious warfare. It is also about political, ethnic, cultural, linguistic, and religious self-determination, and the power of 'the people' as agents of change. The conflict that Žižka and the Hussites were involved in was part of the larger epic struggle between Germans and Slavs. Only a few decades earlier was Prague elevated to an archbishopric by King Karel (Charles) IV, which served to make Prague and the Bohemian crown lands ecclesiastically independent of the German Archbishop of

Mainz. In the thirteenth century, many ethnic Germans colonised the Czech Lands upon the invitation by Czech King Přemysl Otakar II. Granted special rights, these ethnic Germans soon became wealthy and powerful, leading to resentment by the native Czech population. The Hussite wars resulted in a demographic shift in favour of the native Czech population. Liberated from Catholic and German influence, the Czechs were free to practice their form of Christian faith freely and elevate written Czech into a language of literature and law. The Hussite movement later evolved into the Unity of the Brethren, whose major achievement was the *Kralice* translation of the Bible into the Czech language, a work on par with the King James translation into English.

But alas, the pendulum of history swung back into the favour of the German-speaking Austrians and Catholics at the Battle of White Mountain in 1620, whereby the Czech Lands were subjected to 300 years of Austrian Habsburg domination and the re-Catholicisation of the Czech population. The Czech Brethren were either forced to convert to Catholicism or expelled from the country; the Czech language was suppressed by the Habsburg authorities and became the language of the peasantry. The situation remained the same for more than 200 years until the birth of the Czech National Revival, a concerted effort to revive Czech language, culture and national identity. Not until the fall of the Austro-Hungarian Empire in 1918 were the Czechs free of outside influence. The resulting independent nation, Czechoslovakia, was a multi-ethnic state comprising the traditional Czech Lands of Bohemia, Moravia and Silesia, as well as Slovakia and Ruthenia. A mere twenty years later the Czech Lands were once again under German control as the Protectorate of Bohemia and Moravia. After the Second World War, the controversial Beneš decrees forcibly removed nearly 2,600,000 ethnic Germans to Germany and Austria, effectively ending more than 700 years of German presence in the Czech Lands.

Post-war Czechoslovakia was politically fragile, which was exploited by the communists, who in February 1948 managed to obtain complete control over the government in a bloodless coup. The Czech Lands, starting in the late nineteenth century, had gradually become more secular in nature due in part to modernisation and industrialisation. The communists were only too happy to continue this trend through hostility towards all forms of organised religion. Despite the fall of the Czechoslovak communist regime in 1989, more than forty years of indoctrination has resulted in at least fifty per cent of the Czech people claiming to be atheists. Ironically, Žižka is still admired by the Czech people, not for his religious fervour but for championing the Czech national cause. Žižka's legacy continues to have a presence among the Czech people, and continues to be subject to interpretation with each successive generation.

David Muhlena,
Cedar Rapids, Iowa

PREFACE

The modern-day author writing in English about Czech history faces a unique challenge. By what names does one refer to the people and places of the Lands of the Bohemian Crown for Anglophone readers? This is a thornier question than it might appear, involving a centuries-old ethnic struggle between the Germanic and Slavic peoples centred on language. Beginning with the establishment of the Holy Roman Empire, a complex process of Germanisation occurred in Central Europe as detailed by David Muhlena in his Foreword. Czech virtually disappeared as a written language until the nineteenth century. How ironic that the first modern grammar of the Czech language, *Ausführliches Lehrgebäude der böhmischen Sprache* (written in 1809 by Josef Dobrovský) was published in German because Czech was not used in academic scholarship at that time! This linguistic imperialism (as academics call it) inevitably manifested itself in the books and maps of the English-speaking world, which grew accustomed to ostensibly 'Czech' names.

During the nineteenth century, Jan Hus and Jan Žižka came to represent Czechs' aspirations to conduct the full range of civic life in their native tongue. Now, after centuries of foreign occupation, the Czechs are a free people at liberty to choose their own names rather than those imposed upon them by imperial overlords. As Anglophones have come to accommodate the preferences of other, larger countries for post-colonial names such as Mao Zedong or Mumbai, I believe Czechs should be accorded the same respect. For that reason, names will be given in their Czech form with a few exceptions (for example Wenceslaus and Prague) to avoid confusion.

I would like to acknowledge the assistance given to me during this project by numerous individuals and institutions and express my gratitude. First and foremost is David Muhlena, library director of the National Czech & Slovak Museum & Library in Cedar Rapids, Iowa, who graciously consented to write the Foreword for this book. David first introduced me to Žižka's incredible story, and he has served as an invaluable sounding board.

Dean Rod Henshaw and Liga Briedis of Drake University's Cowles Library graciously extended visiting scholar privileges to me, affording access to its rich collection of works of religious history including several vital but out-of-print books. Louise Alcorn of the West Des Moines Public Library assisted in procuring important source books through inter-library loan.

During my brief trip to the Czech Republic, several historical scholars took time from their busy schedules to share their considerable knowledge with me. I regret that circumstances prevented me from meeting Doctor Miloš Drda, Director of the Hussite Museum in Tábor, who generously put his facilities and staff, Doctor Zdeněk Vybíral, Jakub Smrcka and Marta Kratochvilova, at my disposal during my visit there.

Doctor Vít Vlnas, Director of the Collections of Old Masters in the Czech National Gallery, set aside several hours to discuss Bohumil Kafka's monumental statue of Žižka overlooking Prague from Vítkov Hill. Erected in 1950, after decades of controversy and delay, to commemorate the first great Hussite victory over Sigismund's crusaders, it is a singular story in its own right. This statue's subsequent neglect and current restoration illustrate the twists and turns of Žižka's enshrinement in the pantheon of Czech history. As with Dr Vybíral's associates, Dr Vlnas's efforts were made strenuous by the necessity of conducting complex discussions in English – most Czech scholars' third (or fourth) language. Their willingness to do so was most helpful.

Professor David Holeton of Charles University shed much light on the religious history of the Czech Lands, some of its prominent scholars, and life in post-communist Prague.

Preface

Gerry and Misha Griffiths of Cartesian Coordinates are independent filmmakers whose *Blind Courage: The Unique Genius of Jan Zizka* (2005) is essential viewing for anyone interested in this subject. Our conversation gave me the benefit of their experiences filming in the Czech Republic and interviewing notable Hussite scholars.

Professor Peter Gessner, Director of the Polish Academic Information Centre at my alma mater the State University of New York at Buffalo, kindly gave me permission to use background material he has collected about Jan Matejko's 1874 painting 'Battle of Grunwald', another remarkable story in its own right.

Emil Viklický, 'The Patriarch of Czech Jazz', provided insight drawn from his own schoolboy days during the Soviet occupation into how Žižka's story was subsumed by communist iconography. He also assisted with translations and, like my cousin Terry Sasala and his friend Stanislav Simek, helped track down information about museums and art galleries in the Czech Republic. Darcy Baston was my amanuensis *extraordinaire*. Paul Davis, in addition to being a noted historian, is also an accomplished cartographer, and his skills were essential in producing the maps for this book.

And above all, I must thank Kathryn Lappegard, my proof-reader, editor, advisor, and sustaining spirit – without her support and encouragement, I could not have written this book.

Victor Verney
Des Moines, Iowa

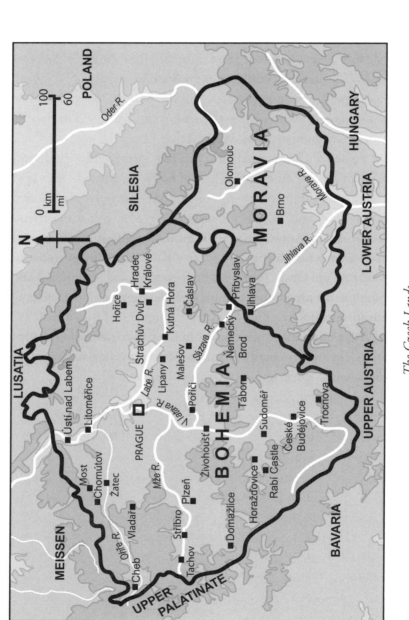

The Czech Lands

INTRODUCTION

Where are now the warring kings?
An idle word is now their glory . . .
W. B. Yeats, 'The Song of the Happy Shepherd'

In the fourteenth century, Europe was in turmoil. Around 1300, centuries of European prosperity and growth came to an unsettling halt. Sweeping upheavals ushered in a new world order. Social structures underpinning an agricultural, feudal, non-national society were becoming obsolete. The Hussite Revolution of 1419 and its avatar Jan Žižka can only be understood in relation to the general crisis of feudalism, then in its death throes. Based on enforced servitude of serfs in bondage to overlords, secular or ecclesiastic, this intertwined religious and political power was unravelling. Complex interlocking forces were shredding the entire social fabric, forces intersecting in the Bohemian lands. The Czechs, who refer to their homeland as 'The Lands Between', sat astride multiple crossroads of financial and cultural exchange. Prague was strategically situated between the Elbe, Oder and Danube rivers. Two main trading routes – north–south from the Adriatic to the Baltic and east–west from the Bosporus to the English Channel – traversed Bohemia. All roads no longer led to Rome. In 1305, Pope Clement V left the 'Eternal City' to escape murderous Italian infighting. Clement needed a location better for his health and found it at Avignon in France. Seventy-five years later, the Catholic Church had three men claiming to be the One True Pope: one in

Rome, another in Avignon, and a third in Pisa. This 'Great Schism' contributed to the secular power of kings and the rise of emerging nation-states.

Urbanisation had steadily increased in Europe. The development of a money economy created a new social class, the burghers, who rose to prosperity and social privilege. Town crafts and trade relations were creating new opportunities for serfs who were becoming merchants, the first incarnation of what today is known as the middle class. However, not all who left the farm enjoyed success. A growing urban underclass overloaded city infrastructures, creating fertile ground for pestilence, hunger and civil unrest. Venetian and Genoese merchant vessels returned from trading voyages with foreign gold, spices, and rats. These uninvited visitors, and their fellow travellers – fleas – brought with them the bubonic plague. Europe's population had outstripped its agricultural capacity. Food shortages and skyrocketing prices led to famine, malnutrition, and disease. The plague passed lightly over the Lands of the Bohemian Crown, comparatively speaking. Bohemia's distance from maritime activity and its mountain ranges did much to insulate the land-locked country. By 1420, plagues, famines, and wars had reduced Europe's population by one-third. Land became more plentiful and labour more expensive. In the Bohemian kingdom and throughout much of Europe, serfs left their fields, the lower gentry lost ancestral holdings, and Jews were evicted wholesale from countries where they had lived for centuries. The Catholic Church's standing was severely compromised, creating a spiritual vacuum and a prevailing sense of desperation.

In Bohemia, a political vacuum was created when the Přemyslid dynasty ended in 1306. During its later stages, ancient Germanic versus Slavic animosities shifted from simple tribal struggles into entrenched authoritarian conflicts. While there had been a sizeable German colony in Prague since the eleventh century, a tidal wave of Germanisation occurred in the thirteenth century. Czech kings, faced with intransigent nobles, enlisted these German burghers as a counterweight. Their prominence in urban trade guilds and churches created resentment among the native Slavs, and this anti-Germanism grew over the next three centuries before erupting in open warfare.

*

When Wenceslaus III, the last male Přemyslid, died without a son, tumult over the Bohemian crown ensued. His sister Elisabeth advanced a claim, while full-scale civil war broke out between German burghers and Czech nobles. After Henry of Luxembourg was elected Holy Roman Emperor, the Czechs made overtures, and he agreed to marry his son John to Elisabeth, while respecting Czech liberties, rights, and privileges. The Czech Diet invited John to Prague for election, and he arrived in 1310. The Luxembourg dynasty had begun. John was never accepted by the Czech nobility, who regarded him as a foreign interloper. Temperamentally unsuited for statecraft, he spent little time or energy on his kingdom, preferring to gallivant around Europe fighting in various crusades and wars. John did not speak Czech, the Czech nobility were disinclined to learn French, and their hostility filtered down to the common people.

After his father's assassination, John had to attend to his native Luxembourg, increasing his absences. The nobles repeatedly fomented insurrection, forcing John to return with foreign armies to dissuade them. Yearning to pursue knight-errantry, John tired of this back-and-forth struggle and made concessions. In the Domažlice Agreement of 1318, he virtually abdicated domestic power, dismissed all foreign advisors and officials, and foreswore bringing foreign troops into the country. The nobles agreed to refrain from insurrection. After that, John was gone most of the time, returning only occasionally to collect money and/or soldiers.

John lost his eyesight from ophthalmia contracted while crusading in Lithuania with the Teutonic Order. This did not endear him to Czechs, who were developing a sense of pan-Slavic brotherhood with the Poles against a common German enemy. Although John (now known as 'John the Blind') was not a model father or king, he had the redeeming trait of courage. John's Francophile ways and his love of the knightly code reached their ultimate, fatal conclusion in 1346 at the Battle of Crécy during the Hundred Years War. At a critical point in the battle, John performed a *beau geste* that ended his reign and redeemed his legacy somewhat. Hearing the panicked French retreat from Welsh longbowmen, John decided there was only one thing to do – tie the horses together and charge. Although his lieutenants pleaded with him earnestly to reconsider, their entreaties were of no avail. John and 500 Bohemian knights were slain.

The tragedy at Crécy ushered in the 'Golden Age of Bohemia' under John's son Charles (1316–78), one of the few Czech warriors to escape the slaughter. The wounded prince returned home and in 1346 was elected King of the Romans. The following year he was crowned King of Bohemia. Born in Prague, he had been named Wenceslaus after his maternal grandfather but chose the name Charles at his confirmation in honour of his uncle, French King Charles IV, at whose Parisian court he lived and studied for seven years. Charles had already shown aptitude and initiative. For a period beginning in 1333, he administered Bohemia as regent due to his father's frequent absences and deteriorating eyesight. In 1334, he was named Margrave of Moravia, the traditional title of the heir apparent, and two years later assumed governance of Tyrol on his brother's behalf. Unlike his father, Charles conceived a deep affection for, and commitment to, his kingdom. He proved an able monarch and today Czechs refer to him as 'Father of the Homeland' (*otec vlasti*). He used his close relationship with Pope Clement to have Prague made an archbishopric and made the city his imperial capital. It bears his name in many spots, notably Charles University, Charles Bridge, and Charles Square. Numerous present-day landmarks including Prague Castle were completed under his patronage, and several other locales in the Czech Republic are named after him, including Karlštejn Castle (Karlstein) and the spa town of Karlovy Vary (Karlsbad, Carlsbad).[1] Charles secured a pre-

---

1. Charles's international renown stretches across the Atlantic to the United States where two cities, Carlsbad, California; and Carlsbad, New Mexico (and the nearby Carlsbad Caverns), are said to be named after him.

eminent position for Prague as the intellectual and cultural centre of Central Europe.

*

Charles's eldest son, Wenceslaus IV (1361–1419) inherited a weak hand, and he played it poorly after coming to power in 1378 at the age of seventeen. Just before his death, Charles had divided his holdings among his sons and other relatives. Wenceslaus retained Bohemia, his half-brothers Sigismund and Jan received Brandenburg and Lusatia (in modern Saxony). Moravia was divided between his cousins Jošt and Prokop, and his uncle Wenceslaus was made Duke of Luxembourg. From the outset Wenceslaus was bedevilled by domestic and foreign enemies, and throughout his reign his grip on power in both Germany and Bohemia was tenuous. This king, incidentally, is not to be confused with Saint Wenceslaus, a revered tenth-century figure immortalised in the Christmas carol 'Good King Wenceslaus'.[2] History has not been nearly so kind to the man who bore that name and title 500 years later.

Charles had arranged his son's unopposed succession as German king – a rare event. Charles accomplished this by revoking privileges he had earlier granted to many imperial cities and by bribing influential nobles. However, Charles had earlier organised the cities into leagues, making it possible for them to co-operate in large-scale endeavours. On 4 July 1376, only two days after Wenceslaus's election as King of the Romans, fourteen Swabian cities, angered by tax increases imposed to pay for Charles's bribery, bound together to defend their imperial status (*Reichsunmittelbarkeit*) against the newly elected Emperor. This league attracted other members and acted as an independent state within the Empire, repeatedly fomenting problems for Wenceslaus until 1389, when he prohibited such leagues while

2. St Wenceslaus (903–29) was taught Christianity by his grandmother St Ludmila, who was murdered by Magyars and an anti-Christian faction that took over the government. Wenceslaus was declared ruler following a coup in 922 and encouraged Christianity. His brother Boleslaus and a group of noble Czech dissenters invited Wenceslaus to a religious festival and killed him in an ambush. The patron saint of Bohemia, his feast day is 28 September.

The Holy Roman Empire

conceding the cities' political autonomy. Wenceslaus also faced opposition from the Archbishop of Prague and was engaged in constant power struggles with the Church hierarchy. Consequently, he was never crowned Holy Roman Emperor by the Pope as would have been customary for a 'King of the Romans'.

Commonly referred to as 'The Drunkard', Wenceslaus had repeated conflicts with the Bohemian nobility. Though his affable, down-to-earth personality endeared him to the common folk, Wenceslaus was disparaged by the gentry as a monarch manqué who neglected his royal duties while indulging in hunting parties lasting for weeks. Following a 1393 rebellion by the Czech nobility, his cousin Jošt was named regent and Wenceslaus was imprisoned in Vienna. His youngest half-brother Jan successfully freed Wenceslaus in 1395, and the following year Sigismund, now King of Hungary, arranged a truce. Preoccupied by continual troubles in Bohemia, Wenceslaus was unseen in Germany for years on end, fostering resentment over this perceived neglect. He faced angry crowds at the Imperial Diets of Nürnberg in 1397 and Frankfurt in 1398. Two years later, the Rhenish electors accused him of failing to maintain peace or resolve the Papal Schism and demanded Wenceslaus appear to answer these charges. Busy with renewed hostilities in Bohemia, Wenceslaus refused. The electors deposed him on grounds of drunkenness and incompetence and chose the Palatine Elector, Rupert III, as king. In 1402, Wenceslaus was again imprisoned and temporarily deposed by Sigismund with the support of the Czech nobility. At the age of nine, Wenceslaus had married Johanna of Bavaria, who died in 1386; three years later, he married her cousin Sofia. He had no children by either wife, presenting Sigismund an ideal opportunity to exact a steep price from his elder half-brother for intervening on his behalf – recognition as heir to the Bohemian throne.

While still an adolescent, Sigismund demonstrated the fondness for shadowy political intrigue that marked his entire career. In 1374, the six-year-old Sigismund had been betrothed to Mary, daughter of King Louis I of Hungary and Poland, who intended them to succeed him. At the age of thirteen, Sigismund was sent to Crakow (modern Kraków) by Wenceslaus (then acting as his guardian), to learn Polish and to become acquainted with the country. Soon, everyone involved regretted it. Sigismund conspired to destabilise Poland by setting its ally Jogaila (or Jagiełło), Grand Duke of Lithuania, against his cousin Vytautas, Prince of Lithuania. Sigismund was expelled and the throne was given to Mary's younger sister Jadwiga. A two-year civil war of succession followed. Louis died the following year, Mary became Queen of Hungary, and Sigismund married her in 1385. However, an opposing candidate for the throne, Charles III of Naples, appeared, and Sigismund fled, leaving behind Mary and her widowed mother, Elisabeth of Bosnia, who was the acting regent. Charles ousted Mary, but Elisabeth had Charles assassinated. Sigismund then plotted with rebellious nobles to have mother and daughter kidnapped. Elisabeth was strangled (allegedly by Sigismund's men) in 1387, but Mary was rescued by sympathetic Venetians. Mary never forgave Sigismund for Elisabeth's death, despite his claim to have punished the murderers. Sigismund then made his own arrangements to be crowned king of Hungary in 1387 and soon had his own troubles with rebellious nobles. After raising money by pledging Brandenburg to Jošt in 1388, he spent nine years struggling for the throne. Sigismund was deposed twice and imprisoned by nobles but skilfully bribed his way out. He and Mary lived apart, and she died in 1395 in a suspicious horse accident when in an advanced stage of pregnancy.

The following year, Sigismund married Barbara, sixteen-year old daughter of Count Hermann II of Celje (Cilly) in modern-day Slovenia. Hermann, a soldier in the Crusade of Nicopolis against the Ottoman Turks, had saved Sigismund's life in battle. He was rewarded with the county of Zagorje, the town of Varaždin, and the royal crown for his daughter, a beautiful, clever and sophisticated noblewoman who spoke several languages. During this time, the Prussian Knights were battling Poland under papal orders on the pretext of fighting heathens. After assuming the Polish throne, Jadwiga in 1386 married Jagiełło, Grand Duke of Lithuania, a pagan empire reaching from the Baltic to the Black Sea. Jagiełło changed his name to Władyslaw and converted to Christianity, accepting the faith for the entire nation. The Prussian Knights were thereby deprived of any legitimate claim for continued hostilities. In 1399, Jadwiga, dying in childbirth, extracted a promise from Władyslaw that he would marry Anna of Celje – Hermann's niece. Władyslaw fulfilled his promise in July 1401, sending a delegation to Celje asking in his name for Anna's hand. Sigismund, smarting from his earlier expulsion from Poland, developed a strong personal hostility towards Władyslaw. Sigismund also recognised that destabilising Poland–Lithuania would aid his territorial ambitions. Moreover, an alliance with the Teutonic Knights could prove helpful in wresting Bohemia away from Wenceslaus under the pretext of fighting heresy.

Sigismund sent them 200 soldiers with the promise to send more as soon as possible.

Barbara and her father were strongly anti-German and made no secret of it. But when Queen Anna invited her uncle Hermann to Poland for an Easter visit, it did not arouse suspicion among German partisans there since he had frequently visited his niece. Sigismund was in northern Hungary at the time, positioned quickly to assemble a large force to aid the Knights. When Hermann arrived in Cracow, he assured Władyslaw that Sigismund's position was so precarious he could not enter the war for fear of losing his throne. This intelligence was of the utmost strategic importance, as Władyslaw could concentrate all his forces northward towards the Teutonic Knights, giving the combined Polish–Lithuanian forces a three-to-two edge in manpower, cancelling the Knights' superiority in materiel and training, and enabling the Poles to win the battle. When the German faction in the Hungarian court learned of this intrigue, they were furious and tried to destroy Hermann's influence. However, his position was unassailable, since Sigismund (correctly) felt he owed Hermann his life. As the Hussite revolution unfolded, German-sympathising Hungarians saw Barbara as their principal adversary. They persistently slandered her as an adulteress, dubbing her 'the Messalina of Germany'.[3] Given his frequent absences from Hungary and the age difference between them, Sigismund was all-too-susceptible to these rumours. Enraged, he banished her and their infant daughter Elisabeth to Varaždin.

One of the participants at Grunwald–Tannenberg was Jan Žižka, who along with large numbers of other Bohemian and Moravian mercenaries fought for the Poles with Wenceslaus's tacit approval. While reluctant to do Sigismund any favours, Wenceslaus was lukewarm towards Poland. However, a rising tide of Pan-Slavism (Poland and Bohemia had been briefly unified at the beginning of the fourteenth century) fostered widespread support among Czechs for an alliance.

---

3. Valeria Messalina (AD20–48), was the third wife of Roman Emperor Claudius. A powerful and influential woman with a slatternly reputation, she conspired against her husband and was executed when the plot was discovered.

Žižka's experience in Poland taught him important lessons about fighting armoured knights with wagon fortresses, put money in his pocket, and garnered him military renown. He returned to Prague a war hero, and Wenceslaus elevated him to a court position as an officer of the palace guard. Frequently serving as royal bodyguard, he regularly escorted Queen Sofia to hear the sermons of Jan Hus then electrifying Prague. For a time, both Wenceslaus and Sofia extended royal favour and protection to Hus (for political and spiritual reasons, respectively). By the time they realised the full import of the movement he was igniting and the dire consequences it held for them, it was too late.

Chapter 1

HUNTER, HIGHWAYMAN, MERCENARY, COURTIER

. . . when thou art king, let us not that are squires of the night's body be called thieves of the day's beauty . . .
William Shakespeare, *Henry IV, Part I*

Little documentary information exists about Jan Žižka's early years for two reasons. First, the original civil records of many Bohemians, including his, have simply disappeared. The permanent loss of church books, land registers, and court records was one of the unfortunate consequences of the Hussite Wars in which he played such a leading role. Secondly, the Counter-Reformation witnessed the intentional destruction of genealogical data. After the Thirty Years War, the Austrian Habsburgs and the Catholic Church (particularly the Jesuits, who burned entire libraries) attempted to eradicate all traces of the leading figures associated with what is considered the first wave of the Protestant Reformation. After extensive archival research by numerous historians, an effort especially vigorous during the quincentary of Žižka's death in 1924, there is today no reasonable expectation of further biographical information coming to light.

The exact date of Žižka's birth is unknown, but the best estimate seems to be *circa* 1360. Documents from 1378 attest to Žižka serving as legal witness to a marriage and a property sale. Another document, dated 10 July of that year, confirms a loan equivalent in the value to a few hundred pounds incurred by him and two friends. Presumably, Žižka would have had to be at least eighteen years old to serve as a legal witness; the loan suggests other plausible inferences. The ability to procure a loan means Žižka was a property holder. This, in turn, leads to the surmise that he was the eldest of his siblings and that his father had passed away while Žižka was still in his teens, if not earlier. His family estate in Trocnova was small and its soil quality poor. Although trading and manufacturing had replaced farming as the prime economic engine in the major towns and cities throughout Bohemia and Moravia, smaller communities like Trocnova were still agrarian, and their prosperity depended on crops and livestock.

In 1384, Žižka sold the last portion of his ancestral manor. Records indicate that Žižka had moved to Prague four years previously to serve in the court of King Wenceslaus, who had assumed the Bohemian throne in 1378. This cannot have been pleasant, since it rendered him landless. In the Middle Ages, property defined one's social standing: for example, the difference between a squire and a knight was that the latter possessed a castle. In Žižka's case, he was reduced to owning nothing – the medieval version of gentility in tatters.

As was common at that time, Žižka initially did not have a surname but was known as Jan of Trocnova. His brother Jaroslav and his sister Agnes were known by the same identifier; by 1378, however, he was being referred to as Žižka, unlike his siblings. This disproves a common misconception that he lost his first eye during the Battle of Grunwald–Tannenberg in 1410. The consensus is that he lost it at a fairly early age while roughhousing with boyhood acquaintances. There has been some dispute about the word 'Žižka', which means 'one-eyed' in Czech. While some have argued that it acquired this meaning in memory of Žižka, linguists and etymologists generally believe the word had that meaning before Žižka's time.

Žižka was a widower most of his adult life. He had two wives, both named Catherine. The first died fairly young. Nothing about her or her background is known beyond that she bore him a daughter, leaving the strong likelihood that Catherine passed away during childbirth.

Even less is known about his second wife. Žižka's daughter eventually made a socially advantageous marriage with a patriarch of one of Bohemia's leading baronial families, Peter of Dubá. Although social barriers between the lower gentry and the upper lords were not as strictly drawn as those with the peasants, it was unusual for a high-ranking baron to marry a squire's daughter. In this case, it may have been a result of Žižka's personal stature. The marriage proved politically advantageous for her father as well, at least temporarily. Originally Royalist Catholics, the lords of Dubá, including Peter, begrudgingly made common cause with the Hussites against Sigismund in the interest of national pacification and reconciliation. It cannot be known whether Peter's co-operative spirit led to his becoming Žižka's son-in-law or was an effect of it, or what influence his wife may have had. Another member of the Dubá clan, Jan Roháč, rose to become one of Žižka's most trusted captains.

The next significant trace of Žižka comes in 1392. An entry in the royal accounts recorded payment of one year's salary to '*Siska, venitor domini regus*' in a small town sixty-five kilometres south of Prague near the royal castle of Orlík. It is reasonable to assume Žižka held the post there of king's huntsman, 'Siska' being a common variant spelling in Latin texts. He was well suited to the job, which afforded a livelihood outdoors on horseback, plying woodcraft and weaponry in woods teeming with bear, wolves, wild boar, and red deer. During Žižka's tenure as royal huntsman, he met and became cordial with some of the great lords who were guests during Wenceslaus's grand hunting parties. But this post had a more significant benefit for Žižka. By all reports, Wenceslaus was comfortable with people of every rank and station, so it is not hard to imagine that an amicable relationship arose between the two men, who were very close in age.

Wenceslaus's over-indulgence in hunting afforded the Bohemian nobility both an opportunity and a pretext to test him with a view to regaining the independence they had lost under his father. In 1395, this simmering insubordination blossomed into outright treason when a league of powerful lords, led by Henry of Rožmberk (Rosenberg) imprisoned the King and held him captive for several months. Two family members – his younger half-brother Sigismund and his cousin Jošt, then Margrave of Moravia and later Brandenburg – joined in with this revolt. Wenceslaus was supported by his youngest brother Jan, Duke of Görlitz, and Jošt's brother Prokop, who succeeded Jošt as Margrave of Moravia. This fraternal strife led to the formation of opposing parties among the Czech nobles. A running feud began, with both sides using bands of mercenaries led by knights and squires of the lower nobility. Given the economic pressures on the men of that social rank, they were predisposed to take up the life of guerrilla fighters, more dangerous but also more exciting and potentially rewarding than the dreary monotony of provincial life. Before standing armies became commonplace, soldiers of fortune constituted a plague as pernicious throughout Europe as the Black Death. The problem was worse in Eastern Europe where it lasted longer. In Bohemia, the distinction between legitimate warfare and simple brigandage became increasingly muddled. Hostilities were directed not so much at the enemy as at his material possessions – crops, livestock, castles, and farms. Although the guerrilla bands operated on the shady side of the law, they were protected by powerful patrons. Hence, these brigands and highwaymen did not suffer general moral or social disapproval.

It has never been determined why Žižka left a congenial and very secure position as the king's huntsman to join in this nasty guerrilla warfare. The band with which he threw in his lot was initially comprised of noblemen belonging to the parties supporting the King. Their primary target was Henry of Rožmberk and his properties. Žižka may have joined this band either due to the King's expressed wish or from a desire to ingratiate himself with Wenceslaus. Žižka's troop was led by another squire known as Matthew the Leader and was sponsored by the lords of Lichtenburg. Those against whom these fighters operated, particularly Lord Rožmberk and his retinue, detested them. The Rožmberk archives give detailed information over a twenty-year period beginning in 1389. Some of the kingdom's leading baronial houses are listed in the Rožmberk records as backers of the brigands. Other records were kept by the town of Jihlava in western Moravia, and both sources make frequent mention of Žižka, revealing that he returned to the Trocnova region some time in 1405–6. When any of these guerrillas were captured by Lord Rožmberk or his partisans, they were tortured to extract information about their cohorts. They were then subjected to a summary trial and, having confessed under torture, executed. This unsavoury fate befell one of Žižka's brothers, and he narrowly escaped it himself.

Žižka evidently distinguished himself as a junior officer, and other influential Bohemian military men took notice of the fierce one-eyed soldier. Among the Czech aristocrats noting Žižka's mettle was a Moravian nobleman, Jan Sokol of Lamberg. A gifted soldier, Sokol was also a man of culture and a familiar face in court circles throughout Europe. There is evidence that Sokol was among the great lords who met Žižka while he served as royal huntsman and the two men were in contact during the years Žižka fought in Matthew's band. More significant was a connection Žižka made with, the Kunštats, a powerful clan throughout Bohemia and Moravia. Among them was Boček, whose possessions included the castle of Poděbrady on the Elbe River. His three sons eventually had prominent roles in the Hussite wars. Two of them, Victorin and Hynek, became close friends of Žižka, and Victorin remained a faithful follower to the very end. Žižka is reputed to have been godfather to Victorin's son George, who later became the first and only Hussite king.

After 1406, the situation changed completely. Prokop died in 1405, and Wenceslaus entered into working arrangements with both Jošt and Henry of Rožmberk. Sigismund was distracted by Turks invading Hungary from the south-east. The guerrilla war in southern Bohemia had spilled over into the internal struggles of Austria, where sibling rivalry flared between the Habsburg princes Leopold and Albert. Sokol, who had been a mercenary for Prokop, now offered his services to Jošt, who in turn forwarded them on to Duke Leopold. The Rožmberk holdings became the objects of attack along with Albert's domains. Farms were looted and burned, cattle driven away, and travelling merchants held up and robbed of their goods. Even royal towns tied to the Rožmberks suffered depredation. Eventually, the Rožmberks and their allied cities became increasingly effective at counter-guerrilla warfare.

One of Žižka's brothers, also fighting as a mercenary, was captured and beheaded at Budějovice (Budweis) some time after 1400. Žižka's leader, Matthew, was captured in 1409, tortured at Budějovice and executed. Žižka was in an increasingly precarious position, and at that juncture, like a *deus ex machina*, Wenceslaus reached out and rescued him from what would have been an inglorious end. In two letters dated April and July of 1409, Wenceslaus directed the town of Budějovice to make peace with Žižka. The second letter reads in part, 'We have received in grace our faithful, dear Jan Žižka of Trucnov [*sic*] forgiving him all single excesses committed against the King and the Crown of the Bohemian kingdom' and instructs the city council to publish an open letter confirming Žižka's amnesty. This royal attention to a squire who had slipped into the nether world between soldier and highwayman certainly would not have happened had there not been a cordial relationship between the two men. It is possible that other powerful friends of Žižka's, particularly Sokol, had interceded on his behalf. This likelihood is suggested by the fact that, only months after the amnesty letters were issued, Žižka was in Poland as a member of a troop led by Sokol. Wenceslaus may have suggested Žižka make himself scarce for a while. Although he would later make Žižka a captain in his palace guard, the king may have felt some fence-mending with Rožmberk was needed before bringing Žižka to the royal court in Prague where the two were certain to cross paths. Given their mutual antagonism, it probably seemed prudent to allow time for the ill-will between them to cool.

Žižka had been hired to fight for King Władyslaw of Poland against the Prussian Order of Teutonic Knights. This expedition was considered extremely important, and Sokol wanted his forces to be as formidable as possible. Beyond his favourable personal opinion, Sokol held Žižka's military ability in high regard. The only way he could have made this assessment was through his previous complicity with Matthew. Those guerrilla wars had taught Žižka a great deal and given him an opportunity to display his abilities as a soldier and leader. By necessity, he had learned how to take the greatest possible advantage of terrain, later regarded as one of his surpassing strengths as a general. He had fought side-by-side with men of the lower social orders with whom professional warriors of the day would not ordinarily have mixed on the battlefield. Consequently, he developed an understanding of, and empathy with, the peasants who had lost their homes, and members of the lower gentry who (like himself) had lost their land. He knew what it was to fight with men who had never had much and had little to lose. His ability to motivate and inspire farmers and labourers was arguably the most vital component of Žižka's spectacular later successes.

While Wenceslaus had been fighting his own nobles, Poland and Lithuania had been waging a series of wars against the Prussian Order. From their capital city, Marienburg (modern Malbork), the Teutonic Knights controlled the eastern Baltic coast and several key seaports. A 1409 peace treaty between the Knights and Poland–Lithuania fell apart after an uprising in the Samogitia region, which the Knights suspected had been encouraged by Władyslaw and Vytautas, Lithuania's Grand Duke. Desiring a land bridge to their northernmost possessions, the Knights professed to doubt the Samogitians were genuinely adopting Christianity, restoring their pretext for invasion. The princes of the German Confederation, the Austrian Habsburgs, and Sigismund were allied with the Knights, encircling Poland on the north, west and south. In previous wars, the Prussian Knights had enjoyed papal support and assistance from the Bohemian kings. This time, however, neither was quite so helpful. There was strong international pressure to avoid another major European conflict. In addition to the Schism and the ongoing war between France and Burgundy, the Ottoman Turks were threatening Austria and Hungary's southern territories, and Christendom badly needed to unify religiously, politically, and militarily. Wenceslaus negotiated a peace settlement but did so with an eye on his brother and the Pope; his proposals clearly favoured the Knights. Rejecting the settlement out of hand, Polish emissaries objected so stridently that Wenceslaus lost his temper and threatened to kill them. The Polish diplomats scurried back to Cracow, and war became inevitable.

Czech participation in that war was telling. Bohemian mercenaries were considered the best available in Central and Eastern Europe, and the Prussian Knights, who had become increasingly dependent on the services of hired fighters, made strong efforts to recruit them. However, only a very modest number of Bohemians and Moravians were willing to fight for the Order, primarily ethnic Germans who had settled in the Czech Lands and still spoke German. In contrast, there were numerous Bohemians and Moravians on the Polish side. The Polish army assembled for the climactic Battle of Grunwald–Tannenberg on 15 July 1410 consisted of fifty banners; two were entirely Czech, three more had considerable numbers of Czechs. Sokol (whose officers included Žižka) was so highly esteemed that Władyslaw reportedly offered him command of the combined Polish–Lithuanian army – arguably the largest army ever assembled on one battlefield during the Middle Ages. This was obviously a political gesture of appreciation to the Slavic brothers-in-arms coming to Poland's aid, but not to be taken literally. Sokol, befitting a well-bred nobleman with a sense of aristocratic politesse, graciously declined the honour, insisting he could not think of accepting the King's flattering offer.

After some cautious manoeuvring, stalling, and feinting by the Prussian and Polish–Lithuanian armies, they came face-to-face in the swampy, lake-filled forests of Osterode (modern Ostróda), east of the Vistula River between the villages of Tannenberg and Grunwald. The battle ended in a total rout of the Teutonic Knights. Beyond that fact, virtually everything about it remains in dispute – including its name – and the facts have been distorted by historians in Poland, Lithuania, Germany, and Russia, where it lives on in popular nationalist sentiment. Notable here is how Žižka's participation was used for propaganda purposes in Germany and Poland during the late nineteenth century. By then, Žižka had become an icon of resurgent Pan-Slavism, and his name evoked strong feelings in both countries, negative and positive. Germans and Poles both exploited Žižka's mythic stature to heighten the emotional power of their appeals to patriotism, and both were guilty of wholesale distortion of the historical facts. Heinrich von Treitschke

(1834–96), an ultra-nationalist German historian and writer, penned an account that is a textbook example of history in the service of ideology. After asserting that 'the Knights joined battle with a force twice as large as theirs', Treitschke wrote:

> The Lithuanians had already been defeated . . . But Wladislaus' [*sic*] commander-in-chief, little Zyndram, seized his opportunity when the Knights' left wing in reckless disorder was pushing its attack. He flung his forces against the main body of the German army, being boldly supported by Johann Ziska [*sic*], leader of the Bohemian mercenaries, this being the first occasion on which Ziska made his name a terror to his deadly enemies, the Teuton.[1]

Along with other inaccuracies, Treitschke flagrantly overstates Žižka's rank and importance. There is no mention of Žižka in any contemporary account of the battle, so it is by no means certain he even fought on the front line, and it is generally believed he stayed with Sokol at Władyslaw's command post.

The year after Treitschke's article appeared, Polish artist Jan Matejko conceived the idea for what would become his painting *Battle of Grunwald*. Matejko (1838–93), a fervent nationalist, created this massive (nearly three metres high and over five metres long) artwork to remind Poles of their former success, lift their flagging morale and motivate them to resist ongoing military aggression and ethnic cleansing by the Germans. In his painting, to the right of the Polish King's banner, Žižka is preparing with great vigour to annihilate Heinrich von Schwelborn, a Teutonic knight. In point of historical fact, Schwelborn was beheaded by pursuing Polish cavalry during the Knights' panicked retreat, not by Žižka during the battle.[2] In the painting's exhibition catalogue, Matejko stated that Žižka was commanding three Bohemian companies before losing an eye, which is

---

1. Heinrich Gotthard von Treitschke, 'Das deutsche Ordensland Preussen' (Berlin: *Preußische Jahrbücher*, 1862); trans. Eden & Cedar Paul as *Origins of Prussianism: The Teutonic Knights* (New York: Fertig, 1969), 115.
2. Stephen B. Turnbull and Richard Hook, *Tannenberg 1410: Disaster for the Teutonic Knights* (Osprey, 2003), 68.

pure fiction. Seen skulking behind Žižka is a dodgy-looking individual casting a baleful glance in his direction. According to Matejko's commentary, Žižka was frequently the target of hired assassins. Hence, his painting depicts this black-clad Teutonic mercenary ready to plunge a dagger in Žižka's side should opportunity arise. This also overstates the actual stature of Žižka, who at that point was simply not important enough to merit assassination (although Sokol was). Matejko appropriated a single incident in Bohemia when Žižka learned of a plot against his life thirteen years later in 1423, and transported it back across space and time to Poland.

Nationalist propaganda and popular mythology aside, what is actually known about Žižka's Polish sojourn can be summed up in one paragraph. After their defeat at Grunwald–Tannenberg, the Teutonic Knights took advantage of a three-day delay by the Polish–Lithuanian forces to secure Marienburg against attack. However, an important castle near the Vistula River, Radzyń, was besieged and taken by Władyslaw and garrisoned with Polish and Czech soldiers under Sokol. The Poles subsequently turned the castle's defence over to the Czechs, who were soon tested when the Knights attempted to win it back. Firm documentary evidence shows Žižka participated in this successful defence. Polish officers returned to secure the castle, but Žižka stayed until it was returned to the Knights in 1411 by the Peace of Thorn (modern Toruń). Although Žižka returned to Bohemia shortly thereafter, he was not accompanied by Sokol, who had been fatally poisoned by parties unknown. Many Czech mercenaries remained, as Poles were disgruntled by the terms of the Peace of Thorn, and the prospect of further warfare promised continued employment. This was no idle hope: three years later, war broke out again between Poland and the Teutonic Knights. Sigismund urged Wenceslaus to recall any Czechs still in Poland, a compliment to their effectiveness, but his injunction did not carry much weight. Many of them fought for Poland once again, while virtually none offered their services to the Knights.

No longer a hunted brigand but now a battle-proven war hero, Žižka was rewarded financially and professionally for his achievements in Poland. When he returned to Prague some time in 1411 the firebrand preacher Jan Hus was becoming increasingly influential, and his sermons at the Chapel of Bethlehem had become incendiary, rabble-rousing events – part religious homilies, part political rallies. Queen Sofia was a regular attendee; she fell under Hus's spell and even took him as her confessor. Church documents record that she was accompanied by Žižka, then acting as royal bodyguard, and he and nearly all of the royal court soon came to be ardent disciples of Hus. As theological debate raged between Hus and his opponents at Charles University drawing uncomfortable papal and imperial attention, Wenceslaus equivocated. He tried to maintain an impossible balance between Hus's Czech adherents and the rest of the Holy Roman Empire and the entire Catholic Church, recognising that either faction was capable of dethroning him. Beset from all sides, he left town and took refuge in a castle at Fosseniez. For a time, he refused even to meet the nobles who came to entreat him to retake the reins of government. Eventually, Wenceslaus was persuaded to return to the capital, and in June 1412 he cajoled Hus into voluntary exile to the castle of Kozí in the southern provinces.

Contrary to a widespread misconception, Žižka did not participate in the 1415 Battle of Agincourt. Official documents show that Žižka purchased a house in Prague's New Town in 1414 for a substantial price. His name appears in the city property register with the title *'portulanis regius'* (king's doorkeeper), a more exalted position than that term would indicate. Reserved for members of the gentry, this was no butler's post, but an officer's commission in the palace guard. Žižka's house was close to the modest palace in the Old Town that Wenceslaus preferred to the grand castle of Hradčany. This endeared the King to his subjects, who appreciated him choosing to live among them in the heart of the city rather than lording it over them from a distance. In 1416, Žižka sold his house and purchased another closer to the King's residence. A different title, *'cliens de curia domini regis'*, is attached to his name on these documents, indicating he was now a full-fledged courtier. This is confirmed by the town secretary Lawrence of Březová, who referred to him on several occasions as '*regis Wenceslai familiaris*', another term indicating courtier status.

Although Hus was gone, he was anything but forgotten by Žižka and the overwhelming majority of the Czech upper nobility. In July 1415, the estates of Bohemia and Moravia convened a diet in Prague and drafted a defiant letter, known as the *protestio Bohemorum*, to the Council of Constance. Signed by 452 of the leading lords and knights, it protested the innocence of Hus, declared his irreproachable character, and proclaimed that anyone accusing the Bohemians of heresy 'speaketh lies as a treacherous enemy of our kingdom and our nation, being himself a malicious heretic, and even a son of the Devil, who is the father of lies'. This provoked a strong reaction from the Council, which summoned the signatories to stand trial for heresy. None of the 452 nobles deigned to respond, and the Council had to settle for burning another radical Czech cleric, Jerome, at the stake the following year. This only stiffened Bohemian resolve, as witnessed by the growing practice of giving communion as both bread and wine to the laity. Although the Council explicitly condemned this practice (which Hus had not originally espoused but endorsed shortly before his death), in March 1417 the masters of Charles University endorsed it. The chalice became the official symbol of the Hussite movement, and its adherents were known as Calixtines from the Latin word *calix* (chalice), or Utraquists, from the Latin phrase *sub utraque parte* meaning 'under both kinds'.

Another Hussite faction that would come to be known as Taborites was emerging. This sect took shape between 1412 and 1414 when Hus preached in the south-central hinterlands to huge crowds (often 40,000 or more) on hilltops under open skies, emulating Jesus' mountaintop sermons. While these were only intended as religious events, any gathering of that size, especially in support of a movement frowned upon by the government, was inescapably political as well. The beliefs of these rural masses eventually coalesced around the rejection of any religious practice not explicitly prescribed by Scripture. Utraquists, in contrast, only wanted to eliminate ritual deemed incompatible with the Bible. The Taborites also embraced chiliastic beliefs in the imminent coming of Christ and the establishment of His kingdom on earth. They incorporated elements of Waldensianism, which had found adherents throughout Bohemia during the previous century, including the rejection of purgatory, prayers for the dead, and worship of the saints, as well as opposition to capital punishment and private property while proclaiming women's right to preach. Although Žižka was fervently religious, he never gave any indication of believing in an imminent Second Coming or other radical tenets espoused by the Taborites. Nonetheless, he soon threw his hand in with a fellow courtier and soldier, Nicholas of Pístny, who first organised the Taborites; and two fire-breathing clerics, Wenceslaus Koranda and Jan Želivský, who brought their rural followers to Prague and sparked the outbreak of the Hussite Revolution.

*

When the Hussite religious movement exploded in southern Bohemia, it generated thousands of willing fighters for Žižka. Swayed by an apocalyptic mood throughout Europe, peasants abandoned their farms and began gathering in five Western Bohemian cities that became the first Hussite enclaves. As Jan Hus and other charismatic preachers held forth under open skies on hilltops, what had started as a religious reform movement quickly acquired political legitimacy and military strength. Žižka drew soldiers from the burgeoning urban underclass, and a segment of the nobility (particularly the lower gentry) supported him. But overwhelmingly, his warriors of God – men, women, and children – were agrarian. They knew nothing of fighting with sword, lance, and armour from horseback – a difficult and expensive skill developed by aristocratic boys from an early age. But if these Bohemian peasants knew nothing else, they knew how to swing a threshing flail and drive a wagon over rough fields; they did so year-round all their lives, and were thoroughly practiced at both. Exploiting these two skills, Žižka turned necessity into a military virtue while making the most of the natural and human resources available to him.

But there were significant difficulties in assembling an army of peasant farmers, beginning with a lack of weaponry. Armouries and foundries were in short supply. Horses, armour, swords, and halberds were prohibitively expensive even where available, far beyond the reach of an aspiring Hussite soldier. So, when new recruits came in from the surrounding countryside bringing their flails and wagons with them, Žižka armed them with their own implements. These converted farm tools, fundamentally simple but engineered for maximum effectiveness, became the signature weapons of Žižka's Hussites. The flail's blunt head, attached to a handle with a short chain, was enhanced with iron sheathing and spikes, yielding an inexpensively manufactured, easily maintained weapon – no sharpening required.

Žižka and his followers then turned their attention to the wagons. He did not invent the war wagon. Its use as a primitive military weapon is recorded in the annals of Alexander the Great: an encounter with the Thracians at Mount Hæmus predated the Hussite Revolution by seventeen centuries. However, Žižka perfected its use. His Hussites made numerous ingenious alterations to them, and wagons become the central element of the Hussite army around which all others – infantry, cavalry, and artillery – were centred. Žižka's introduction of mobile fortresses that could be rapidly deployed and assembled had multiple effects that outlasted him and the Hussite Revolution. During the Middle Ages, disciplined infantry tactics perfected by the ancient Romans had all but disappeared. For a thousand years after Rome's fall, the Germanic style of heavy cavalry ruled European battlefields. In pre-national European society, the concept of fighting for one's country was non-existent. Medieval armies were largely comprised of mounted armoured knights gathering retinues under their own banners. War, to a large extent, was a matter of these knights meeting in pitched cavalry charges. The armies of that era usually had no training as a unit, and tactics were crude: horse and infantry were massed and simply charged each other.

Knights, independent-minded lords of their own fiefdoms, were loath to submit to what modern-day military thinkers would regard as battle discipline, formation of tactical bodies, or rules of battle organisation. Often, knights would pick and chose who they were going to fight based on whim or personal animosity. Infantry consisted of ill-equipped, untrained, and disorganised mobs. When such a mob could be induced to venture forth unprotected onto the battlefield, opposing knights would slaughter them like cattle. Leading an army of this sort was like trying to herd cats. There was little opportunity for rational leadership or inspired generalship. Hence, most medieval battles degenerated into uncontrollable free-for-alls. The creation of the battle wagon fostered not only tactical planning and battle discipline, but a well-defined military organisation as well. Žižka's peasants initially had no more idea of tactics, discipline, and organisation than their social betters on horseback. Although they would have deferred to their officers, who were noblemen, in all likelihood this would not have been sustained for long in the course of a heated battle. However, these peasants were pragmatic and well aware of what had happened to previous European uprisings, when poorly armed, untrained peasants were obliterated when set upon by heavily armoured, well-armed knights. They realised that if they did not do something different, the same thing would happen to them. This consideration, as much as any religious zealotry, nationalist fervour, or personal charisma on Žižka's part, made them willing to submit to his rules, drills, and a harsh code of discipline. Unlike the medieval knight but very much like the Roman legionnaire, the Hussite soldier operated under strict discipline in which stern punishment – very often death – was threatened for any breach of orders, misconduct, or shirking of duties.

The Hussite force was organised under four captains: one each for wagons, infantry, artillery, and cavalry. Each captain was responsible for his assigned troops and trained to respond to battle drums and signal flags. On the march, Žižka's basic formation consisted of a central core of baggage wagons and infantry, flanked on either side by columns of war wagons. According to some sources, Žižka used this same formation tactically when meeting an enemy force head-on. Except for whatever mounted cavalry he might have had at his disposal – a component that fluctuated greatly in size – his entire force was stationed within the wagons, with a certain percentage retained for the defence of each in order to secure the flanks and the rest drawn up in front of the formation for battle. As the enemy drew near, a signal from Žižka and his lieutenants directed the two outer columns to advance while at the same time wheeling inward. As these two columns met, the enemy would be trapped and often completely annihilated. When deemed necessary, the rear of the outer wagon columns would also pivot inwards and join together, and the inner columns would follow suit, forming two concentric rings. To let the cavalry in for defence or permit the infantry out for attack or pursuit, flag signals directed the wagons to open a portal quickly and without confusion.

While the Hussites occasionally took the offensive with their war wagons, it was not standard operating procedure. As a general rule, Žižka favoured strategic advance coupled with tactical retreat; the exceptions only serve to prove this rule. Doubtless, the capabilities and feats of Žižka's wagoneers have been overstated and even mythicised by chroniclers who never actually witnessed them. Accounts of complex evolutions executed at a rapid gallop should be viewed with some scepticism. Horses drawing the wagons would have been extremely vulnerable to being killed or disabled by archers, quickly bringing manoeuvres to an abrupt halt. It seems unlikely that Žižka, unless he had no choice – as was the case on a couple occasions, would have failed to realise this. (Horses were not a factor at the pivotal Battle of Malešov in 1424, when Žižka launched boulder-laden wagons down a hillside followed by an artillery barrage and general charge to exploit the ensuing mêlée.)

When sufficient cavalry were available, Žižka deployed them on the outer flanks of the war wagons as a scouting screen, minimising vulnerability to surprise attack and allowing a '*tabor*', or defensive formation, to be set up very quickly. On the battlefield the roles were reversed, with the wagon formation providing protection for the cavalry, who usually deployed inside it so as to prevent their more numerous opponents from overwhelming them. Initially, the Hussite armies lacked effective numbers of cavalry, given their comparatively few noblemen, who traditionally provided the mounted contingents for a medieval army. However, the Taborites were able to form small cavalry contingents made up from men who had served in the retinues of nobles, and hence had at least some familiarity with mounted warfare. In his early campaigns, Žižka created a small force of crossbowmen mounted on draft horses, but they usually did not participate in pitched battles against their numerically superior, better armed and more skilled counterparts. These crossbowmen later became more effective when they were able to re-mount on captured Royalist warhorses and assumed a larger, albeit still limited, battlefield role. While many of the lesser nobility and gentry joined the Hussites as the movement grew, they tended to affiliate themselves with the moderate Utraquist faction rather than Žižka's Taborites. As a result, the Hussites usually fielded the largest cavalry forces when the various Hussite factions were fighting in alliance – frequently not the case. Cavalry never became a formidable element of Žižka's armies, and generally the infantry outnumbered them by a ratio ten to one.

Žižka's battle wagons were built with uniform wheel sizes and axle lengths, perhaps the first instance of mass-produced, standardised military vehicles. The basic body structure was a rectangle of stout planking about a metre high. Hanging planks were suspended from the top of the wagon on one side, functioning like armour. Some wagons had storm-roofs on the top providing additional cover from arrows and other missiles descending at steep angles. Another large hinged plank pierced with firing slits was slung below the wagon body. The wagons were also cleverly fitted with mantlets, or wings, which could be slid out and joined to an adjacent wagon, forming a continuous bulwark. Other movable boards were used to protect the wheels against damage. On the wagon's inside wall, a ramp was fitted which could be dropped down during battle, allowing crew members quick passage in and out of the wagon. A large container of stones, either attached to the rear or inside the wagon body, provided stability as well as missile ammunition. Several ballast wagons were completely filled with stones and placed at the corners and 'gates' of the formation, providing even further stability. The wagon wheels were large and usually iron-rimmed, with the front wheels projecting out slightly in front of the body, permitting them to be chained to the rear wheels of the wagon ahead. With this interlocked structure, the wagons were virtually impossible to manhandle aside or tip over.

The basic battlefield tactic of the Hussites was to start in a defensive square of wagons. If time permitted, a ditch would be dug around it. Large pavises were used to cover any gaps in the structure and sometimes to construct a second line of defence behind the wagons. The inside of the square held cavalry, baggage, horse teams for the wagons, and any infantry not assigned as wagon defenders. The infantry were used either as a ready reserve to shore up faltering defences or to spearhead a counter-attack. Ideally, they played no role in the early stages of the battle so they were well-rested and fresh. After the initial use of the massed firepower of the missilemen and artillery to repulse attacking forces, the pole-armed infantry would counter-attack while the cavalry swept out from the sides of the square to strike the enemy's flanks. It is testimony to the discipline instilled by Žižka that there is no record of his mounted forces pursuing a defeated enemy to the point where they put themselves at risk or left the wagon formation vulnerable to flanking counter-attacks. Ten years after Žižka's death, this very breach of battle discipline resulted in disaster at the 1434 Battle of Lipany, a severe setback for the Hussite movement.

Žižka consistently used the terrain to the greatest advantage. If possible, he tried to form his wagons on high ground for several reasons. Struggling uphill slowed down and tired out attackers, and if the ground was sufficiently steep effective cavalry charges were precluded altogether, forcing the Royalists to dismount and making them far less formidable. Equally important, an elevated deployment negated enemy missile and artillery fire, both of which could prove deadly to the Hussites, their wagons, and their horses. If possible, the Hussites preferred to deploy 'hull down', with only the top part of the wagons being visible from lower ground. This made it difficult or impossible for high-velocity weapons with flat trajectories, like handguns and cannons, to target the wagons from close range. Enemy crossbowmen had either to fire from further away, reducing force and effectiveness, or move in close and attempt to drop shots into the Hussite camp at a very steep angle. The latter option was not practicable with cannon, so gun batteries had no choice but to fire from long range where the viable angle of fire was only marginally better while power and accuracy were decreased. When high ground was not available, Žižka formed his wagons using impassable topographical features, such as rivers and lakes or man-made structures like dams and city walls, to secure one flank. This freed up additional wagons, enabling him to extend the formation's front and maximise the firepower that could be brought to bear on the enemy.

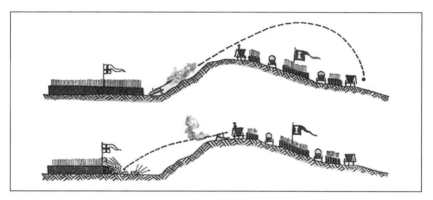

Advantages of high ground

Wagon crews had specialised tasks and responsibilities. This promoted battlefield effectiveness and created a strong group mindset, unfamiliar and somewhat daunting to the Hussites' enemies. The imposition of specialised tasks fostered the recognition that each soldier was a part of a larger, interdependent machine, creating a powerful *esprit de corps* and smooth battle co-operation. The standard wagon crew consisted of twenty members: two armed drivers, two handgunners, six crossbowmen, four flailmen, four halberdiers and two pavisiers. Wagons were arrayed in basic tactical groups of ten and assigned to a combat line commanded by a line master (*zeilmeistern*), with the number of wagons per combat line varying from fifty to a hundred, depending on the size of the army. Hussite missilemen were permanently assigned to the wagons; there is no evidence of them being used as a separate body of troops.

Under Žižka's leadership, the crossbow was the wagon crews' predominant weapon, although by the 1430s one missileman in four was likely to be armed with a handgun. Crossbows and handguns required very little training to use and hence were ideal weapons for creating an effective fighting force in a very short period of time. The biggest problem was their slow reload time – when users were most vulnerable. However, within the shelter of the wagons, fighters were protected during the reloading stage and were able to sight and fire through loopholes provided for the purpose. Bracing their weapons inside these loopholes steadied their aim and made their fire more effective. To lessen further the vulnerability of the missilemen and the wagons themselves, Žižka turned part of his infantry into 'support' squads. These elements, like the main infantry contingent, were equipped with a mixture of close-combat pole arms which, given their long reach, could be used effectively from within and behind the wagons. The two most widely used pole weapons – and unquestionably the ones that made the greatest impression on their enemies – were the flail and an improvised equivalent of the halberd. The flail became closely identified with Bohemia and for many years after the Hussite wars was still used by Bohemian infantry. It was a brutally effective weapon against those wearing 'soft' armour such as leather and chain mail; the concussive blunt trauma of a well-delivered blow could incapacitate a man. The Hussite approximation of the halberd, like the implement upon which it was modelled, was designed to allow an infantryman to pull a cavalryman to the ground or, failing that, hamstring his horse.

At Žižka's direction, Hussite weaponsmiths fabricated a number of different artillery pieces with which to support the infantry. Most common was the *tarasnice*, essentially an overlarge handgun with a bore of about five centimetres and 1.2–1.5 metres in length. They were usually mounted on a free-standing framework within the wagon, often with a swivel mount. The other main type was the *houfnice* (from which comes the word 'howitzer'), a short-bodied cannon with a bore of

20–30 centimetres mounted directly on wagons braced against recoil. Both were used to deliver shrapnel (consisting of small stones) at point-blank range. The Hussites also had an early handgun called the *píšťala* – a Czech word meaning 'whistle' from which comes the term 'pistol' – which fired multiple shot at point-blank range. An important advantage of these guns was the relative ease with which they could be manufactured. Their small calibre and short length made the casting process less complicated and required fewer raw materials. Both the *tarasnice* and the *píšťala* could probably have been made by a skilled gunsmith rather than a cannon forger. One other cannon in the Hussite arsenal was the bombard, which was of limited usefulness in open battle due to its long reload time and lack of manoeuvrability. Additionally, these larger cannon were usually in short supply as they were extremely hard to cast. The Hussites did capture some and used them to good effect during several sieges against Royalist castles.

If the signature weapon of the Hussite army was the flail, and its primary logistical technology was the gun-carrying battle wagon, its backbone was the foot soldier – the close-combat trooper armed with flail and halberd, and organised into 'rotas' of 100 men. Although Žižka's men initially had little or no background in warfare, they proved ideal for Žižka's new methods of fighting, since they had no preconceived ideas. Moreover, Žižka, like other leaders of rag-tag insurgencies throughout history, had little choice but to employ all willing and able-bodied people at his disposal. This included women, who were accepted as full battlefield equals and not just nurses and cooks, and even adolescents outfitted with slings with which they hurled stones from behind the wagons. Hussite foot soldiers understood just how hideously effective their opponents would be if they attempted to fight a conventional battle. Žižka was able to impose discipline and training that would have been impossible to enforce on the more traditional feudal hosts of the time. He created a well-trained army willing to adopt weapons and tactics which the nobility would have regarded as beneath their dignity, one versed in new tactics and capable of resisting far larger enemy armies.

Chapter 2

PREACHERS AND POPES

... let us build a city and a tower ... and let us make a
name, lest we be scattered abroad ...

Genesis 11.4

There can scarcely be a greater irony than the Czech Republic's
current status as one of the most irreligious countries in Europe. In
2001, fifty-nine per cent of the citizenry considered themselves
agnostics, atheists, non-believers, or unaffiliated with any organised
religion. In 2005, thirty per cent of Czech respondents stated they
did not believe in God, spirit, or life forces, while only nineteen per
cent claimed to believe in God.[1] This was second-fewest in Europe,
surpassed only by Estonia's sixteen per cent. Six centuries ago, things
were very different indeed.

As the Hussite Revolution can be understood only in the context of
the religious conflicts that swept fifteenth-century Central Europe, Jan
Žižka's story cannot be told without recounting that of Jan Hus. A
gentle soul with great generosity of spirit, Hus gave his name to the
uprising regarded as the defining moment in the history of the Czech
people. Hus and Žižka were the pen and sword, respectively, of the
Hussite Revolution, although many have wondered whether Žižka's zeal
took him a great deal farther than his friend and religious master would
have approved. Given the prickly relations between Žižka and various

1. These statistics are distinct from Slovakia where 68.9 percent of the population identify
themselves with Roman Catholicism.

leading Hussite clergy, which on at least one occasion turned violent, it is altogether likely these two strong-minded leaders would have clashed eventually.

While many biographical details about Žižka are obscure or simply lost, much is known about Hus, born to well-to-do Czech peasants between 1369 and 1374 in the small farming community of Husinec (Czech for 'goose-pen') in southern Bohemia. He later dropped all but the first three letters of the village's name, shortening his surname to Hus ('goose') and creating a self-deprecating joke of which he was fond. Eventually, the goose, along with the chalice, became a symbol on the flags of Žižka's 'warriors of God'. Hus showed intellectual brilliance at an early age, obtaining a quality elementary education with support and encouragement from a local priest. He was accepted into the Charles University in 1390, an achievement for someone of his social class. He became a bachelor of arts in 1393, bachelor of theology in 1394, and master of arts in 1396. Two years later he was chosen for a University post and began lecturing. Among his textbooks were the writings of English religious reformer John Wyclif.

Hus was ordained in 1400 and named dean of the faculty the following year. Hus's account of his initial motivation for entering the clergy reads:

> Before I became a priest I often, and gladly, played chess. I wasted my time. I bought fashionable gowns and robes with wings, and hoods trimmed with white fur. I thought that I would become a priest quickly in order to secure a good livelihood, and dress well, and be held in great esteem. Alas! The goose was plucked of its virtue by the devil.[2]

In October 1401 Hus became dean of the philosophical faculty, and from October 1402 to the following April he was University rector. That year he became curate (*capellarius*) of Bethlehem Chapel, built and endowed in 1391 by zealous Prague citizens to foster

---

2. Theodore K. Rabb, *Renaissance Lives: Portraits of an Era* (New York: Pantheon, 1993), 20.

preaching in the Bohemian tongue. This deeply influenced Hus, who experienced a spiritual awakening some time around the age of thirty, regretted his materialistic ways, and committed himself to serious theological pursuits. Although Hus was a Catholic priest, he is usually pictured bearded and without tonsure. Even though he described himself as small and fat, he is invariably depicted in Czech iconography as tall and slender. These artistic liberties evoke the lean and hungry look of a man who thinks too much, rather than the jolly monks and wanton friars of Chaucer and Boccaccio. A driving force of the Hussite movement was outrage at the drunkenness and ribaldry of decadent clerics. Evidently, his disciples considered it unhelpful to depict an image resembling those they were trying to de-legitimise and overthrow.

Hus drew heavily from the ideas of John Wyclif (1325?–84), known as 'The Morning Star of the Reformation'. Both reformers espoused translation of the Bible into the vernacular, asserting its final authority. Both proclaimed the pope's fallibility and endorsed limiting Rome's temporal power and clerical wealth – themes later picked up by Martin Luther. Wyclif and Hus originally received protection from their respective kings owing to power struggles with the papacy. Considered useful – temporarily – for political reasons, both fell out of favour when they became too controversial. Both had their views denounced and were condemned to burning at the stake, in Wyclif's case forty-six years after his death!

The Protestant Reformation is said to have begun when Luther nailed his ninety-five theses to the door of Wittenberg chapel in 1517. But Luther's ideas were hardly the first challenge to Catholicism in Europe. Luther expressed astonishment at finding so many points of agreement between Hus and himself. Writing to a former teacher, Luther declared 'I have hitherto taught and held all the opinions of John Huss [*sic*] unawares . . . we are all Hussites without knowing it.'[3] There were differences between them, but the parallels are numerous

---

3. Preserved Smith, *The Life and Letters of Martin Luther* (Boston: Houghton Mifflin, 1911; repr. New York: Barnes and Noble, 1968), 72.

and meaningful. Both were college professors and priests who drew huge public crowds when preaching in their university chapels. Both promoted local religious autonomy and helped establish their national language. Luther translated the Bible into German to make it more accessible to ordinary people, significantly contributing to the emergence of the modern German language. Hus also espoused a vernacular Bible and preached in Czech instead of Latin; he also introduced diacritics (especially the háček)[4] into Czech spelling.

The two men focused on another issue: transubstantiation. This integral tenet of Roman and Orthodox Catholic theology holds that during Mass the consecrated bread and wine of the Eucharist are changed, in substance, into the flesh and blood of Christ although they appear to remain the same.[5] Hus and Luther espoused an alternative concept, 'consubstantiation' (also termed 'remanence'), asserting that the substance of Christ's Body and Blood exists concurrently with that of the bread and of wine. Since Luther, while most Protestants have more or less broken with the belief that the bread and wine are actually transformed, many adhere to the belief that a 'Real Presence' comes to exist after consecration. Wine had been reserved exclusively for priests since the late thirteenth century and this became the defining issue of the Hussite revolution. The argument in Bohemia (which Hus himself tended to avoid until just before his death) was whether the benefits of the Eucharist were garnered by only receiving the bread. Many Czechs believed they were not. Though Hussitism was a fractious movement that splintered into several groups, they agreed on this point. Catholic ecclesiastics and theologians countered Hussite assertions with the doctrine of 'concomitance'. This posits that participants receive the entire Christ – body, blood, soul, and divinity – even if they receive communion under only one form. The practice of distributing the bread alone to

4. Also known as a caron, wedge, inverted circumflex, or inverted hat, a háček looks similar to a breve but has a sharp tip, unlike a breve which is rounded.
5. This doctrine, which has no explicit basis in Scripture, first appeared in the early ninth century, was formalized at the Council of Trent (1545–63), and was reaffirmed at the Second Vatican Council (1962–5).

Roman Catholic laity remained in effect until the Second Vatican Council of 1964–5, when the ancient custom was restored.[6]

Before being burned at the stake, Hus declared 'You are now going to burn a goose, but in a century you will have a swan which you can neither roast nor boil.'[7] Copies of Wyclif's writings were used to kindle the fire. One hundred and two years later, Luther posted his theses, and today the swan is a symbol of many Lutheran churches. The seeming prescience of Hus's remark, served to heighten his saintly stature with subsequent generations of Bohemians, and Protestant iconography commonly connects Wyclif, Hus, and Luther. Had Hus lived longer, he would have presided over difficult times for his followers, and his memory might be less revered. Some feel that Hus left the historical stage at the proper time and in the proper manner to ensure everlasting fame and respect. A living Hus would have been a valuable voice for the movement, but the dead Hus embodied a spirit of pride and resistance, inspiring the Hussites and steeling them for the coming doctrinal and military assault upon their beliefs.

*

After the papal seat moved to Avignon in 1305, it remained there seventy years. This period has been called the 'Babylonian Captivity of the Papacy', referring to the Jews' deportation from Jerusalem. The Catholic Church developed a reputation for corruption and predominant French influence, and the papal curia's efforts to extend power and increase revenues estranged major parts of Christendom including England and Ireland. In September 1376, Pope Gregory returned to Rome, provoking continuous rioting and forcing him to remove to Anagni the following

6. Since 1978, the distribution of communion under both forms has been permitted in all dioceses of the United States. On 7 April 2002, the U.S. Conference of Catholic Bishops approved a document entitled *Norms for the Distribution and Reception of Holy Communion under Both Kinds in the Dioceses of the United States of America* encouraging the practice.

7. John Fox, 'An Account of the Persecutions in Bohemia under the Papacy', in William B. Forbush (ed.), *Fox's Book of Martyrs: A History of the Lives, Sufferings and Triumphant Deaths of the Early Christian and the Protestant Martyrs* (London: John Day, 1563; repr. Grand Rapids: Zondervan, 1967), 143.

May. After Gregory's death, rioters demanded that a Roman pope be elected. Fearing the mobs, the cardinals elected a Neapolitan, Urban VI, when no viable Roman candidates presented themselves. Urban had been a respected papal administrator, but as pope he proved suspicious, overbearing, and prone to violent outbursts of temper. The cardinals soon regretted their decision; the majority left Rome and elected a rival pope, Clement VIII, who re-established a papal court in Avignon. The second election threw the Church into turmoil. The conflict quickly escalated into a diplomatic crisis dividing Europe. Secular leaders had to choose which pope they would recognise. In England, Bohemia, and the rest of Europe, this fracture of the Rock of Peter cast further doubt in the popular mind about papal infallibility. The existence of two popes meant that one – and perhaps both – were illegitimate and not to be obeyed.

Wyclif's influence upon Hus – and by extension Bohemia – was a direct result of the Schism. In 1379, Wenceslaus (then Holy Roman Emperor) made overtures to England's King Richard (then twelve years old) regarding a dynastic marriage with the Emperor's half-sister Anne. The proposed marriage was unpopular in England, but Urban sanctioned it, favouring any alliance that might strengthen him against the French and Clement, their preferred pope. In January 1383, rings were exchanged, and Anne was crowned Queen. Their respective families had not always lived in peace. Anne's grandfather, blind King John, was slain at Crécy in 1346 fighting with the French. Edward the Black Prince, Richard's father, was present when John was found dead, and according to family tradition Edward took three of the eight plumes on John's crown. A highly educated woman, Anne (1366–94) was instrumental in spreading Wyclif's views to the Czech Lands. She favoured his doctrines and extended patronage on his behalf. Wyclif, noting that Bohemia and Germany already had vernacular Bibles, decried the 'foolishness' of opposition to an English-language Bible as heretical, noting '. . . it is possible that the noble queen of England . . . might have a gospel edited in . . . Bohemian, Teutonic, and Latin, and it would be devilish presumption to consider her a heretic implicitly for that reason'. Moreover, Wyclif added, 'though a stranger and foreigner, she was diligently meditating a translation of the Gospels into English'. Many nobles had French translations, and Wyclif implied that national honour required an English translation. Along with her tri-lingual Bible, Anne brought to England Central Europe's court culture, the side saddle, and numerous Bohemian followers. Under King Charles V, Paris was uncongenial for Bohemian scholars wishing to study abroad. A close connection therefore grew up between the universities in Prague and Oxford when scholarships at Oxford for Bohemian scholars were created with Anne's encouragement.

Many Bohemian Oxford students, notably a young cleric named Jerome, brought home Wyclif's books. Returning to Prague in 1408, Jerome found that Wyclif's doctrines had attracted growing numbers of adherents. Jerome introduced these books to Hus and became one of his chief followers and most devoted friends. The two were a study in contrasts. Jerome (1379–1415) was a cosmopolitan born to a wealthy Prague family. His beliefs caused him a great deal of trouble and forced him to move frequently, often one step ahead of the ecclesiastic authorities. 'Young men and students', Jerome said in a public disputation, 'who did not study the books of Wyclif would never find the true root of knowledge.' Hus became rector of Charles University a second time in 1409 as a pawn in the power struggle between Wenceslaus and the Church. As Jerome travelled through Europe facing charges of heresy, suffering imprisonment, and barely escaping death, Hus continued teaching and preaching. He became increasingly bold in admonishing the Church and became a leading representative of Czech national aspirations. Consequently, German clerics in Bohemia turned the Archbishop of Prague against him.

When Charles IV founded the university bearing his name, he envisioned it as a universal institution in which no nationality was dominant. He divided its administration into four 'nations': Czech, Pole, Saxon, and Bavarian, which were to share power equally on a rotating basis. In practical effect, however, the latter three factions became a hegemonic German bloc. The growing number of Czech students resented their collective power. After Hus's first term as University rector in 1402–3, the German who assumed the post convoked a University congregation, banned Wyclif's books as heretical, and prohibited their teaching – moves obviously aimed at Hus. Czechs protested but were outvoted three to one, and they began demanding the University charter be changed to grant them more equitable representation. They found an unlikely ally in Wenceslaus.

After Wenceslaus's deposition as Holy Roman Emperor in 1400, his replacement, Rupert, did not fare well. Wenceslaus disputed Rupert's title, and many princes and cities were slow to acknowledge him. Rupert had little to fear from Wenceslaus, but his position was jeopardised in 1408 when he supported Pope Gregory XII against the vast majority of German prelates, who wished to summon a general council to end the Great Schism. Wenceslaus shrewdly supported the powerful pro-conciliar faction, which agitated openly for Wenceslaus's restoration as German king. However, the Archbishop of Prague, Zbyněk Zajíc, and most of the Charles University hierarchy opposed the King's scheme to have Bohemia observe neutrality between the rival popes Benedict XIII (Clement's Avignon successor) and Gregory XII (Urban's Roman successor). Only Czech members of the University supported Wenceslaus, who needed its endorsement. In 1409, Wenceslaus issued the Decree of Kutná Hora reversing the University's balance of power: the Czech 'nation' now held three votes and the others only one. He also re-named Hus rector. After ineffectual protests, German professors and students left Prague, most relocating to Leipzig and founding a new university there. Others went to universities in Heidelberg, Vienna, and Cologne, spreading rumours of rampant heresy in Prague. Charles University lost its place as an international body of learning and became the spiritual centre of the Czech nation. Archbishop Zbyněk protested too, but Wenceslaus forced his acquiescence by withholding clerical pay and threatening to confiscate church property.

The Council of Constance unexpectedly deposed both popes and chose the short-lived Alexander who was installed at Pisa. Zbyněk summoned Hus before the Czech inquisitor and denounced him to the

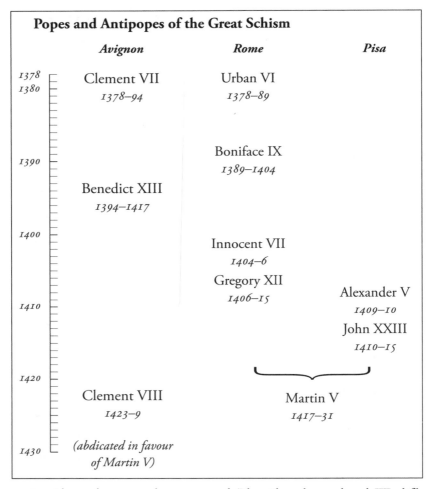

Popes and Antipopes of the Great Schism

	Avignon	*Rome*	*Pisa*
1378 *1380*	Clement VII *1378–94*	Urban VI *1378–89*	
1390		Boniface IX *1389–1404*	
	Benedict XIII *1394–1417*		
1400			
		Innocent VII *1404–6*	
		Gregory XII *1406–15*	Alexander V *1409–10*
1410			John XXIII *1410–15*
1420	Clement VIII *1423–9*	Martin V *1417–31*	
1430	*(abdicated in favour of Martin V)*		

curia. Alexander strongly supported Zbyněk, who ordered Wyclif's teachings suppressed and forbade Hus from preaching in Bethlehem Chapel. Disregarding the Archbishop, Hus continued preaching and appealed to Pope John XXIII, Alexander's successor. Many Czechs began to revere Hus as a divinely sent leader. The Archbishop ordered Wyclif's books burned in the episcopal palace courtyard and excommunicated Hus and his followers, provoking widespread rioting. Hus again appealed to John in Pisa; Zbyněk appealed to Gregory who summoned Hus to Rome to answer charges of heresy. Hus haughtily refused and expressed contempt for Gregory:

What reason have I . . . to put myself through the extraordinary difficulty of going a great distance, passing through the midst of my enemies, to place myself before witnesses and judges who are my enemies? What is still worse, I would be compelled to worship the Pope on bended knee!

The representative sent to plead his case, added Hus later, had been imprisoned and ill-treated.

For a time, Hus was supported by Wenceslaus and Sofia, albeit for different reasons. Wenceslaus, who pointedly remained 'neutral' in the showdown between Benedict and Gregory, suggested that the latter's opinion of Hus carried little weight in his kingdom. 'If anyone wishes to accuse him of anything', he disdainfully wrote to Gregory,

> let them do so in our country, before the University of Prague or another competent judge. Our kingdom does not see fit to expose so useful a preacher to the judgement of his enemies, to the great disturbance of the whole population.

Queen Sofia had long been under the sway of Hus, even taking him as her personal confessor while continuing regularly to attend his Bethlehem Chapel sermons escorted by her bodyguard, Jan Žižka. Unlike Wenceslaus, her motivation seems to have been genuinely religious. Her plea to Pope Gregory on Hus's behalf stressed piety and the common welfare:

> An order has recently been given which has caused great upheaval among our people and confusion in our kingdom. We request that, for the honour of God and the welfare of our people, you will establish as soon as possible the liberty of Jan Hus, faithful preacher in our chapel, so as to end the popular commotion over his condemnation. We cannot endure so great an assault on the teaching of God's word in our palaces and cities. The word of God ought not to be hindered but rather preached in the streets, from the rooftops, and anywhere it has listeners.[8]

8. Rabb, *Renaissance Lives*, 25–6.

But the political landscape shifted, and Hus's unwillingness to adjust cost him his royal support. Often accused of arrogance, self-righteousness, and hot-headedness, Hus over-estimated the willingness of highly placed friends to support him unconditionally. The popular enthusiasm his lectures generated may have contributed to a sense of invulnerability. If so, it was an illusion soon shattered. In 1411, 'Antipope' John proclaimed a crusade against King Ladislaus of Naples, and a papal emissary urged Praguers to buy indulgences. Hus openly denounced the papal bulls against Ladislaus and preached against indulgences sold in support of a crusade against Christians. This displeased Wenceslaus, who received a percentage of sales in his kingdom. Hus had gone too far, and Wenceslaus warned him: 'Hus, you are always making trouble for me. If those whose concern it is will not take care of it, I myself will burn you.' All of Prague, which continued to harbour Hus, was laid under interdict; a general excommunication closed churches, ended baptisms, marriages, and burials, and threatened residents with eternal damnation. Hus's excommunication was renewed after he refused to obey the papal summons to Rome. The interdict was expanded to include any place giving him any succour whatsoever, and it was more strictly enforced.

Sigismund began pressuring his half-brother to do something about Hus. Wenceslaus knew that inaction on his part could provide Sigismund with a pretext to invade Bohemia. Attempting to calm things down, Wenceslaus demanded that not only Hus but some of his more vociferous opponents leave Prague. Hus went into voluntary exile at a supporter's castle in Kozí Hrádek, seventy kilometres south of Prague. Over the next two years, Hus also spent time at another castle near the capital, Krakovec, occasionally engaging in open-air preaching, maintaining a copious correspondence, and composing the treatise *De Ecclesia* ('On the Church'), which furnished material for the capital charges later brought against him. Wenceslaus grew exasperated with Hus and decided he had no option but to turn the matter over to Sigismund, who had endorsed convening the Council of Constance in 1414 to settle the Schism once and for all. In the interest of putting dissension and dispute to rest, Hus accepted Sigismund's imperial summons to the Council, probably urged by Wenceslaus. He demonstrated a fair amount of naiveté: sermons he brought with him show that he intended to convert the assembled Church fathers to his doctrinal positions, a hopeless prospect. The safe-conduct promised to him by Sigismund, a secular ruler, had no weight in a papal court, as the Emperor found to his chagrin and embarrassment. The curia held that promises or pledges of honour extended to heretics were not binding. While Hus was surely aware of this legalism, he probably saw the safe-conduct as a sign of royal patronage and believed he could rely on the support of Sigismund and Wenceslaus during the proceedings. However, some have noted that Hus made his will before setting out for Constance in October 1414, seeing this as an indication that he foresaw his fate and even sought it.

On arriving, Hus saw the announcement of his trial as a heretic – not the learned disputation he had anticipated. After a rumour spread that he intended to flee, Hus was turned over to the Archbishop of Constance and brought to his castle, spending more than two months chained, poorly fed, and increasingly ill before being placed in a monastery dungeon. Although witnesses against Hus were heard, he was not allowed an advocate for his defence, common practice at such proceedings. He was accused of heresies he had never endorsed, including communion under both kinds. After a series of trials lasting seven months, thirty-nine charges were read against him. A prelate pronounced sentence upon Hus, who protested loudly that he did not wish anything but to be convinced of his errors from Holy Scripture. He then fell upon his knees asking divine forgiveness for his enemies. At the execution site, he knelt and prayed aloud. Suggestions that he be given a confessor were rejected as unmerited by a heretic. After being undressed, Hus's hands were tied behind his back and his neck bound with a rusty chain to a stake surrounded by a pile of wood and straw up to his chin. At the last moment, he was offered one final chance to recant and (ostensibly) save his life, but Hus declined. 'God is my witness that I have never taught that of which I have by false witnesses been accused,' he declared. 'In the truth of the Gospel which I have written, taught, and preached, I will die today with gladness.' As the flames engulfed him, he sang a hymn until the smoke choked him into silence. His ashes were scraped up and thrown into the Rhine.

When Hus left for Constance, Jerome had assured him that, if events warranted, he would come to give whatever assistance he could. He kept his promise after hearing increasingly dire reports. Unlike Hus, he arrived without an imperial safe-conduct, and his friends persuaded him to return to Bohemia. On his way back, he was arrested, imprisoned, and returned to Constance. He was immediately arraigned on charges of fleeing a citation; unbeknown to him, one had been issued against him. The rest was a foregone conclusion, and Jerome did not even get the pretence of a fair hearing. Recognising that no accommodations or compromises would spare him the same fate as Hus, he opted to go out in a blaze of glory. On his trial's second day in late May 1416, he boldly renounced a previous recantation, and a week later he was condemned and immediately burned at the stake.

Arguments persist over Sigismund's alleged treachery at Constance. Some accuse him of complicity in Hus's death; others assert he was powerless to prevent it. Undisputedly, the execution triggered the first great flash-point of the revolution that took Hus's name, galvanising rebellion-prone Bohemian radicals and enraging even the most conservative Czech nobles. The outraged sense of betrayal, usurpation of local judicial prerogatives, and besmirching of national honour was shared by Czechs of all social classes, temporarily overshadowing political and religious differences that later re-emerged. In the aftermath of the deaths of Hus and Jerome, the conflict which had been prepared for centuries and simmered many years finally came to full boil.

Historian John Mears, writing in 1879, presented as documented fact an apocryphal episode that first appeared in print a century after it allegedly occurred, which has become an entrenched part of Žižka's legend. Mears recounted how Wenceslaus one day noticed Žižka stalking the palace courtyard, lost in thought.

'What is it', asked the king, 'that so intensely occupies your thought?'

'The grievous affront', he answered, 'which has been offered to the Bohemian nation in the punishment of John Huss [*sic*].'

'Neither you nor I', said the slothful monarch, 'are in a condition to avenge the affront; but if you can find means to do it, take courage and avenge your fellow-countrymen.'[9]

This episode, whether factual or not, accurately highlights defining attributes of Žižka and Wenceslaus: the single-minded truculence of the one, the *laissez-faire* statecraft of the other.

Sigismund, now Holy Roman Emperor and with the full weight of a reunified Catholic Church behind him, became increasingly bellicose about the Hussites, expressing impatience at Wenceslaus's inaction and Sofia's complicity. Although she had been a fearless advocate for Hus, Sofia realised a foreign invasion would not only unseat her and her husband but would unleash devastation throughout the kingdom. In late February 1419, Sofia prevailed upon Wenceslaus to issue a decree restricting Hussite services to three Prague churches. Many clergymen left Prague to join the Hussites along with an important courtier, Nicholas of Pístny, whose departure was involuntary. Like Žižka, Nicholas (also known as Nicholas of Hus after a southern Bohemian castle of which he had been burgrave during the first decade of the fourteenth century) was a courageous and capable soldier with a dominating personality. A staunch supporter of the Hussites, he had also been squeezed economically from his ancestral manor and forced to enter the royal court. When Wenceslaus imposed these new restrictions, Nicholas took strong exception and engaged in a lengthy and heated argument with Wenceslaus, who suspected Nicholas might be fomenting a palace coup. He suggested that if Nicholas could not maintain a civil tongue he could have him strangled into silence. Nicholas, unwilling to back down, left Prague and re-located to Bechyně in rural southern Bohemia.

Wenceslaus was reluctant to suppress the Hussites completely. His solution only fostered hilltop, open-air services limited by neither seating

9. John W. Mears, *Heroes of Bohemia: Huss, Jerome and Zizca* (Philadelphia: Presbyterian Board of Publication, 1879), 281.

capacity nor civil authorities. When Nicholas stormed out of Prague, he (like Hus) was able to transplant his ideas and influence to a less confined environment where he soon demonstrated the ability to understand, motivate, and organise the peasantry. Wenceslaus's measures did persuade Archbishop Konrad (Zbyněk's successor) to lift the interdict. The King was anxious to re-establish Catholic orthodoxy. Many anti-Hussite priests, primarily Germans, had left the city under threats of violence, and Wenceslaus urged them to return. On 18 June 1419, a solemn church re-consecration was interrupted by a Hussite crowd led by cleric Jan Želivský. The Hussites prevented a ceremonial procession and took over the church. A former monk who had been preaching at St Mary's in the Snow, one of the three remaining Hussite churches, Želivský was a fiery, eloquent and outspoken orator with a particularly strong effect upon women. As spokesman for the 'little people' of Prague's New Town, he had assumed political leadership of its craftsmen, artisans, and labourers.

This spurred Wenceslaus to more drastic measures. On 6 July 1419, he ordered the New Town government purged of suspected Hussites and replaced them with opponents of the movement. The new city councillors implemented police actions against the Hussites and closed all schools refusing to return to a strictly Roman curriculum. Over the next three weeks, resentment throughout the country grew. On 22 July, Nicholas organised a mass gathering near Bechyně that drew 40,000 people, many from distant parts of the kingdom. This event saw the first use of the biblical term 'Tábor', giving the radical Hussite movement its name. In Prague, Želivský fanned the embers of popular discontent, sensing the time was ripe for action. He recruited an experienced, dependable military man committed to the Hussite cause – Jan Žižka.

After his argument with Nicholas, Wenceslaus decided he could not trust his other courtiers either. He summoned them to surrender their arms, and Žižka showed his boldness. On 15 April 1419, he is said to have led a large body of heavily armed Hussites into the palace to answer the royal summons. 'Sire', declared Žižka to the flabbergasted King, 'behold a body of your faithful subjects. We have brought our arms as you commanded. Show us your enemies and you shall acknowledge that our weapons can nowhere be more useful to you than in the hands which now hold them.' The monarch could only gasp a directive to 'Take your arms and use them properly.'[10] Three months later, when Želivský took to the streets in armed rebellion, he knew there were arms available for his followers, and a competent soldier ready to lead them.

On 30 July, Želivský preached to a packed church, fiercely denouncing the city council's police actions. He called on his disciples to follow him in a procession through the city streets, having ensured that many of them were armed. Behind a monstrance held aloft displaying a Eucharistic wafer of bread, Želivský led the crowd to another Romanist church waiting re-consecration. Finding the doors barred, they stormed it and hanged a resisting priest. After celebrating Mass with no apparent sense of inconsistency, they re-formed the procession and marched back towards St Mary's in the Snow. It was no accident that Želivský chose a route leading past the New Town city hall, which was also barred by frightened city functionaries. The crowd demanded admission to present its demands to the city councillors, who chose to talk from the supposed safety of an upper-storey window. During some contentious parlaying over imprisoned Hussites, a stone was allegedly thrown from a window, striking the priest leading the procession. The enraged crowd broke down the doors and threw the councillors out the windows. Those who survived the fall were dispatched by the mob below. They were buried without their fine robes and jewels, which were piled in a heap and burned, an expression of contempt and a demonstration that the Hussites were not motivated by base impulses of plunder. This incident became known as 'The First Defenestration of Prague'. After the slaying of the councillors, Žižka took charge, garrisoning the building against the inevitable reaction from Wenceslaus loyalists. A small troop of royal horseman was sent to retake it, but seeing the huge numbers of insurrectionists – many well-armed – they quickly withdrew. A new city council of stalwart Hussites was

10. Frederick G. Heymann, *John Žižka and the Hussite Revolution* (Princeton: Princeton University Press, 1955; repr. New York: Russell & Russell, 1969), 60 n.

elected, and a militia was organised under the leadership of several captains, Žižka first among them.

Neither rioting mobs, rebellious nobles nor invading crusaders caused Wenceslaus's ultimate demise, but rather an impertinent remark. Learning of the rebellion, Wenceslaus flew into a towering rage. A courtier suggested that the King's failure to take decisive action against Nicholas and Žižka was responsible. Wenceslaus had endured a lifetime of insults and indignities, many from his inner circle, and this snide remark was too much. Furious, he fell upon the advisor with his dagger and would have run him through if not restrained by others present. A massive stroke brought on by this angry fit left his left side partially paralyzed. More vulnerable than ever, Wenceslaus felt deserted by his friends, subjects, and even the Queen. After dispatching a message to Sigismund imploring his speedy assistance, he agreed to a compromise brokered by the Old Town city councillors whereby the New Town would ask the king's forgiveness, pledge him their loyalty, and promise to respect and maintain the rule of law. In return, Wenceslaus recognised and confirmed the Hussite-led New Town city council. But this last chance for a peaceful resolution disappeared on 16 August when Wenceslaus suffered a second stroke and (in the words of the city scribe Brežová) expired 'roaring like a lion' in pain.

*

After Wenceslaus's death, whatever calming effect he had had evaporated, and the prospect of Sigismund as king further roiled rebellion. Turning to the Book of Revelation, Želivský declared that Sigismund was the Great Red Dragon cast from heaven. Only 'by the blood of the Lamb' (meaning the chalice) would true believers defeat this beast of Satan, he exhorted his spellbound audiences. On 21 August, the Queen, who had not dared risk exposing Wenceslaus's embalmed body to a procession through Prague, finally transferred it (under cover of darkness) from the Vyšehrad castle, where she had taken refuge with a garrison of loyal soldiers, to the Hradčany. Even so, she was unable to bury him for another three weeks. Sigismund, who shared his late brother's tendency to procrastinate, did as little as possible as slowly as possible. Appointing Čeněk of Wartenberg as regent until he himself could formally assume the Bohemian crown, Sigismund also conferred upon him the Order of the Dragon, although Čeněk was as heretical a Hussite as anyone else. Sigismund recognised Čeněk's influence among the leading Czech nobles and was willing to go to great lengths to win their support. However, he was not prepared to come to Prague just yet despite urgent pleas from Sofia, panicked over mass assemblies organised by Nicholas that kept getting larger and closer to Prague.

On 17 September, at a huge hilltop gathering near Plzeň, a fiery priest named Wenceslaus Koranda emerged as a leader. Another hilltop assembly took place on 30 September near Benešov, only forty kilometres from Prague. It drew thousands of people from throughout Bohemia and Moravia, and thousands more (including Žižka) came from the capital. Koranda brought a large contingent from Plzeň. The agenda was no longer just religious, but political as well. The assembled multitudes heard Koranda's call to revolution against the servants of Antichrist. 'God's vineyard is flourishing', he warned, 'but the goats are nearing. The time to wander with the pilgrim's staff is over. Now we have to march, sword in hand.' The following day, led by Nicholas and supported by Žižka, Koranda, and Želivský, the Taborites met with the Prague Calixtines and pressed for immediate action, including the election of a Hussite bishop. The Calixtines, led by the University masters, refused; they still regarded themselves as faithful followers of the Catholic Church, and they knew that such an act would effectively cut all ties with Rome.

As rural and urban Hussites became acquainted, some untoward incidents revealed there were already deep divisions between the two groups. The rural folk, seeing the magnificent churches of Prague for the first time, were deeply shocked and offended. They wanted a return to the simple modes of worship practised by early Christians, and they regarded decorative art displays as papist decadence. Like their leaders, they were far more inclined to take direct action than to engage in theological debates. Indignant, they destroyed several paintings and statues in the Old Town Church of St Michael. When the Taborites left Prague, it was on a much less harmonious note than when they entered. Moderate Utraquists, likewise shocked and offended at the outlanders' uncouth barbarism, began having second thoughts about their newly forged alliance.

Arrangements were made for another mass meeting in Prague on 10 November to bring together Hussite representatives from the entire kingdom. Upon learning this, Sofia and Čeněk forbade any and all such meetings in hopes of stemming any further unrest. They also called a conference of the high nobility and Old Town dignitaries on 6 November, who pledged to defend the Queen against anyone attempting to seize power. Large numbers of German mercenaries reinforced the Hradčany garrison and occupied several strategic buildings on the Vlatava's left bank and Charles Bridge, a main artery from Prague to the west. The Old Town leaders hired additional mercenaries, and strict orders were given to prevent Taborites from entering the city. The New Town authorities were deeply alarmed by these ominous measures. Žižka, seeing the Old Town and the Vlatava's entire east bank, including the Hradčany, strongly held by hostiles, knew the Royalists' next step would be to reinforce the Vyšehrad castle, cutting off communication with southern Taborite strongholds and establishing a dominant position over the New Town, the Hussites' stronghold. On 25 October, he led the New Town's militiamen to the Vyšehrad, where the small garrison, commanded by courtiers who knew and sympathised with Žižka, turned over the castle without resistance. This freed the New Town's rear from any threat and counter-balanced the Royalists' occupation of the Hradčany.

As 10 November drew close, both sides prepared for a showdown. Hussite bands from Plzeň, Domažlice, Klatovy, and Sušice totalling some 4,000 took a common route to Prague, escorted by a baron who had joined the Hussites and two young knights. However, another group of pilgrims from Sezimovo Ústí were not so fortunate. At a narrow pass of the Vlatava River near Živohoušť, they were ambushed by a large force led by Lord Peter of Sternberg, a Catholic noble in Sigismund's pay.

Heavy losses were inflicted on the pilgrims, and many were taken prisoner and transported to Kutná Hora to be tortured and thrown down the shafts of the city's silver mines. Kutná Hora was a predominantly Catholic community where fervent German nationalism and religious feeling combined to create fanatical hatred of the Hussites. An accusation was sufficient for execution; without trial, alleged heretics were thrown down the shafts of its silver mines, source of the city's wealth and prestige. If the fall did not kill them, they slowly died from hunger, dehydration, shock, and infection. It is estimated that some 5,000 men, women, and children died during the Hussite wars in this gruesome manner.

News of the ambush reached Prague, arousing fierce passions, and the Hussites temporarily forgot their differences. Moderate Old Town Calixtines were as indignant as New Town radicals. Nicholas, seizing the moment, offered his services. The Old and New Town militias were united under the joint leadership of Nicholas and Žižka. They agreed that the first thing to do was to open up Charles Bridge for Taborites coming from the west. A five-day battle to drive the Royalists from the Lesser Town and establish a bridgehead on the west side of the river succeeded in capturing the Saxon House, archiepiscopal palace, and other strongholds. The Royalists took refuge in the Hradčany, while Sofia fled to the castle of Kunratice. Royalist efforts to re-take the Lesser Town were rebuffed, and the protracted battle levelled the entire district and compelled the residents, mostly Germans, to evacuate. This served the Hussites by denying the Royalists both cover and collaborators. Nonetheless, the victory was inconclusive. Čeněk remained entrenched in the Hradčany and soon received reinforcements. On 6 November, the Royalists issued a challenge of war to the Praguers. Behind the scenes, however, influential moderates in both camps were attempting to prevent a mutually destructive clash. Three days later, a truce was arranged, and four days after that an armistice to last until 23 April 1420 was ratified. Terms stipulated that the Queen and her supporters would hold themselves bound to ensure freedom of Hussite worship; the Praguers agreed to suppress attacks on Catholic monasteries, churches, and statues, and to expel Taborites responsible for such acts. Although the agreement seemed fair, the Royalists pressed for one more condition that was granted with a willingness that probably surprised them – the return of the Vyšehrad.

It was a serious mistake, and Žižka knew it. Prague was now sandwiched between two strong fortresses in Royalist hands, and the balance of power was drastically shifted in their favour. Žižka recognised the ramifications, but his objections were over-ruled by those longing for peace. Disgusted by the surrender, he left the capital and joined the Taborites at Plzeň at the invitation of a sympathetic Koranda. Plzeň, the 'City of the Sun', had become the leading centre of Hussitism. It was one of the 'five towns' to which the hilltop preachers, invoking the Biblical cities of refuge, had urged their followers to flock in order to escape the coming of Antichrist.[11] Žižka knew Plzeň controlled all major roads west to Bavaria and Franconia and would make an ideal Hussite bulwark. Upon arrival, he was immediately appointed Plzeň's militia captain. Shortly thereafter, Žižka led a sortie against local Royalists who, unable to attack Plzeň itself, had been conducting small-scale war against its outlying domains, inflicting considerable damage and death. Their leader, Bohuslav of Švamberg (Schwanenberg), attempted to trap Žižka at a nearby fort named Nekměř. Bohuslav had strong numerical superiority and confidently attacked Žižka, who had seven war wagons 'on which there were those snakes [guns] with which they destroy walls'. Bohuslav's men and horses were taken aback by the unfamiliar noise and smoke and were repulsed with heavy losses. Otherwise insignificant, this skirmish was the first recorded instance of Žižka's use of this new weapon.

Elsewhere, a major development occurred in Sezimovo Ústí, a town belonging to a noble family divided over Hussitism. One local lord, Ulrich, tried to suppress the new beliefs, but a large number of Taborites defeated him. The Taborites realised the town's location in the river valley

11. Josef Macek, *The Hussite Movement in Bohemia* (London: Lawrence & Wishart, 1965), 31. The others were Slaný, Žatec, Louny, and Klatovy. The Biblical passage alluded to, Numbers 35:6–34, actually lists six towns, so Písek was sometimes added to the group to make it accord therewith.

made defence impossible. An old deserted fortress nearby, named Hradiště (meaning 'bulwark'), seemed a much better spot. Located on a steep hill surrounded on three sides by the Lužnice River and a tributary, it belonged to another anti-Hussite Ústí lord in the process of rebuilding it. Aided by his brother, a Hussite, in January and February 1420 the townspeople took the fortress and relocated to it after burning Sezimovo Ústí to the ground. Provisional shelters were erected, and that year's mild winter aided their progress. The community's leading priests believed it would become the new centre of Hussitism and renamed it Tábor. The settlement's elders had been impressed by Žižka during their ill-fated pilgrimage to Prague the previous November. They sent a respectful message to him at Plzeň, informing him of the settlement of Hradiště and asking his assistance in securing their new community. Žižka had a ready and generous response, sending his most trusted officer and a large contingent of fighters.

Meanwhile, differences of opinion between Žižka and Koranda had already occurred. Plzeň was effectively a theocratic dictatorship, and Koranda pulled rank on his new captain. Without consulting Žižka, the headstrong priest destroyed some monasteries and churches built in honour of saints – whose worship was banned by Taborite ideology – and forcibly expelled monks and anti-Hussites from the town. Žižka, who felt war should be conducted by soldiers, not clerics, was troubled. In early February 1420 he wrote to the University masters in Prague, asking their opinion. They answered that under no circumstances could priests fight in battles, adding that laymen with no other option might fight a purely defensive war for their creed. Žižka took both parts of this answer to heart. Throughout his career, he did not participate in any overt aggression against Bohemia's neighbours, acting only in defence when foreign incursion left him no choice. His inquiry demonstrates scruples and lack of arrogance. While asserting command in military matters, he always deferred to the University masters on spiritual questions.

By the end of February 1420, the situation in Plzeň had deteriorated sharply. Its moderate and conservative contingents suffered in silence after seeing what Koranda did to those who dared speak out. However, they began grumbling after mid-month, when Koranda had declared Christ's Second Coming would take place. The date came and went with no divine visitation, and his credibility was undercut even among his most loyal followers. Royalists had blockaded most roads to the city, and the sullen mood of Koranda's opponents became openly hostile. In early March the enemy invested the city and tightened the ring. Žižka, who had resisted any suggestion of surrender, now realised it was only a matter of time before the city fell. Žižka's disappointment was compounded by the recognition that the loss of this strategic city would be a major setback. Reluctantly, he took another look at Tábor's invitation. Twice, he had seen half-hearted popular support subvert military planning and execution. But Tábor's citizenry, unanimously and enthusiastically committed to the Hussite movement, were unlikely to have the mood changes he had seen in Prague and Plzeň – having burned their home town, they had nowhere to go. Hearing of the dire situation at Plzeň, Žižka's friends in Prague advised him to negotiate with the Royalist commander, Wenceslaus of Dubá, and he took their advice. Dubá, a reasonable sort, was not averse to gaining Plzeň by negotiation instead of costly battle. On 20 March, the two commanders agreed to terms. Plzeňers could freely take communion in two kinds without sanction or retribution. Those wishing to leave the city, soldiers or civilians, would be allowed to do so unmolested. Terms would be binding on all Royalist forces, not just those under Dubá's command. Given the guarantee of Utraquist worship, most of the city's Hussites decided to remain. Approximately 400 disciples chose to follow Žižka and Koranda to Tábor, many burning their belongings in the town square before departing on 22 or 23 March.

Žižka has been criticised for his intransigent refusal to negotiate with Royalists when it would have seemed rational to do so. While he scrupulously adhered to his written agreements, time and again Žižka's enemies failed to do likewise. They often rationalised their treachery by asserting that promises made to heretics were not binding. After leaving Plzeň, Žižka suffered the first of many such betrayals when Royalists immediately violated the armistice. Secret messengers sent out by anti-

Hussites in Plzeň had informed Sigismund's allies of Žižka's forthcoming march. First to respond was the fanatic Nicholas Divoký, leading a powerful Kutnohorian contingent. While heading west, they were joined by two smaller bands led by barons Jan Městecký of Opočno and Peter of Sternberg. They proceeded to Písek, through which Žižka's caravan had to pass, and took control of it. Three leading Catholic barons, Bohuslav of Švamberg (Žižka's previous adversary at Nekměř), Hanuš of Kolovraty, and Henry of Hradec, joined them, making their total force about 2,000 men, mostly mounted and heavily armoured lords, knights, and retainers.

On 25 March, Žižka's band forded the Otava River near Sudoměř. After passing the village heading south, he saw the enemy approaching in two columns. Although he would have preferred high ground for a defensive stand, there was none to be had in the wide, flat river valley. Wooded hills to the south were too distant to be reached in time. However, there were empty fishponds nearby, and Žižka situated his troops with one flank against one's dam. He covered his other flank and rear with twelve war wagons. Concentrating his infantrymen in a short but rather deep front, he kept the Royalist cavalry from fully exploiting their superior numbers. The battle began in mid-afternoon and lasted several hours. The first mounted charges were repulsed, and the Royalists were forced to dismount and fight hand-to-hand. They almost breached the wagons and severely damaged three of them before darkness fell with preternatural suddenness. The disconcerted Royalists began striking each other in the confusion, broke off their attack, and retreated.

This battle, minor in conventional military terms, was nonetheless significant. Had Žižka not reached Tábor, the Hussite Revolution would have been nipped in the bud. Instead, Žižka's prestige at Tábor and throughout Bohemia was enhanced by repelling a superior force led by those known as the 'Iron Lords'. This renewed the confidence of those already committed and persuaded others to join. Equally significant was the emerging role of the war wagons. At Nekměř, they had served as an emergency fallback structure; at Sudoměř, they were employed as a calculated tactic, one that would reverse the long-standing superiority of cavalry over infantry. In the battle both sides fought with ferocity and determination, and leading officers on either side were killed. Before retiring, the Royalists captured approximately thirty Hussites, and Divoký ordered them sent to Kutná Hora for torture and execution.

The next morning, Žižka's force headed east and camped to await the Tábor escort that would accompany them on their journey's final leg. Žižka's entrance was a joyous occasion. Standing in front of their tiny makeshift wooden huts to greet the one-eyed man who had just defeated the seemingly invincible 'Iron Lords', the Taborites felt a renewed assurance of success.

Theoretically, Tábor was democratic and egalitarian. Leading representatives, including military leaders, were elected by popular vote. Social divisions and hierarchical structures were eliminated, rents and wages forbidden, debts discharged, taxation abolished, and private property outlawed. Citizens called each other 'brother' and 'sister'.[12] Newcomers were required to deposit superfluous belongings into tubs in the town square. These community chests were administered by clerks who parcelled out the contents according to need, a practice emulated by other Hussite towns. This egalitarianism attracted not only disaffected Bohemians but peasants and urban poor from Austria, Styria, and Poland. However, equality was a relative term, and certain types of individuals rose in the community while others did not. Priests held supreme power and some (including Koranda) behaved like tyrannical dictators. Although women were allowed to preach and even occupy limited leadership roles, patriarchalism was never seriously challenged. Preferential treatment in housing was given to established Taborites at the expense of newcomers. Inevitably, favouritism, corruption, and exploitation arose. Minus stringent bookkeeping or public accountability, some embezzlement, fraud, and pilfering occurred.

But with the question of immediate survival looming, these were not matters of primary concern to Žižka, who left civil administration to the priests. On or around 8 April 1420, the Taborites selected four

12. Thomas A. Fudge, '"Neither Mine nor Thine": Communist Experiments in Hussite Bohemia', *Canadian Journal of History*, April 1998, 4.

captains (*hejtmen*). They elected Nicholas of Pístny (not yet arrived) as first captain by dint of age and stature, followed by Žižka, Zbyněk of Buchov and Chval of Machovice. Nicholas and Žižka functioned as senior officers while Zbyněk and Chval served as deputies. Eventually, Nicholas became the main political leader, in effect prime minister. Žižka took charge of all military affairs. He led drills and battles, settled recruitment policies, determined the selection of enemies and timing of attacks, chose whom to assist or take on as allies, and arranged armistices. He also assumed responsibility for all external political relations, essentially becoming Tábor's foreign minister as well. Žižka began organising, equipping, and training his soldiers under a military principle every bit as revolutionary as the Hussites' religious tenets. Refusing to be bound by conventional wisdom or accepted practice, he calculated how to use his available manpower and resources most effectively. From late March until mid-May 1420, Žižka led small-scale sorties into the surrounding countryside for 'real-world training'. Military education by simulated exercises was then unheard of, and soldiers of that era would have found the notion ludicrous. These 'little wars' – quick, limited strikes at which Žižka had garnered expertise as a highwayman – were perfect for developing tactical cohesion, battle discipline, and aptitude with wagons and weaponry. Rather than push raw, untested troops immediately into full-scale battles, he brought them along gradually with operations within their capabilities. This fostered an incremental sense of confidence in his men that they could go toe-to-toe with professional soldiers. With a series of successful forays, Žižka not only built up morale but also acquired enemy crossbows, handguns, and bombards, which the Taborites could not yet manufacture.

On 5 April, he raided the town of Vožice, sixteen kilometres north-east of Tábor, where Divoký had retired under the protection of a royal castle after the Sudoměř battle. Attacking just before dawn, Žižka's troops forced Divoký 's surprised men to retreat to the castle, but not before Žižka had taken a large number of prisoners. After transporting them to Tábor, he was able to exchange them for the thirty-odd Hussites taken at Sudoměř, sparing them death at the bottom of a mine shaft. He

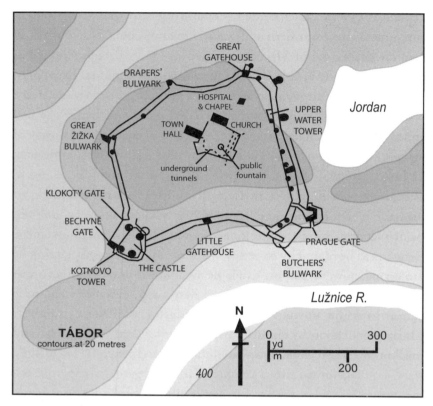

GREAT
GATEHOUSE

DRAPERS'
BULWARK

HOSPITAL
& CHAPEL

GREAT
ŽIŽKA
BULWARK

TOWN
HALL

CHURCH

UPPER
WATER
TOWER

Jordan

underground
tunnels

public
fountain

KLOKOTY GATE

BECHYNĚ
GATE

LITTLE
GATEHOUSE

PRAGUE GATE

KOTNOVO
TOWER

THE CASTLE

BUTCHERS'
BULWARK

Lužnice R.

N

TÁBOR
contours at 20 metres

0

yd
m

300

200

400

Tábor

also captured arms and riding horses, valuable commodities in short
supply. He immediately began training young townsmen and peasants
in mounted warfare, disregarding the convention that only nobles fought
on horseback. A few days later, Žižka led a raid against Sedlec castle,
home to Ulrich of Ústí, the lord who had attempted to prevent
Sezimovo Ústí's residents from joining the Taborites. Many of Žižka's
fighters were former townsmen, and they fought with a vengeance.
Ulrich and all his retainers were killed, and six prisoners were told that
if any one of them was willing to behead the other five, he would be
spared – an offer taken up by a man named Pinta.

Next was the liberation of Písek. Žižka's men had little difficulty
putting the Royalist garrison there to flight, an important achievement.

Písek was one of the first towns to join the revolution, and its re-conquest demonstrated that Royalist victories could be reversed. It became the strongest and most important Taborite settlement west of the Vlatava River. In late April, a final sortie was undertaken against Prachatice, only thirty-two kilometres from the Bavarian and Austrian borders. The town's mostly Germans inhabitants fled when the Taborites approached, and Žižka, lacking sufficient men to garrison the town, demolished part of its wall so it could not be used as a defensive position by future enemies. Then, it was vital to make Tábor an impregnable fortress, and Žižka did it masterfully. He ordered a triple wall built on the narrow neck between the two rivers east of the town, strengthening the town's position atop a steep peninsula nearly surrounded by water. Rough hexagonal, the fortress was enhanced by tower bastions at all six projecting corners, and only one gate leading to the bridge over the Lužnice. The final result was so strong that when an urgent request for help arrived from Prague on 16 May, Žižka did not hesitate to answer, taking several thousand Hussite warriors while leaving behind a relatively small number of fighters to defend Tábor in his absence.

Chapter 3

THE EMPEROR STRIKES

Resistance to the organised mass can be effected only by
the man who is as well organised in his individuality as
the mass itself.

Carl Gustav Jung, *The Undiscovered Self*

In late 1419, Sigismund finally came to Bohemia. Arriving in Brno on
15 December, he called the Diet of the Bohemian estates together, then
informed various German princes, the Teutonic Knights, and King
Władyslaw of Poland that he would hold court in Breslau (modern
Wrocław) in early 1420. He then briefly returned to Hungary to meet
his long-estranged wife, Barbara. Though she had been accused of
adultery, they finally reconciled following Władyslaw's repeated urging.
Sigismund was not the forgiving type, but her father still governed
Celje, and she had many friends and supporters in Hungary, where his
position was still weak, and Poland, where her late sister had been
Queen. He then returned to Brno, where the highest-ranking clergy
and lords of the kingdom had gathered. At this time Queen Sofia told
Sigismund that, given the turmoil sweeping the country, she could no
longer perform her royal duties. Sigismund confirmed Čeněk as regent
and appointed two Catholic barons to the next highest positions.

Although the Czech nobles hoped for a clear resolution to the
questions raised the previous September, Sigismund remained evasive,
implying he would not prevent anyone from receiving communion in
the two kinds. Although vague, this satisfied the nobles, and they paid

him homage as their rightful ruler. While only a formal coronation could officially make him king, this established feudal allegiance and was therefore a political victory for Sigismund.

The next matter was unrest in the royal towns, especially Prague, and representatives from the capital city appeared on 27 December. The Emperor kept them waiting two days before deigning to see them. They knelt before him, asked forgiveness for their city's disobedience, and requested a public hearing to explain themselves. Sigismund was stern, keeping them prostrated while flinging fierce invective. They were finally allowed to rise to their feet, given no promises, and told that Prague would not be forgiven until all chains and rails barricading the city streets were removed and its fortifications demolished. They were also told that all harassment of Catholic priests must cease immediately and those driven out must be allowed to return unmolested.

In early January 1420, the representatives returned to Prague and made their report. The councils of both the Old and New Towns felt they had no choice but to submit. The barricades were removed, and many Catholic priests immediately returned to Prague along with Germans who had also fled. The Germans triumphantly declared that the Hussite heresy would soon be wiped away. The Prague Hussites were understandably fearful for their immediate prospects. Sigismund then purged all the pro-Hussite royal officials, particularly burgraves of the royal castles, and it seemed he would quickly and easily dispose of the Hussite problem.

But the last centres of resistance had to be subdued, particularly Plzeň, before Sigismund could assume the crown. Plzeň was besieged successfully, yet he still did not go to Prague. His Bohemian advisors argued against bringing foreign soldiers, insisting it would arouse nationalist sentiment and imperil any deal. Sigismund disregarded their advice and proceeded to Breslau where he conferred with various German princes and Roman prelates. He apparently decided against any compromise and displayed far more intolerance. On 5 January 1420, a royal decree was read in every town marketplace throughout the kingdom. Bohemians were to cease assisting the three towns still actively opposed to him (Plzeň, Písek, and Hradec Králové), submit to all orders from the Catholic Church, and desist from gathering in large groups, spreading rumours, or criticising him.

Sigismund then arbitrated the lingering dispute between Poland and the Teutonic Knights, and his decision strongly favoured the Prussians. The Poles were temporarily allowed to occupy the disputed territory but could not fortify it. After the deaths of Władyslaw and Vytautas, the territory would revert to the Order; both rulers were livid when they learned of this. Sigismund wanted good relations with the Knights, but he turned Poland and Lithuania into mortal enemies.

After two months of routine civil administration, Sigismund took further strong action. A prominent Prague merchant in Breslau on business, Jan Krása, was denounced for speaking disrespectfully of the treatment and execution of Hus and Jerome by the Council of Constance. Arrested and taken to court, he was tortured to make him recant and admit that communion in two kinds was sinful heresy. Krása refused and was dragged by horses through the town streets. Still defiant, he was burned at the stake. When news of this incident spread, it became clear that any peaceful assurances by Sigismund were not to be trusted. It seemed obvious he intended to eliminate not just the Taborites but all Hussites. This perception was confirmed on 7 March, when he issued a call to arms throughout Silesia and Lusatia; the next day a papal legate declared a crusade against the Bohemian heretics. On 15 March, Krása was executed, and Sigismund declared heresy a capital offence entailing the loss of all possessions of the family of anyone so accused. Sigismund knew very well that his German mercenaries would take this as a licence to kill and rob at will.

Although Sigismund had discarded his tactic of telling different Czechs different things, he was determined to divide them as much as possible before setting out against them militarily. He hoped to convince the nobility, including the Hussites among them, not to support rebellious townspeople and peasants. After subduing the lower classes, he could then deal with the nobles. Sigismund had brought Čeněk, the ranking Hussite, to Breslau, treating him with great pomp and bestowing numerous honours upon him to win him over. Possessing ingratiating manners that gave the impression of great sincerity, Čeněk was one of the most two-faced men ever to hold high office in Bohemia. As one of society's upper echelon, he wanted to join the King in keeping with his upbringing. However, he had genuine feeling for the Czech nation and sympathised with many religious reforms the Hussites advocated, and he had protected them during the movement's early days. Čeněk was horrified by Sigismund's determination to exterminate the Hussites but realised he could not be dissuaded. Consequently, he said nothing, and Sigismund believed Čeněk had rejoined the fold. On 10 April 1420, the king left for Schweidnitz in Lower Silesia, and Čeněk headed to Prague, where Krása's execution had hardened attitudes. That episode and the newly declared crusade made it clear that Sigismund would settle for nothing less than total abandonment of Hussitism by all Czechs. Even conservatives were dismayed, and radicals were re-energised. Želivský had been quiet, but he now re-emerged with fierce new sermons against Sigismund, rallying Prague to a renewed spirit of resistance. On 3 April, councillors and magistrates of the Old and New Towns, University masters, and all Hussite priests met at the Old Town's city hall. They pledged mutual defence and swore to fight for their religion, if necessary at the cost their lives. They reorganised the city's military structure, electing four captains from both towns, each with ten sub-captains. They strengthened the city defences and dug a deep moat south of the New Town as fortification against any attack from the Vyšehrad.

By these actions, Prague became the leading city of Hussite resistance, and its leaders sent messages to all other Bohemian towns requesting delegates to arrange for mutual defence. They condemned the papal bull and pronounced the Church an evil stepmother to the Czech people. Appealing to nationalism, they added a reminder that Germans had exterminated the Slavs of eastern Germany centuries earlier and intended to do the same thing to Bohemian Slavs. In all, 1,400 German families and many Catholic clerics from both towns departed. Allowed to take their movable goods, some took refuge with the Hradčany and Vyšehrad garrisons. Others fled into the hinterland to be safely removed from the anticipated attack on Prague.

Čeněk returned from Breslau on 15 April. He had been in touch with the city authorities and informed them he would adhere to their resolution of 3 April. He then took several sweeping measures that surprised Sigismund. First, Čeněk secured the Hradčany, arresting two devoutly Catholic lieutenants in charge – even though they were his relatives. He posted officers upon whom he could rely throughout the castle and evicted the priests and Germans who had taken shelter there. Less considerate than the Prague authorities, Čeněk made them leave their money and jewellery behind. He rallied most of the Hussite nobility against Sigismund by renouncing allegiance to him and returning the prestigious Order of the Dragon medal. On 20 April, he addressed a manifesto to all Bohemians and Moravians co-signed by Ulrich of Rožmberk, although Rožmberk's name was probably attached without his permission.

This manifesto included the first version of the revolution's most important document. It directed Czechs not to submit to Sigismund or obey him, declaring he had been neither elected nor crowned and was in fact the Bohemian kingdom's enemy. Ten specific accusations were made, including the insult of heresy and Sigismund's complicity in Hus's death, the Kutná Hora atrocities, and the papal crusade. Sigismund, the document stated, intended to destroy the Bohemian nation and exterminate its people. Invoking the ancestral spirits, it warned that anyone following Sigismund would forfeit honour, life, and property, while declaring that no true Czech would commit such a transgression. The manifesto closed by listing what eventually became the 'Four Articles of Prague'. The declaration was rapidly disseminated throughout Bohemia, even reaching several foreign countries. It electrified everyone by announcing that the highest-ranking Czech nobleman, the country's regent, had sided with Prague against Sigismund and the Holy Roman Empire. Čeněk had recently come from the Emperor's court, so his accusations carried tremendous weight and roused the population to action.

The Hussite revolution now had a clear and concise statement of its aims. The Four Articles declared the freedom of all Czechs to take communion in two kinds, the right to free preaching of God's word in Czech throughout the kingdom, the obligation of priests to live holy lives free from materialism and sensuality, and the denial of all charges against Czechs as heretics. Although wording and order were changed over time, these articles remained essentially constant, basic tenets of faith upon which all Hussites, from conservatives to radicals, could agree. As a core set of beliefs, this document fostered a new sense of unity across the movement.

On 23 April, the previously arranged armistice expired, and scores of Hussite nobles, lords, and knights issued challenges to Sigismund. Most of these noblemen, although politically conservative, had become practicing Hussites, and many had begun taking communion in both kinds. They had been reluctant to oppose Sigismund, feeling that he was their 'natural lord'. However, Čeněk's reversal allowed them to renounce their loyalties. This new coalition immediately took diplomatic and military action. Čeněk knew that Poland and Lithuania were now fierce enemies of Sigismund and would be likely to support anyone hostile to him. He dispatched a Hussite nobleman, Werner of Rankov, to offer Władyslaw the Bohemian crown. Although the Polish King did not say yes, he did not refuse, either, though his ambivalent reply did not reach Prague for several weeks, and by then there had been significant developments. However, the door remained open to this option and would later be revisited.

A community similar to Tábor, known as Oreb, had been established in and around the town of Hrádec Králové in eastern Bohemia. Their spiritual leader, a priest named Ambrose, mobilised a large number of followers for a march to Prague. These Orebites were commanded by Lord Hynek Krušina, who was subsequently elected captain-general of Prague's military forces. His troops reinforced the ongoing siege of the Vyšehrad, which was unsuccessful despite repeated efforts. Although Krušina accepted the appointment, he soon left Prague without explanation, so the city was without expert military leadership. His departure may have been related to wavering on the part of Čeněk and more especially Ulrich of Rožmberk. In addition, Žižka had been carrying on small-scale warfare in southern Bohemia, burning castles and monasteries. Although this was the most effective action being taken against the Royalists, it displeased Čeněk. He may have been disturbed by some atrocities committed by the Taborites, or perhaps he was discouraged by the repeated failure to take the Vyšehrad. What seems fairly certain is that, although Čeněk was drawn to the religious elements of the Hussite revolution, he recoiled from its political implications. As a nobleman and courtier, he was horrified by the peasant revolutionaries threatening to overturn the established social order.

Sigismund left Schweidnitz in late April 1420 with approximately 20,000 men, mainly Germans. He entered Bohemia on or about 1 May and learned that Ambrose and Hynek Krušina had taken Hradec Králové's militia to Prague. The town was virtually defenceless and, though most residents were Czech, resistance was impossible. Its German minority enthusiastically welcomed Sigismund, who dismissed all Czechs on the city council and replaced them with Germans. The papal legate, Ferdinand, declared that anyone renouncing Hussitism would be forgiven. The Emperor had tempered his attitude in light of the national front unexpectedly formed against him. He had been sure that the Hussite nobility was with him, and dividing his enemies seemed more important than ever. Learning of Čeněk's about-face, Sigismund treated it as an opportunity rather than a setback. He had two trusted Bohemian advisors covertly approach Čeněk and offer a two-week armistice. Negotiations soon revealed Sigismund would be able to do better. Čeněk's only insistent demand was freedom for Bohemians to take communion in both kinds. If Sigismund agreed to that, he would turn the Hradčany over to the Emperor – whom he had denounced as the Czech nation's deadliest enemy two weeks earlier. Sigismund quickly agreed. The arrangement, actually a betrayal, was kept secret for the time being.

Sigismund's ambassadors also contacted both Prague city councils, assuring them the Emperor desired a peaceful solution. He had apparently softened his hard stance at Breslau, returning to the willingness to compromise he displayed at Brno. The diplomats informed Prague's leaders that Sigismund would receive a delegation for the public hearing they had requested at Kutná Hora. The councillors, aware of Sigismund's unreliability, were sceptical. However, Čeněk urged that the Emperor's offer be accepted, claiming nothing could be lost. The councillors, as yet unaware Čeněk had betrayed them, were persuaded by his smooth eloquence. The city was shocked and outraged the next day when it learned Čeněk had surrendered the castle and opened its gates to 4,000 German troops. Both of Prague's great castles were again in enemy hands due to treachery by the man they had praised as a national hero. The furious Praguers' first impulse was to take vengeance on the traitor, but he was beyond their reach. In angry frustration, they tried to storm the castle anyhow. Although the poorly organised assault failed, it compelled Čeněk to leave town quickly. However, the newly reinforced garrison inflicted heavy casualties on the Hussite attackers. An equally ill-planned attack on the Vyšehrad also failed and provoked a counter-attack on the New Town which inflicted serious damage.

Prague was demoralised, and things looked dire. With Sigismund less than a hundred kilometres away and both castles in enemy hands, it was difficult to see how the city could hold out. A defeatist mood prevailed, and the radicals advocating continued resistance were outvoted as letters of challenge from Royalist and Catholic lords and knights kept arriving. Again, submission seemed the only option. An emissary was sent to the Royalist commanders at the Hradčany. They were willing to grant an armistice, so on 12 May a six-day truce was instituted while a Prague delegation went to Kutná Hora to plead their case with Sigismund. As this was occurring, Sigismund triumphantly entered Kutná Hora. Many Catholic refugees were there, including Germans who had fled Prague and clerics from churches and monasteries destroyed by the Hussites. They were overjoyed, confident Sigismund's huge imperial army camped outside their city walls would soon inflict a fatal blow on the Czech heretics.

Two days later, the Prague delegation arrived. Everyone including Sigismund assumed they would ask for surrender terms and meekly accept. The audience he granted resembled the one five months earlier at Brno. Again, six elderly men including two University masters knelt before Sigismund and implored forgiveness. Again, Sigismund scowled furiously and did not present his terms before covering them with a lengthy, violent stream of humiliating abuse. However, it was not a complete reprise. This time, in return for one concession – the freedom to take communion in both kinds – the Praguers offered not only to open the city gates but to destroy a section of the city wall through which Sigismund might enter as lord and master. But this was not enough for Sigismund, who stipulated more drastic conditions without even acknowledging the religious issue. All barricades and fortifications would have to be completely removed, and the citizens completely disarmed. All weapons were to be collected and delivered to either the Hradčany or the Vyšehrad. Upon fulfillment of those conditions, Sigismund declared, he would enter Prague and grant its citizens whatever grace he deemed fit.

It was all too clear to the stunned residents of Prague what this meant – total and unconditional surrender. They would be completely defenceless against any measures the Emperor might inflict on Hussites unwilling to renounce their faith – which might include being dragged through the streets and publicly beheaded. The news eliminated any indecision or internal debate. By taking an unrelenting hard line and disdaining the advice of his Bohemian councillors, Sigismund overplayed his hand and lost his last best opportunity for a peaceful solution. Overnight, the vast majority of Prague's citizens united in the conviction that surrender on Sigismund's terms was unthinkable. Moderates and radicals, University masters, and the urban poor spoke with one voice. Rather than disarm and dismantle their fortifications, they immediately strengthened their defences and re-doubled all barricades and fortifications. However, they knew that without help their position was hopeless. The enemy was simply too strong. Despite continual friction between Prague moderates and Tábor radicals, any objections to re-forming their alliance were now insignificant. There was no time to waste in debate. The city sent messengers to all potential allies, particularly the Hussite towns of southern and western Bohemia, requesting help with as much speed and strength as could be mustered. The most important of these requests was received at Tábor on 16 May by Žižka.

*

Žižka left Tábor for Prague with a much different force than that he took from Plzeň less than two months earlier. He had approximately 9,000 men, many accompanied by wives and children. Weaponry included guns and crossbows for the wagon crews, and lances, maces, and flails for the foot soldiers. A few hundred were mounted, and he had a large number of war wagons and others for supply. Prague had urgently requested Žižka make all possible speed, and he did. The normal speed of a medieval army was a maximum of 24–30 kilometres a day. Žižka's Taborites covered forty kilometres by forced march in one day, reaching Benešov, halfway to Prague, early on 19 May. Like all generals, Žižka knew that speed was often the difference between victory and defeat.

The Royalists, naturally, did not want Žižka's troops reinforcing Prague. They knew their best chance to stop him was before he crossed the largest obstacle in his way, the Sázava River, but they missed that opportunity. At Benešov, six miles short of the river, a weak force of 400 cavalry was all that stood in Žižka's way. After being reinforced by some infantrymen from the town, the Royalists prepared for battle. Žižka sent some men around the Royalist flank and set fire to the town in their rear. Seeing that, the Royalists retreated to a strongly walled monastery. Žižka made a cursory attempt to storm it but did not waste time on repeated attacks, recognising that his priority was getting to Prague as quickly as possible. Having neutralised the enemy forces as an obstacle, he forded the Sázava near the village of Poříčí.

While making camp near the river's north shore, Žižka's scouts informed him that two strong enemy columns from Kutná Hora and

Hradec Králové were approaching, as well as a smaller force from the south-west. Combined, they were considerably stronger than the Taborites. The Hradec Králové troops were commanded by Wenceslaus of Dubá; the Kutná Hora contingent signalled the first appearance of Florentine Count Philip (known as Pippo Spano), one of Europe's most highly regarded mercenary generals. At late evening, Žižka formed his wagons on a hill overlooking the Sázava valley and had a ditch quickly dug around the formation. The battle began shortly after sundown and was a Taborite victory. Though Royalist losses were light, it was evident they could not take the entrenched Hussite formation. They retired, leaving their dead and many battle standards behind. In a sense, Poříčí was a repetition of Sudoměř: after an initial Royalist charge failed, no attempt was made to continue the battle. Medieval fatalism had caused even an acclaimed *condottiere* to give up after one repulse without even considering other options.

The road to Prague was open, and after another day's march Žižka's force arrived at the capital on 20 May. They were given a tumultuous welcome. Large crowds greeted them at the gates, and once safely inside they were feted with food and drink to a degree these rustic peasants must have found overwhelming. Taborite women were lodged in a monastery, and Žižka took his men to a large island north of the city, today called Štvanice. It was the safest location; a surprise attack on it was virtually impossible. Žižka gave his troops one day of rest, which many spent touring Prague. They were again scandalised by the luxurious fashions of affluent residents – ladies' fine gowns, jewellery, and veils; gentlemen's elegantly groomed beards and moustaches. Some became so indignant they forcibly attempted to cut off these latter displays of personal vanity. Angry complaints about unwanted barber service were registered, and Žižka's commanders strictly forbade further molestations and tightened discipline generally, stressing the need for constant readiness.

On 22 May, Žižka took a strong detachment to the Vlatava's west bank after learning a large supply convoy was being escorted to the Hradčany by Royalist troops. With little difficulty, Žižka's raiders ran off the escort, captured several prisoners, and took nineteen wagons heavily loaded with supplies including badly needed food. The following day, Hussite troops from Žatec, Louny, and Slaný arrived, and there were many mouths to feed. Although Sigismund did not yet move against Prague, he tried to intimidate its residents with a show of force, hoping to convince them to surrender. He left Kutná Hora on 21 or 22 May, and after two days camped near Litožice, fifteen kilometres east of Prague. Told of the Hussite ambush of the supply train intended for the Hradčany garrison, he elected not to risk open battle, and when a strong Hussite force approached, he retreated to Kutná Hora.

Žižka had not yet been given overall command of Prague's military forces. However, his experience, leadership skills, proven bravery, and recent victories, along with his strength of personality, gave him decisive influence in Prague's war councils. Unlike prior raids and small-scale sallies, his focus now was defensive. Protecting Prague was essential to the Hussite movement's survival. But Žižka was not a man simply to wait, using what time he had upgrading Prague's disadvantaged position. With both royal castles in enemy hands, Praguers were vulnerable regardless of any defensive measures. Žižka could not engage both strongholds simultaneously, so he concentrated on the Hradčany. He may have been influenced by lingering bitterness, remembering that after taking the Vyšehrad the preceding October, that accomplishment was undone by timid Prague authorities. Instead of the light force holding it then, the Vyšehrad was now heavily garrisoned under Lord Všembera of Boskovice, a competent and highly regarded Moravian officer.

Nonetheless, the primary factor influencing Žižka's strategic thinking was the Hradčany's food shortage after his capture of its re-supply convoy. He could starve out the garrison without a direct assault. However, he could not ignore the Vyšehrad. The moat dug to defend the New Town from it had been partially filled in during the fighting in May. He gave orders to dig a new moat – deeper, wider, and further north, hence less susceptible to attacks from the castle. Prague women, Taborite and Hussite wives, young boys, priests, and Jews did most of this fortification building. They worked willingly, knowing that if

Sigismund's German mercenaries took the town, none would be spared. On 30 May, after several days of strenuous effort, the fortifications were manned by Prague militiamen and Orebite soldiers. Two days earlier, Žižka's Taborites had begun besieging the Hradčany, forcing Sigismund to act. The Emperor realised that losing the Hradčany would be a significant defeat. He made some diversionary attacks to draw away Hussites assisting Prague. He marched north-east in a wide arc around the city and convinced the town of Louny to surrender, falsely claiming Prague had already done so. Zajíc of Hasenburg had successfully pulled the same trick a few days earlier on the nearby town of Slaný. While it surely distressed the militia from these towns to learn of this, the ploy failed. The men from Louny and Slaný, recognising Sigismund's strategy, did not abandon their stations in Prague.

The Hradčany's food shortage grew worse, and Hussite guns inflicted serious damage. The garrison was reduced to eating horsemeat and grew increasingly disgruntled. Large numbers of Czechs deserted to the Hussites. Sigismund, after camping briefly south of Prague, approached the Hradčany on 12 June with his entire force and another food supply train. He knew Žižka was eager to do battle and cleverly took advantage. Drawing up his army in battle formation, he waited while the Hussite troops formed to accept his challenge. This distraction allowed the convoy to slip through. As soon as this was accomplished, Sigismund quickly retreated. Although Žižka gave pursuit, the Royalist army escaped with only light casualties to its rearguard. Sigismund had outfoxed Žižka. Now, the Hradčany's garrison could not be starved out before the main crusading army arrived. Consequently, Žižka broke off the siege on 14 June and focused entirely on strengthening Prague's defences.

Clearly, civic and military reorganisation was needed. There was continual friction between rural Taborites and urban Hussites. Although Taborite commanders attempted to restrain their forces from unauthorised acts of violence, Taborite women (unlike the men, not sequestered outside the city) burned the monastery of St Catherine in the New Town after forcibly evicting the resident nuns. This was one of several episodes of women-on-women violence during the Hussite wars. Most Hussite women travelled with the army as unofficial auxiliaries, and they felt less bound to obey commanders, though Žižka made it clear that all members of his army, including its female camp followers, were to observe military discipline under threat of severe penalties. This incident evoked memories of previous Taborite vandalism of Prague religious sites, and the city council complained stridently. While Taborite leaders had tried to prevent such acts, many secretly sympathised, having grown critical of a perceived lack of zealous reformism on the part of the Prague authorities. Mutual finger-pointing became so pitched that a meeting of the New and Old Town leaders, University masters, and representatives of the city's allies was called.

The imminent danger facing them all helped the assembled leaders quickly resolve their squabbles. New city councils were elected in both towns in which radical elements had stronger voices. Both councils carried out a full-scale purge of all 'enemies of the law of God', the term for those unwilling to accept communion in both kinds, including many German Catholics still in the city. Officials went door-to-door, asking the head of each family (or the wife if the husband was not at home), to sign a solidarity pledge to the cause of the Chalice. Any refusing, including wives and children left behind by German men who had fled earlier, were expelled from the city. Their houses were confiscated and given to Taborites and other allies. While serving as a 'religious cleansing', this also left the city relatively free of potential traitors. The term 'Fifth Column' would not appear until five centuries later, but Praguers were quite familiar with the concept.

The assembled leaders also made the first of several refinements to the 'Four Articles'. Originally, the fourth point had only demanded that Bohemia be cleared of the accusation of heresy. This article now emphasised the punishment of all deadly sins, a result of increased Taborite and Orebite influence in the city councils. The Four Articles, with some changes, stood throughout the Hussite wars as the revolution's defining principles, and the over-riding purpose of these long and arduous conflicts was their preservation and defence.

Žižka insisted that the military command structure should also be overhauled. Twelve captains were elected, four each from the Old Town, the New Town, and from Tábor and the other allies. This helped integrate the various groups by blurring local and regional distinctions. Although troops designated for mobile operations like sallies maintained their original grouping, defensive forces manning the battlements came to have a sense of collective identity, damping down intramural bickering. While undocumented, it seems likely Žižka had again been named Prague's captain-general, given his dominating influence in determining general strategy and the organisation of the city defences.

Two events elsewhere affected Prague's preparations. On 31 May, Sigismund ordered Ulrich of Rožmberk to attack Tábor, the second most powerful Hussite stronghold after Prague. He considered this mission so important he gave Ulrich some elite Austrian troops commanded by Leopold Krajíř, Budějovice's royal governor. This force besieged the fortress city while Ulrich personally visited Sigismund, solemnly renouncing Hussitism for himself, his vassals, friends, retainers, and subjects. The Taborite commanders at Prague could only dispatch Nicholas of Pístny with 350 cavalrymen to Tábor's aid. This small mounted contingent, probably all the Hussites had, was of little value in Prague and hence easily spared. As Nicholas approached Tábor, he sent a messenger to sneak into the city. The defenders were told that Nicholas would attack shortly before dawn on 30 June and instructed to sally out at that time. This co-ordinated attack was completely successful. Squeezed between the two forces, Royalists besiegers suffered heavy losses and hastily retreated, leaving behind large supplies of food, money, and armaments, including heavy siege guns. Infuriated, Rožmberk could do little except order all Hussite priests he could get his hands on imprisoned and starved to death. After this, he became one of Žižka's most implacable and dangerous enemies.

The Hussites had another significant victory in eastern Bohemia. Hradec Králové, strategically situated where the Elbe River becomes navigable, had been taken by imperial forces after Krušina marched its militia to Prague's assistance. There, like Želivský in Prague and Koranda in Plzeň, Ambrose had agitated against the Catholic Church even before the outbreak of the Hussite Revolution, and he was the acknowledged reformist leader in the upper Elbe valley. There, as in southern Bohemia, large-scale hilltop religious assemblies were held, mainly at a hill near Třebechovice, a few kilometres east of Hradec Králové. Like the Taborites, Ambrose and his followers gave their favourite hill a new, biblically-inspired designation, the militant name 'Oreb' from the books of Isaiah and Judges.[1]

The Orebite community espoused the same puritanical beliefs and rituals as Tábor. They also shared a hatred of German monks living in luxury at the expense of the Czech peasantry, and en route to Prague in May the Orebites destroyed the great monastery at Hradiště, which had dominated the region. However, there were significant differences between the Taborites and Orebites. The latter did not go quite as far in rejecting Roman Catholic teachings and practices, and they did not develop the chiliastic fanaticism that characterised Tábor radicals. Generally speaking, they were more pragmatic, largely due to Ambrose. Energetic and determined, Ambrose was nonetheless cool under fire and a far better politician than most other Hussite priests. Suspended by Queen Sofia as Hradec Králové's parish priest in early 1419, Ambrose became the region's undisputed Hussite leader after the revolution erupted. He was in Prague in November 1419 and participated in the five-day battle in Lesser Town. It was then, if not before, that he and Žižka probably met, and their acquaintance developed into a close and life-long friendship.

Ambrose got along with people from all stations and walks of life, and he was able to recruit several important barons and knights to the Hussite cause. These included the aforementioned Hynek Krušina of Lichtenburg, Aleš Vřešťovský of Riesenburg, and Diviš Bořek of Miletínek, each of whom became a significant figure in the movement.

1. Isaiah 10: 26 and Judges 7: 25, named as the location where Gideon defeated the Midianites. Mount Tabor is mentioned in Judges 4: 6–16 as the site where Barak organized ten thousand men for a decisive military route of Sisera, captain of Canaanite King Jabin's army.

Ambrose recognised the strategic importance of Hradec Králové and would not resign himself to its capture and occupation. He then displayed the rationality, initiative, and courage which endeared him to Žižka. While he very much wanted to retake Hradec Králové, he did not wish to weaken Prague's defence by taking his troops there, realising that if Prague fell all other Hussite cities were doomed. On his own initiative, he sneaked out of Prague, eluding Royalist patrol lines, and met with Lord Aleš and two squires near Pardubice. They collected and armed some local peasants and early on 25 June assaulted Hradec Králové, overwhelming the surprised German garrison. Aleš was well prepared for Sigismund's counter-measures. After several unsuccessful attacks, the Emperor decided his troops were needed more urgently in Prague and lifted the siege in early July. Hradec Králové became a solid Hussite stronghold and the centre of the Orebite movement. Under Ambrose, it maintained close co-operation with Žižka until the latter's death.

As the first great anti-Hussite crusade marched towards Prague, most of the country was still dominated by the Emperor's royal castles and towns and those of the anti-Hussite Czech nobility. The pending attack on Prague began to take definite shape. The city's strength would require a well-planned and organised assault, and the defenders anticipated a prolonged siege. The Royalists held the two great castles dominating the city north and south, the Hradčany and the Vyšehrad. These positions controlled all roads to the north-west, west, and south. From the hill on which the Hradčany sits, a high plateau runs east, overlooking the city and dominating most of the Vlatava's west bank and any approach from the north. In addition, the Royalists would easily be able to occupy the hills south of the Hradčany, choking off the only other possible route on the river's west bank.

On the east bank, where the main part of the city was located, the situation was somewhat better, although the south was completely closed off by the Vyšehrad. An unfortified expanse nearly five kilometres wide lay between the castle and the New Town's walls, dominated by two natural elevations. Some soft hills rise in the district later called the 'Royal Vineyards' (or Vinohradský, the name by which this Prague area

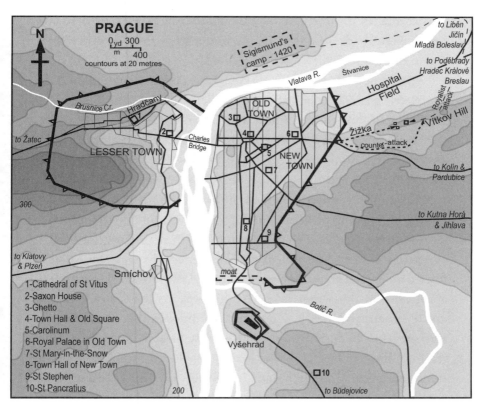

Prague and the battle of the Vítkov, 1420

is known today). Further north, a long, steep, narrow ridge known as Vítkov (St Vitus Hill) runs parallel to the river, which turns sharply east after flowing past the Hradčany. North of the Vítkov is a narrow strip of low-lying flood plain. Now the Karlín district of present-day Prague, it was then known as Hospital Field (*Špitálské pole*) after a thirteenth-century cloister, church, and hospital built by the Knights of the Cross with the Red Star.[2] Through it ran the main road from Prague to the north-east and the towns of Brandýs, Mladá Boleslav, and Nymburk. To the south of the Vítkov, through what today is Prague's Žižkov

2. The name Karlín was established in 1717, when authorities in what was then a Prague suburb requested it be called Karolinenthal (the Karoline Valley) in honour of the Austrian Emperor's new bride. After some clumsy translations – perhaps intentionally so – into Czech, it eventually crystallised into Karlín.

district, ran the main road to the east and the towns of Český Brod and Kolín. Both roads were vital supply routes from the rich agricultural region of the Elbe valley.

Žižka knew that, if the Vítkov were taken, Prague would be completely encircled, choked of all supplies, and eventually forced into submission. As long as the Vítkov was held and those two supply routes were maintained, the less risky option of a blockade combined with a low-level siege would be foreclosed to the Royalists. Just as Sigismund had stymied his attempt to starve out the Hradčany garrison, Žižka could thwart any attempt by the Emperor to do the same to Prague's defenders. The only structure on the Vítkov was an old watchtower at its crest built to protect vineyards on its south slope. Just north of it, closer to the steep northern slope, Žižka erected two small wooden forts, a moat, and an earthen wall reinforced with rocks. He garrisoned approximately thirty men in each fort to ensure the hill would not be taken by surprise attack. Žižka had confidence that the Taborites stationed in the forts would hold off any assault long enough for reinforcements to be sent. Other measures included cutting down some trees and levelling a few houses impairing sight lines. Just after all conceivable steps had been taken, huge masses of enemy soldiers, horses, and tents began appearing on the plateau across the river north of the city.

*

Sigismund had assembled a vast international army, approximately 80,000 strong, drawn from thirty-three nations across Europe from Spain to Russia. Along with nobles, knights, and squires were numerous clerics up to the rank of archbishop, as well as retainers, townsmen, and peasants. They had been promised forgiveness of their sins and exemption from purgatory, but they were professional mercenary soldiers who nonetheless expected pay for their efforts, and they had been told there would be much plunder to be had in the sack of Prague. Assembled on the plateau high on the Vlatava's west bank, they looked down at Prague and taunted the defenders with chants of 'Ha, Ha! Hus,

Hus! Heretic, Heretic!' Any Czech unfortunate enough to fall into their hands was burned to death, even non-Hussites. Most of them were driven by hatred: they did not want merely to defeat the Hussites and conquer Prague, but were intent on wiping out every last man, woman, and child within its walls.

Sigismund realised that even with his four- or perhaps five-to-one numerical superiority, an all-out siege of the city was not going to be easy. But he knew that with the Vyšehrad and Hradčany in his control, he had but to secure the two roads heading north-east and east from Prague to seal off the city. This would turn the large number of defenders from an asset into a liability, since they would quickly consume their food supplies. However, because this strategy was so militarily sound and rational, Žižka anticipated it. On 14 July 1420, shortly after noon, several thousand cavalrymen from Meissen, Thuringia, Silesia, and Hungary crossed the Vlatava north of the city where it turns towards Libeň. Proceeding south, they started up the east end of the Vítkov, which rises in a long, gradual slope. The main force in Prague did not notice them until they had already begun assaulting the wooden bulwark. After crossing the moat and taking the old watchtower, they attacked the earthen wall. There were only twenty-six men, two women and one girl defending it, but they did not flinch. Without guns, they were reduced to hurling stones and lances. One woman showed special courage and led a counter-charge, reportedly shouting 'No true Christian must ever retreat from Antichrist!' She was killed and has passed into the realm of legend.

The narrowness of the ridge favoured the defenders, who would have quickly been overwhelmed otherwise. The cavalrymen's large numbers were of little benefit to them, as they could neither attack across a broad front nor flank and surround the two forts. Seeing the attack from the city walls, Žižka mobilised Taborite and city militia and ordered them to attack from the south slope, steep but not nearly so steep as the north slope. He then hurried to the scene with an elite force of troops comprised of his personal bodyguards and long-time comrades. Žižka plunged into the fight as things had become critical.

Defeat seemed imminent until the main body of attacking Hussites crested the ridge from the south, shouting battle cries and singing the hymns that subsequently intimidated many other opponents. Led by a priest carrying the sacred host aloft, a front line of archers was followed by peasants armed with flails and pikes bringing up the rear.

There has been much discussion about the Royalist cavalry's panic at this sudden rush from their left flank. They were products of their time: superstitious and prepared to attribute divine or demonic intervention to anything out of the ordinary. The nobility, for all their power, wealth, and social status were not particularly enlightened or educated. It has been suggested that the stories these impressionable men had heard about Taborite devil-worship may have made them jumpy. The Hussites were certainly anything but ordinary, and amidst the mêlée, with men shouting, horses rearing, arrows flying, and all the city's church bells ringing, chroniclers partial to both sides have theorised that the Royalists may have feared they were being attacked by the Prince of Darkness himself. The element of surprise clearly played a role; the steepness of the Vítkov's south slope prevented the Royalists from seeing the attacking Hussites until they had reached the crest. Even had they seen them coming, the narrow ridge would not have allowed them room to form a flank against them. The Royalist force was an undrilled collection of several contingents who had not previously fought together. They were fighting on unfamiliar ground, and like most medieval troops were flummoxed when forced from standard procedure. With only the loosest of battle plans, the Royalist horsemen were incapable of implementing quick adjustments. They recoiled from the Hussite attack and were forced to the north crest of the hill, beyond which was a nearly vertical, 75-metre drop.[3]

Any horseman going off this northern edge would fall five or ten metres before hitting the ground, and he would likely bounce and continue falling, slamming into trees and boulders along the way with his horse rolling and flailing on top of him. Looking at the spot today,

---

3. I am grateful to Jiri Cajthaml of the Department of Mapping & Cartography at Czech Technical University in Prague for this information.

even an experienced climber would want an abseil rope to descend safely. As the Hussites pressed their flank, the Royalists, whose horses had been caught up in the panic and confusion of their riders, were forced over the lip. Encumbered by armour and weapons, many broke their necks, backs, and limbs. Within an hour, 300 cavalrymen were dead, either from the fall or at the hands of Hussite soldiers who scrambled down after them; others were chased across Hospital Field to the river where many drowned attempting to swim across. Carrying away their wounded, the remaining Royalists retreated in disarray. The Prague soldiers assembled on Hospital Field for hymns of divine praise and thanks.

The Royalists lost some 500 men, including their general, Count Henry of Isenberg. Since this was a small portion of their total force, this setback alone does not explain why they were so thoroughly demoralised, or why there was no follow-up attack or modified blockade. They had lost any of hope of surprising the Hussites, but that did not prevent them either from re-grouping for a second attack on the Vítkov or imposing a blockade further from the city with somewhat thinner lines. They had more than ample manpower for either option. Žižka expected a second attack, and immediately had the fortifications strengthened. The moat was deepened, the original bulwark rebuilt with stone, and additional ones erected. The women of Prague and Tábor, their children, and the city's Jews again performed most of this labour.

The answer to the puzzling lack of persistence or follow-up by the imperial forces, given the effort and expense committed to Prague's conquest, lies in the nature of the army Sigismund drew together. Like the Hussites, it had problems with internal dissension, and parallels can be drawn between the opposing forces. Like the Hussites, the Emperor's multi-national army was a fractious assemblage, and there was severe friction between its Czech and German nobles and knights. On several occasions Sigismund had to intervene personally to prevent bloodshed. As the Taborites had accused the Praguers of lacking sufficient zeal, the German Royalists grew indignant at a suspicious lack of intensity on the part of Sigismund and his Bohemian retinue.

In all likelihood, Sigismund never really contemplated an all-out siege of Prague, believing a show of overwhelming force, coupled with an encircling ring of blockading soldiers, would quickly persuade the city to surrender. He knew his foreign troops would unleash wanton slaughter and destruction upon a defeated Prague. While he was unconcerned by any potential loss of Czech life, the city's destruction was another matter. One chronicler recorded the reaction of Sigismund, not especially sentimental, when he first laid eyes on the city of his birth and childhood after an absence of many years. 'Oh, Prague', he reportedly sighed, 'my own parental heritage, how do I find thee!' This wistfulness did not extend to the people of Prague. He was operating as both Holy Roman Emperor and temporal swordbearer of the Roman Catholic Church, and hence bore a double enmity towards the Bohemian Hussites as rebels and heretics. But Prague had been built into a crown jewel by Sigismund's father, Charles IV, and doubtless he wanted to take possession of this inherited masterpiece in all its glory, instead of riding into a smouldering city in ruins. This notion seems to have eluded the Royalist crusaders, particularly the Germans. Driven by centuries-old tribal enmity for the Slavs, they were eager to slaughter every Czech they could grab, regardless of religious creed, and burn the city to the ground. Their fury was further stoked when an angry mob of Praguers and Taborites stormed city hall and took away seventeen German prisoners whom they marched to the riverbank. There, where they could be seen by the enemy across the Vlatava, they were burned alive in retaliation for Royalist atrocities – except for a priest who promised to give communion in both kinds.

Many crusaders had travelled great distances to win fame and fortune by their swords, and they were frustrated at being held back by Sigismund within sight of the hated heretics. The day following the Vítkov battle, Sigismund's commanding officers ordered the heavy siege guns set up on the plateau overlooking Prague to commence firing on the city. Sigismund intervened and explicitly prohibited any bombardment. This fed rampant speculation that there was collusion between Sigismund, the Czech Royalists, and the Hussites. Many believed

Žižka's readiness for the Vítkov assault was not due to acuity on his part, but rather treachery by Bohemia's Catholic Royalists, who allegedly tipped off the Hussites to prevent their churches and monasteries from being sacked. It was not a far-fetched suspicion given the secret negotiations between the Emperor and his Czech lords, although some Royalist soldiers went so far as to accuse Sigismund of being a secret Hussite himself!

A portion of the Czech nobility fighting for the Emperor may have been genuinely concerned at the prospect of an impending slaughter. Most, however, were scarcely more humane than Sigismund, and would have shed few tears over the Hussites, whom they regarded as a barbarous rabble they would gladly be rid of. Like a squabbling family, they reserved for themselves the right to fight with their fellow Czechs and resented outsiders presuming to do so. But they were horrified at the thought that the prestige and grandeur of 'Golden Prague', which reflected its glory on them, might be obliterated. The Bohemian and Moravian Royalists had other, more venal motives as well. They had enjoyed increasing autonomy under Wenceslaus's weak rule, and they recognised that an imperial conquest of Prague in which they played little part would marginalise them politically and threaten a return to the weakened status they had had under Charles. They also feared that wholesale German occupation and despoliation of Prague might spread through the land, including their own estates. Moreover, they shared the Hussites' belief that the Catholic clergy were altogether too wealthy and saw the reform movement as an opportunity to acquire some of that wealth – provided no foreigners were meddling.

Contrary to the Germans' and Hungarians' beliefs, the Czech Catholics were not in collusion with the Hussites. They were, nonetheless, making strenuous efforts to convince Sigismund to discharge the foreign troops, arguing that the territorial integrity and political viability of the Czech Lands would be fatally compromised were the Germans allowed to possess it. They promised Sigismund that, if he sent the foreign troops home, they would deliver Prague to him in a month. The Emperor, suspicious by nature and doubtless recalling

Čeněk's duplicity, was sceptical. The Czech nobles played to his vanity and ambition, knowing how badly he wanted to be crowned as Bohemia's king. They, not the peasant riff-raff, were the true representatives of Bohemia, they insisted, and they would see him crowned and swear fealty to him. On 28 July, they did so at a solemn coronation held in St Vitus Cathedral in the Hradčany. Looking on as Archbishop Conrad placed the crown on Sigismund's head were ten princes and a large body of prelates and barons. Prague's city fathers and many peers of the realm, however, were notable by their absence, a fact observed on all sides. Mollified for the time being and hoping the Czech Catholics might spare him the trouble and expense of dealing with the Hussites, Sigismund now had to work out how to disperse the numerous high-ranking princes and prelates of his imperial army without loss of face either to them or himself. A thorny matter at best, it had taken on new urgency.

The vast size of the Royalist army had created health and hygiene problems. The sprawling camp was an improvised affair, with little planning or regard for sanitation. The crusaders' disregard for the basic necessities of camp life stemmed from the belief they would enjoy a swift victory and then ride home, leaving whatever trash and debris they had generated as a farewell gift for the Czechs. Consequently, sanitary conditions soon became unspeakable. The summer of 1420 was particularly hot, and accumulating garbage, human waste, dead horses, livestock remains, and rotting food created a health nightmare. Some 200 Czech captives had been hacked to pieces and left unburied in the German encampment. While the killers may have wished to gloat over them briefly, they probably did not plan on spending an extended period of time in close proximity. Inevitably, flies, mosquitoes, and vermin proliferated, followed by the usual diseases, including typhus and cholera. Many Royalists died without coming close to a battle. Morale plummeted, aggravated by inactivity and the rampant rumour-mongering universal among disgruntled and restless soldiers.

Many German princes and other commanders were disgusted and began agitating to leave. However, there was the issue of money.

Sigismund had counted on Prague's rich booty to pay his thousands of mercenaries. Desperate to disperse what was rapidly becoming a major problem, Sigismund plundered the jewels and precious metals of the Hradčany's churches and monasteries, promising to restore them after the war. This seriously damaged Sigismund's standing with Prague's moderates. While dismayed by the Taborites' destruction, they were willing to concede it was motivated by principle (however misguided), in contrast to the crass expedience of paying off foreigners who had been bent on their destruction.

On 30 July, after getting paid, the invaders struck camp and headed home. Sigismund had been humiliated, while the Vítkov battle had enhanced Žižka's stature at home and abroad. His genius at organisation, strategy and tactics had been displayed and noted by friend and foe alike. He had melded a fractious coalition with competing loyalties and ideologies into a unified fighting force, intuitively anticipated the enemy's most likely and dangerous moves, and shown tactical brilliance during battle. His personal bravery had inspired incredible fortitude and courage in his followers. Žižka also bought the Hussites, especially the Taborites, valuable time to strengthen themselves against subsequent crusades. Although anti-Hussite invaders returned in wave after wave, they never again gained the heights overlooking Prague to hurl invective on its citizenry and threaten its grand architecture with their guns.

Chapter 4

PRAGUERS AND PIKHARTS

Things fall apart; the centre cannot hold;
Mere anarchy is loosed upon the world,
The blood-dimmed tide is loosed, and everywhere
The ceremony of innocence is drowned . . .
W. B. Yeats, 'The Second Coming'

The first great crisis was over. However, Sigismund was still in Bohemia. He had gone to Kutná Hora, accompanied by many of his Bohemian and Moravian nobles, hoping to enter Prague without military action. But the Catholic lords who promised they would deliver the capital city provided he hold his foreign mercenaries at bay could not fulfil that promise. Sigismund was furious, his suspicious nature fully aroused. He now believed his Czech nobles were secretly Hussites and had conspired against him. While these lords had made their pledge in good faith, there was simply no way Prague's citizens and their leaders were going to accept Sigismund as ruler. Correspondence dated 10 July 1420 sent to Venice by the Prague government makes this crystal clear, calling him 'our principal foe, our cruel enemy, and the intolerant persecutor of the Bohemian nation', followed by a litany of complaint, including over the murders of Hus, Jerome, and Krása. The newly-crowned king was charged with harbouring the intention of completely destroying the Czech Lands, accusations previously levelled at him. This was the first official act of foreign policy by Prague's revolutionary government, seeking an alliance with the Venetian Republic, which bore its own grudges against the Emperor.

The first order of political business was finding a new king. Democracy and the notion of republican government were as yet unknown in Bohemia except for the primitive, small-scale version practiced by the Taborites – one of several reasons they were regarded as fanatics. More realistic than his Taborite followers, Žižka believed a new king was needed for two reasons: first, only a universally acknowledged figure could unify all of Czech society; second, he felt the selection and coronation of a new king would pre-empt Sigismund from making further attempts on the Bohemian throne. Given Bohemia's brief unification with Poland the previous century and the cultural similarities of the two countries, it was natural for the Hussites to look in that direction. Overtures had already been made to the Polish King Władyslaw. The matter was taken up again during the late July meeting of Prague's leaders and their allies at which Žižka acted as Tábor's official representative. Nicholas of Pístny, at one time regarded as a likely candidate to replace Wenceslaus, had lost stature. The decision to make this initiative was made without him, and eventually he opposed it.

The meeting's participants decided that a new diplomatic mission, headed by Hynek of Kolstein, would more accurately reflect the changed political make-up of the Hussite movement. Hynek would be charged with presenting the Polish King with the Hussite grievances against the Emperor, familiarising him with the Four Articles of Prague, and requesting that he accept the Bohemian crown. Žižka, who carried the official seal of Tábor, affixed it to the document signifying his complete agreement. Hynek left Prague for Poland in late July 1420, travelling by way of Silesia. The Breslau councillors learned of the initiative and informed Sigismund who instructed them to capture Hynek, but they were unsuccessful. Hynek met Władyslaw in early August, stayed briefly, and returned to Prague in mid-September.

Hopes that the political situation could be stabilised and a strong government established were soon dashed. The two main Hussite parties began fighting each other. The Taborites, both clerics and peasant laity, still felt the Praguers were uncomfortably removed from their puritan principles. Praguers, especially the middle and upper classes, felt the radical ideas of the Taborites were too drastic, and they resented the attempt to impose provincial values on their sophisticated worldview and lifestyle.

On 6 August, one week after the Battle of Vítkov, a Taborite crowd gathered in front of one of the New Town's most beautiful monasteries and burned it to the ground. This event coincided with the issuing of a twelve-point list of demands to the councillors of the Old and New Towns: unless the people of Prague agreed to observe the points stipulated, the Taborites and their allies would withdraw their support and leave the city. They wanted the abstract points of the Four Articles put into immediate, concrete civil and administrative practice. They called for immediate nationalisation of all church property, closing of all public drinking houses and brothels, criminal proceedings against all known adulterers and prostitutes, and punishment of dishonest merchants or craftsmen. They did not neglect to add a prohibition against their running *bête noire* – wearing expensive and luxurious clothing. Another point stipulated that the University masters should also behave in accordance with this Law of God and that their preaching and teaching ought to be closely supervised. Moreover, anyone who took exception to these or any other Laws of God was to be expelled from the city. But the most staggering provision demanded that all monasteries be destroyed along with 'unnecessary' churches and their elaborate altars, ornaments, and sacred objects of gold and silver. This went to the very heart of Prague's collective self-image since the city was renowned throughout Europe for the beauty of its Gothic church architecture. Even the most fervent Prague Hussites recoiled from this barbarous puritan fanaticism.

While Prague pondered the implications of this stunning document, the Taborites burned three more monasteries in the Old Town. This section of the city had more glorious religious buildings than the New Town, and the Taborites encountered serious resistance. Learning that the Taborites intended to burn the St James monastery, the Old Town's butchers armed themselves with the tools of their trade, forming a human wall to prevent it. The Old Town council, in a brilliant stroke, decided to use the monastery, long since deserted by the monks, as a warehouse. This cleverly managed to hold the Taborites at bay with the claim that the buildings were necessary to store food and arms. Another church had been similarly threatened, and it was set aside by the city council for all Germans who had signed the Hussite pledge of loyalty and professed their acceptance of the communion in both kinds. In light of their willingness to convert to Hussitism, these Germans were permitted to conduct religious services in their own language, a noteworthy exception to the Hussites' insistence upon universal use of the Czech vernacular. The Taborites' fanaticism was motivated by aversion to idolatry, but there were other factors. The Taborites were restive in Prague, an unfamiliar and unsettling environment for them. However, it reflects poorly upon their priests that they encouraged their destructive impulses.

On 10 August, a group of Taborites and citizens of the New Town, led by Koranda, marched south to Zbraslav, site of a Cistercian monastery that was one of Bohemia's most glorious religious buildings. The sacred burial place of the kings, it held the deceased Wenceslaus, who had been buried there one year earlier. The monastery was deserted, but the wine cellars were full. Displaying flagrant hypocrisy, the Taborite soldiers – the same people demanding that all drinking establishment in Prague be shut down – helped themselves to the wine and became thoroughly drunk. They broke into the royal tomb, disinterred Wenceslaus's body, placed it on the altar and put a straw crow on his skull. They poured wine on the remains, exclaiming, 'If thou wert alive, thou wouldst fain drink with us', mocking the late King's reputation as a drunkard. Bored with this macabre diversion, they set the buildings on fire and returned to Prague. Along the way, still thoroughly intoxicated and egged on by their priests, they attempted to storm the Vyšehrad. As can be imagined, this was an utter failure and provoked a counter-attack by the castle garrison. Lord Všembera and his Royalist soldiers were not about to miss the opportunity to inflict punishment on an impaired and disorganised mob that had foolishly placed itself within reach, and the Hussites suffered considerable loss of life.

This repugnant incident, particularly the desecration of a grave (however hated its occupant) greatly damaged the reputation of the Hussite movement domestically and abroad, feeding an already widespread opinion that they and their priests were out-of-control terrorists. It is definitely known that Žižka, likely preoccupied with high-level discussions of the twelve-point ultimatum, was not present at these events, and he certainly would have intervened had he been. Žižka was all for the destruction of monasteries, but he had a strong puritan streak as well. Widespread drunkenness of Catholic priests and monks had been a significant factor in provoking the reformist spirit of the Hussite movement. Now, the Taborites themselves had gone even further into bacchanals of wanton destruction. Another long-term repercussion of this incident was further to alienate Žižka from Koranda, whom he held responsible and whose leadership he had surely begun regarding as dangerously unsound.

Although relations between Žižka and the Taborite priests were becoming increasingly strained, he nonetheless agreed fully with the twelve-point programme submitted by the Taborite leaders. Yet another hand was behind this document as well – that of Želivský and his New Town council. Those councillors had been quick to sign on to the Taborite programme. The Old Town administration, however, was not nearly as amenable. They scrutinised the twelve points, joined in the process by the Charles University masters, who were represented by the English expatriate Peter Payne. An early disciple of Wyclif, Payne had fled Oxford in 1417 and found a new home in Prague. Commonly known as 'Master English', he became a leading theologian, teacher, and diplomat in his new country. Payne discussed the twelve points with the Old Town councillors, and they decided to delay any answer as long as possible, perhaps hoping that either by negotiation or main force the Taborites' attitude might be softened.

The Taborites, however, had grown accustomed to forthright and direct civil administration, with matters settled in most cases on the spot by popular vote of a general assembly. They had little tolerance for the Prague aristocrats and intelligentsia who seemed to be stalling. They waited two weeks before deciding enough time had elapsed and then took matters into their own hands. On 18 August, Želivský, a rabble-rousing demagogue of the first order, assembled a large crowd before the Old Town city hall, vehemently attacking the councillors. He pointed out that Prague was in imminent danger of losing its Taborite allies as long as the present, non-compliant government held office. In what was effectively a coup d'état, he called upon the assembled multitude to replace the present councillors on the spot with a new group of candidates. Želivský then nominated new candidates for mayor and the city council, who were quickly endorsed by the crowd. This hasty election, and the show of strength behind it, intimidated the city councillors into resigning and handing over the town seal to Želivský, who immediately passed it to his chosen replacements. From this point on he exercised control of both towns and began acting like a dictator.

Four days later, on 22 August, the entire Taborite contingent marched out of Prague without bothering to give an official explanation. It is not difficult, however, to guess what may have led Žižka and Koranda to take this step. The immediate danger to Prague had passed, and there was no pressing need for the Taborites' continued presence. A more concrete reason was that it was harvest time. Many of the fighters in Žižka's 9,000-strong force were not permanent residents of Tábor but farmers from the surrounding countryside. Their grain was ready for harvest, and the horses pulling the wagons were needed for working the fields. Tábor would not survive without a reliable food source, and Žižka later instituted provision for sufficient people to remain in Tábor to ensure adequate agricultural resources. A considerable number of Žižka's men returned to their farms. He therefore arrived in Tábor with a somewhat smaller force than that which he had left and immediately began a running guerrilla war against Sigismund's strongest ally in the region, Ulrich of Rožmberk.

Less than a week after leaving Prague, Žižka travelled to Písek and reinforced his depleted ranks with volunteers. The residents of anti-

Hussite Vodňany, eighteen kilometres further south, were alarmed and sent an urgent plea for help to the Rožmberk grandees administering the town. Vodňany's soldiers had fled upon learning of Žižka's approach, testimony to the fear the one-eyed general had begun to instil in his enemies. Ulrich's help was not forthcoming, and two days later Žižka took the town. A bit further to the south-west, Prachatice surrendered to Žižka a second time, promising to adhere to the Four Articles. The cumulative effect of these small conquests gave Žižka relatively stable control over most of south-west Bohemia nearly to the Bavarian border. It also posed a direct threat to Rožmberk's main city, Krumlov. Žižka had no intention of assaulting this strongly fortified place, knowing it would be difficult and costly. Instead, he returned to Tábor and after a brief rest marched up the Lužnice valley and took the town of Soběslav without resistance.

Ranging further south, Žižka besieged Lomnice, which surrendered on 16 September, despite being strongly fortified. This location was judged sufficiently important by Žižka to warrant a permanent garrison, and he appointed Jan Roháč as its captain. Roháč belonged to a branch of one of the great baronial families of Bohemia, the Dubás, and he may have been the brother or cousin of Žižka's son-in-law Henry of Dubá. Although little is known about Henry, Jan became a leading figure of the revolution and one of Žižka's closest friends and most loyal followers. Žižka then moved east from Lomnice, conquering the town of Nová Bystřice near the Moravian border and its castle. He took prisoner the wife and daughter of the town's owner, Leopold Krajíř, formerly a 'robber baron' who had fought as a highwayman against the Rožmberks, who was now Sigismund's burgrave and governor at Budějovice. Žižka left the two women unharmed but burned down the castle. He then set out for Tábor by a circuitous route which took him to his home town of Trocnova. He conquered the nearby town of Sviny Trhové and garrisoned its castle, creating another outpost from which to threaten Krumlov.

Žižka's war of harassment against Rožmberk greatly resembled the guerrilla campaigns of his younger days as a brigand. Not limiting himself to conquering towns and castles, Žižka inflicted whatever economic damage he could on the great baron, burning or destroying his fields and crops and driving away his cattle. Ulrich managed one victory, overwhelming the castle of Kamenice belonging to Prokop of Ústí. Ulrich's retainers also captured Koranda, who was travelling from Tábor to Bechyně in late September just as Žižka was returning from Sviny Trhové. The loss of Tábor's spiritual figurehead and founding father resulted in significant political changes there.

The next decision made by the Taborites was one their reluctant allies in Prague were not ready for – electing their own bishop, a priest named Nicholas of Pelhřimov. All priests were ordered to obey him and told that no one could preach without his permission; he was also placed in charge of Tábor's finances. The significance of this step cannot be overstated. While it was by no means the first time that various heretics had declared a bishop for themselves, such moves had until then been essentially underground. The men of Tábor had openly declared their independence from the Catholic Church and severed all ties to Rome, something Prague moderates were loath to do. The Taborites announced they no longer considered themselves subject to the Pope or his procedures of priestly ordination. This Taborite episcopate was, in fact, the first in the history of Protestantism. This episopate was abolished during the period when Tábor was an autonomous republic in the Bohemian kingdom. However, after the city lost that status it resumed electing its own bishops under the aegis of the Taborites' spiritual successors, the Church of the Brethren, a tradition which has endured to the present day.

The new bishop was a young man still in his middle thirties. Educated at Charles University, Nicholas had been ordained in 1415 and become associated with the reform movement early in his priestly career. He was one of the very first to join the Taborite community but had kept a relatively low profile as long as Koranda was around. Nicholas had a reputation for strong religious fervour, keen knowledge of theological issues, and the gift of eloquence. From May until August 1420, in the absence of Koranda's domineering persona, his reputation had grown, and he was elected when Koranda seemed unlikely to return. His selection was spurred by other issues as well. Tábor had become a hothouse of ideas far beyond anything Jan Hus would have considered, and increasingly radical credos began to grow. Even at Tábor, limits would have to be established and distinctions made between the teachings of Hussitism and the increasingly outlandish proclamations of spiritual fanatics – some of whom had even begun challenging the symbolism of the chalice itself. This free-thinking theology was offensive to Žižka, a devout believer in the sacred properties of the chalice. Some twenty years senior to the new bishop, Žižka took on new weight as a leading figure, and there is evidence that he played a decisive role in Nicholas's election and backed him with his personal influence. Over the next year, the two men worked to rein in and subdue various mystical fanatics and the perceived threat they posed to the Hussite faith. This would not be the only time Žižka would take steps against Tábor's more extreme splinter groups. In the short term, the election of Nicholas was instrumental in building smoother relations between Žižka and the Taborite priesthood.

Nonetheless, war not politics was Žižka's main concern, especially his campaign against Rožmberk which he resumed at Bor Panský (today Bor Malý), a small town and castle in the upper Otava River valley. It had strategic value, located halfway between the Taborite outposts of Strakonice and Sušice and guarding the road between Rožmberk's southern lands and Plzeň. When the citizens of Bor Panský and Ulrich called for help, they were answered by German regulars from Budějovice under Krajíř, German mercenaries commanded by Henry of Plauen, and additional troops led by Bohuslav, whom Žižka had fought at Nekměř. Both Henry and Bohuslav were elements of the Plzeň *Landfrieden* (German for 'peace of the land'), a powerful coalition of the region's towns and nobles.[1] When the three Royalist commanders arrived, Žižka had already taken the town and castle, but seeing that their combined forces greatly outnumbered his, they attacked.

---

1. A similar, somewhat less powerful Landfrieden was centred in Loket, near present-day Karlovy Vary.

Tactically, the ensuing battle was not especially significant as it essentially replicated those of Sudoměř and Poříčí. Žižka deployed a wagon fortress near a hilltop church, repulsing several cavalry charges and eventually forcing his enemy to withdraw. The Royalists suffered heavy losses, while Žižka's troops also sustained significant casualties.

Strategically, the battle prevented the forces of Rožmberk and the Plzeň Landfrieden from taking part with Sigismund in the struggle for the Vyšehrad. Žižka did not participate in this battle either, but his absence was a voluntary one. Perhaps nursing his grudge over the earlier giveaway of the castle, Žižka, when asked for assistance, only sent a token contingent of forty horsemen on 4 October 1420. A week later, he still limited his aid to a small number of additional troops and did not accompany them to Prague, engendering some comment.

*

In Žižka's absence, Prague's forces were led by Hynek Krušina, originally the military commander of the Orebites. had He begun besieging the Vyšehrad in mid-September 1420 with an army supplemented by several Hussite nobles including Hynek of Kolstein (after his return from his diplomatic mission to Poland), Diviš Bořek, and Victorin Boček, who became one of Žižka's best officers and closest friends. Twelve thousand strong, the Hussites camped south-east of the castle, blocking its supply route and cutting off its food supply. The garrison, like that of the Hradčany earlier in the summer, was reduced to eating horsemeat. The Royalists attempted to re-supply the castle by way of the Berounka River, a tributary of the Vlatava south of Prague, but the Hussites anticipated this move and prevented it. The siege forced Sigismund into action, as had the previous one against the Hradčany. The Emperor, leading some 16,000 men, first employed standard tactics of diversionary feints against smaller, unprotected towns, hoping to draw the Hussites out, but they did not move from their blockading position. By 28 October, the castle's food shortage had reached a critical point, compelling its commander, Všembera, to meet Krušina under a flag of truce. They agreed that, if the castle did not receive assistance within three days, the garrison would surrender; they would be permitted to depart freely with their hand weapons but would have to leave behind all the heavy armament.

Sigismund was reluctant to do battle without possessing overwhelming force, and this cost him the Vyšehrad. While he waited for 2,000 additional Moravian reinforcements under Henry of Plumlov to arrive, the three-day grace period expired. Všembera, a man of principle, insisted upon honouring the surrender terms he had signed. Sigismund, who had no such scruples, was already angry with Všembera (also a Moravian) and grew furious when Henry arrived and warned the Emperor that a frontal assault under the circumstances would be suicidal. Sigismund, influenced by his Hungarian and German advisors, saw divided loyalties, if not outright treachery, on the part of all his Bohemian and Moravian nobles. In a rage, he ordered Henry to charge into the teeth of the Hussite guns while giving less dangerous assignments to the Hungarian and German contingents.

The ill-considered assault was repelled, and in the counter-charge Henry and 500 of his men were killed and many more taken prisoner. This fit of pique cost Sigismund in other ways. Another Royalist casualty was Peter of Sternberg, whose attack against the pilgrims from Sezimovo Ústí had been the first open clash of the war. His death allowed his wife, a secret Hussite, to declare her beliefs openly, bringing two strong castles and the town of Benešov into the Hussite domain. After Všembera officially surrendered, the German mercenaries of the castle garrison marched off unmolested, while as many as 1,500 Moravian Royalists, doubtless shocked by Sigismund's flagrant disregard for their lives, deserted to the Hussites. The Praguers then dismantled the Vyšehrad, a process that continued for several centuries until today nothing is left of the once-magnificent castle but the foundations.

The Vyšehrad's fall greatly strengthened the capital city and the revolution in general. It carried special significance for the Praguers, who had not only eliminated a Royalist stronghold dominating the New Town but had demonstrated military strength and efficiency in their own right, as opposed to the events at Vítkov, where the Taborites and other allies had been the decisive elements. It also exacerbated divisions among the Royalists. Sigismund's goal of subjugating the Bohemian Hussites was now even more remote. He singled out his Czech nobles as scapegoats, nearly causing bloodshed between them and the Hungarian nobility at the imperial court. Although the Moravian nobility, with their close proximity to Hungary, had been reluctant to rebel openly, their support began wavering. Sigismund was also compelled to visit Kutná Hora and Čáslav to shore up the loyalty of the Bohemian nobles there, loyalty he himself had done the most to weaken.

On 5 November, four days after the battle, a message was sent by the Hussite leaders to all of Bohemia. It was addressed primarily to those Czechs still feeling some loyalty to Sigismund, either for dynastic or religious reasons. Nationalist arguments were made to convince conservative Czechs that this loyalty was misplaced. Sigismund was accused of shaming the Czech nation with the undeserved charge of heresy and attempting to supplant native Czechs with Germans and Hungarians. At the Battle of Vyšehrad he had wantonly sacrificed Bohemian nobility, while protecting his German and Hungarian warriors, and was accused of fomenting civil warfare between Hussites and Catholics to weaken the Czech nation and hasten its extermination with the help of his foreign friends. A quotation ascribed to Sigismund – declaring he would give away all of Hungary if only he could kill every Czech – was particularly effective in stirring nationalist feeling in conservative Catholic nobles.

The message achieved its desired effect. More Czech noblemen joined the revolution during the autumn of 1420, and even those not joining weakened in their support of the Emperor. This included Ulrich of Rožmberk, whom Sigismund had considered his most important Bohemian vassal. Ulrich was constantly subjected to attacks by Žižka's Taborites and never received the aid Sigismund kept promising. On 4 November, the Emperor wrote Ulrich an uncharacteristically apologetic letter. Sigismund tried to assuage him with the excuse that losing many able-bodied soldiers at the Vyšehrad prevented him from sending assistance, which he pledged to dispatch as soon as possible. Nonetheless,

Ulrich seems to have been recalculating where his best interests lay, and Žižka helped him decide.

In November, Žižka moved against Prachatice. He had taken this town twice previously, its citizens swearing both times to submit to Tábor and adhere to the Four Articles. They did not keep their promises. Feeling they could depend on Ulrich's protection, its citizens had now purged all Hussites, expelling some, imprisoning others, and burning a few at the stake. When Žižka arrived, the town was prepared for battle. He called on the defenders manning the walls to open the gates and permit his Taborites to enter. He promised that, if they complied, no harm would come to them or their belongings. The citizens replied that they already had the body of Christ and all the priests they needed, a sarcastic answer that cost them dear. Outraged, Žižka declared that when he conquered the town not a single inhabitant would be spared. Men began scaling the walls at several locations while archers drove the defenders from the ramparts. The first Taborites over the wall opened the gates, and it was over very quickly. A hundred and thirty-five townsmen were killed on the walls and in street fighting while ninety-two surviving captives were marched before Žižka. Seven Hussites were set free, and the remainder herded into the parish vestry, the doors barred, and the building torched. Žižka spared the women and children, but they were ordered to leave town immediately. Taborite peasants then settled into the newly vacated houses, and from then on the town was an important satellite of Tábor and yet another threat to Ulrich.

Things were not going well for Ulrich. One of his strongest castles was Příbenice, a strategic site in the Lužnice valley and a base of operations against Tábor. Koranda was imprisoned there with some other Taborites, and in the dawn hours of 13 November he and his fellow prisoners overcame the guards in the tower where they were held. Koranda sent word to Zybněk, the captain in charge at Tábor, who quickly arrived with a troop of Taborites. Between Zybněk's men outside the walls and Koranda in the tower, the castle was rapidly taken along with the smaller fortress of Přibničky across the river. Mercenaries sent by Ulrich arrived too late and were routed by Zybněk's men. Koranda did not mind sending Hussite enemies to their death as long as he did not do the work himself; during the battle, however, he threw stones from the tower, one of which he believed killed a man. In consequence, he refrained from ever celebrating Mass again as he had broken the Fifth Commandment and felt his now-bloodstained hands were unworthy of the Eucharist – a literal adherence to religious law common at that time and likely to strike the modern observer as hypocritical.

Following these reversess, Ulrich made his decision. Žižka's lengthy guerrilla war had inflicted a severe toll on his towns, villages, fields, herds, orchards, and fishponds. His influence on his fellow nobles, which had risen after Čeněk's defection, began to fall again, particularly after Sigismund's defeat at the Vyšehrad. Ulrich had no desire to fight on the losing side. If nothing else, he wanted a truce. Informed of this wish, Žižka and the Taborite leaders agreed that it was in the Hussites' best interests to make this armistice. Tábor would gain freedom of movement to more distant parts of Bohemia without worrying about its southern front. It also suggested that Ulrich had begun to doubt Sigismund's strength. However, it was the religious element of the armistice agreement which led Žižka to accept it. On 18 November 1420, a document was exchanged, the first of a handful written by Žižka that have been preserved. The armistice stipulated high indemnities in the event it was broken by either party, and Ulrich pledged to adhere to the Four Articles of Prague and permit their observance throughout his domains. This armistice, which was to last until 4 February 1421, gained Hussite freedom of worship throughout most of southern Bohemia – more important to Žižka than any military or political success. This document was the last recorded instance in which he referred to himself as 'Jan, called Žižka, of Trocnova'. His name was the first of four Taborite captains listed; Žižka's superior Nicholas of Pístny was conspicuous by his absence. The city of Písek, where the negotiation was held and finalised, was appended as a fifth collective signatory.

By late November 1420, Žižka could take satisfaction in the events of the preceding weeks and months. A shadow on this otherwise upbeat picture was the continuing friction between him and the Taborite priests, but Žižka had every reason to think this could be addressed, particularly with the co-operation of Tábor's new bishop. There were parallel frictions back in Prague involving the previously dominant Želivský, whose political power-base had been undercut by the recent victory at the Vyšehrad. That battle had been won by several noblemen who were no friends of Taborite radicalism. The military representative of the Taborites during that battle was Nicholas; he commanded a small troop and did not impress Prague's citizenry as Žižka had. However, he carried himself with the same haughty arrogance that had got him into trouble with Wenceslaus. Nicholas was as problematic an ally as he was an enemy. During the negotiations with the Vyšehrad commander, Krušina had consulted all Prague and allied leaders regarding terms of surrender for the castle garrison. Everyone agreed with them except Nicholas, who thought they were much too generous. Despite being in a minority of one in this opinion, he obstinately held to it and withdrew his troops from the island near the Vyšehrad which he had occupied to prevent supplies from reaching the castle by way of the Vlatava River. After marching his men to Prague in a temper, he was persuaded to sign the armistice and rejoin the Prague army.

Problems again developed between Praguers and Taborites – who were as obsessed as ever with clothing. This time, the issue was the ornate vestments originally worn by Catholic priests and still used by moderate Utraquist priests in Prague. Dubbed the 'struggle over the ornates', this difference of opinion led to bad feelings on both sides.

More important, however, was the matter of finding a new king, and on 14 November the New and Old Town councils called a meeting to address this question. Most in attendance favoured renewing the previous offer to the princes of Poland–Lithuania in a more formal manner. One voice was raised in protest – Nicholas's. His objection, which he presumed to make on behalf of all of Tábor, was that it was impermissible for anyone but a native-born Czech to be considered for the Bohemian crown. Hynek quickly proved him wrong, producing the credentials from his previous mission to Poland. In plain view was the seal of Tábor duly affixed by Žižka. Nicholas was in no position to disavow Žižka, who had so recently saved Prague from destruction. But he was resistant and observed muttering under his breath. It seems likely that Nicholas's objections were based less upon political principle and more upon personal ambition, which Wenceslaus (correctly, it would seem) had believed was nothing less than the royal throne itself. Nicholas's objections were over-ruled by the assembly, which was in no mood to put up with further obstructionism on his part, and the question of religious ritual was then addressed.

The proceedings quickly became a condemnation of Taborite practice. A resolution was proposed forbidding new teachings in the city unless they were found to be in accordance with Holy Scripture or predicated on irrefutable logic. All such teachings were to be approved by a committee of four University masters elected by the citizens of Prague. In addition, Prague priests were to wear traditional vestments. This proposal was loudly opposed by Nicholas, who was once again over-ruled. It was not only a defeat for Tábor but Želivský as well. Although he does not seem to have been particularly concerned with the issues of the vestments, Želivský was displeased by diplomatic overtures being sent to the Polish King. A populist, Želivský was opposed to a foreign king who could be expected to align himself with the upper nobility. It is unlikely he had democratic government in mind, but was probably motivated by a preference for a king unbeholden to the lords and more prone to recognise the forces underpinning the Hussite movement. The most important thing, from Želivský's perspective, was to consolidate Prague's radicals with the Taborites to garner decisive influence in the new king's selection. The 14 November agreement was reached by circumventing Želivský despite his political power. Further undercutting his position was the ban on unapproved 'new teachings', many of which happened to resemble his own. Želivský was in no position to raise objections. The aristocratic commanders who had led the Vyšehrad victory, combined with the University and Old Town patricians, were far stronger than he. The Prague conservatives then decided that the city councils elected to placate the Taborites need not continue in office. On 19 November, the Old Town's citizens elected a new council comprised of individuals more aligned with the city patricians. Even the New Town, Želivský's power-base, elected more moderate councillors and a new mayor.

While Želivský was willing to bide his time, knowing political fortunes ebb and flow, Nicholas had no patience whatsoever and could not accept even a temporary setback. He realised, however, that his protests alone would avail him nothing. He recognised that his political leverage depended on the military strength of Tábor and its effective use on behalf of Prague and other Hussite communities. Attempting to restore his influence, he decided to launch military expeditions against castles and towns in the Prague region still in Royalist hands.

The first of these, the town and castle of Říčany belonging to a lord named Diviš, was twenty-two kilometres south-east of Prague. In late November, Nicholas moved against it. Though reinforcements were sent from Tábor, his forces were still weak. He asked Prague for help, pointing out that a victory over Říčany would benefit Prague much more than Tábor. Hynek, unmoved, declined to participate on the excuse that his own domains were threatened by Sigismund, after which he resigned his position and left the city. His claim was not untrue, but most felt it was a pretext to avoid working with Nicholas, whom he heartily detested.

On 24 November, some Prague troops did join the Taborites to besiege Říčany. As was customary, a pre-battle Mass was held. But as soon as it started, the ornate vestments worn by the Prague priests provoked the Taborites, who attempted to halt the service. Swords were drawn and clubs raised, but the leaders intervened and decided for the time being that each contingent would celebrate Mass separately, deferring a final solution until after the campaign. Nicholas returned to Prague and continued his attempts to reinvigorate Taborite influence. Going before the new city councils, he insisted the agreement of the preceding May be observed, specifically referring to the assignment of joint responsibility for Prague defence. The Prague authorities replied that those measures had been provisional ones, taken under duress in the face of civil emergency, and, as the crisis was now over, there was no compelling reason to renew the agreement. Dismissed once again and angrier than ever, Nicholas went back to Říčany.

Žižka returned to Prague and brought with him four Hussite noblemen: the brothers Peter and Purkhart of Janovice, Peter Zmrzlík of Svojšín and Ulrich Vavák. While sharing Žižka's hatred for Sigismund, they were by no means Taborites. Devout Hussites and committed revolutionaries, they were likely candidates to bridge the growing divide between Tábor and Prague. En route, Žižka's troops stopped off at Říčany and joined the siege while the four lords continued on to Prague to carry out their diplomatic mission. On 4 December, Diviš surrendered Říčany. The terms permitted him, his family, and his followers to keep their lives and any possessions they could carry. This agreement, however, was not honoured and, as Říčany's womenfolk left their homes, Taborite women fell upon them and took their possessions, clothes, and jewellery. They got off more lightly than seven priests from the town whom Žižka had burned to death.

On 6 December, the combined troops of Prague and Tábor returned to the capital, and two days later a meeting was convened at the behest of the four lords at the monastery of St Ambrose. Fearing that mobs might disturb the meeting, the organisers implemented rules which (among other things) excluded women and priests. At its conclusion the only unresolved issue was the issue of the vestments. Deemed a matter of ritual, it was decided the question would be submitted to public debate between the clergymen of Tábor and Prague, moderated by Ulrich Vavák, the highest-ranking of the nobles. The disputation would be held on 10 December at the University. To foster goodwill, leaders of all groups concerned were invited to a banquet beforehand. Žižka and his colleagues accepted, but Nicholas, still sulking, declined with the ludicrous excuse that the banquet would provide his enemies an opportunity to murder him. After making this outlandish statement, he left Prague, vowing never to return. Scarcely out of the city gates, his horse stumbled and he was thrown him, breaking a leg and sustaining a severe chest injury. His companions took him back to Prague despite his protests which – yet again – were over-ruled.

The banquet went well, but problems arose before the disputation started. The Taborite clergymen suddenly objected to the location, which they felt gave home advantage to the University masters. Vavák, after discussions with the University masters and Žižka, placated the Taborites by changing the locale to a large home in Old Town. The event drew a capacity crowd with both contingents in full force. Also representing Tábor were Žižka, Chval and Roháč. Roháč had allied himself with Tábor and would eventually become one of its military captains. Although the Taborite clergy were expecting an immediate and specific discussion of the vestments issue, Prokop of Plzeň, the University rector, insisted that the entire structure of Taborite teaching be examined, holding that it was a danger to Christianity and the Czech people. At his behest, a master named Peter of Mladeňovice read a list of alleged errors and heresies espoused by the Taborite clergy, along with other blasphemies allegedly held by 'some' Taborites. In addition Prokop mentioned the Taborite prediction of Christ's second coming (which, of course, had not occurred) as well as their blanket prohibition of any religious teachings drawn from outside the Bible. Other items included Taborite opposition to the worship of saints and the destruction of their pictures, statues and associated churches and chapels deemed 'unnecessary', and the questioning of the doctrine of transubstantiation. Prokop did not neglect to toss in the election of their own bishop, ordination of laymen as priests, undignified holding of Mass in ordinary clothing, and several instances of Taborite priests marrying. A final point was the inherent contradiction between the Hussite doctrine prohibiting priests from holding worldly power and the almost total political control exercised by the Taborite priests.

Peter closed by assuring all present that he had no intention of indicting or incriminating anyone but rather intended to point out the error of the Hussite ways while warning the Czech people against their misguided teachings. The Taborites became increasingly restive as this list was being read. After Peter concluded, Chval angrily jumped up and denounced the condemnation of the Taborite creed. Chval was out of his element. An excellent soldier, he was no theologian and rather clumsily declared his whole-hearted support for each of the seventy-two alleged heresies read. Roháč followed by unfavourably comparing the University masters to the leaders of the Council of Constance, where Jan Hus had only been charged with forty heretical articles.

The first Taborite priest to respond was Martin Houska, commonly known as 'Loquis' in light of his skill as an orator. More intellectually adept than Chval, Houska insisted that many of the seventy-two points were distortions or misrepresentations, and he was backed up in this assertion by Bishop Nicholas. In response, the University masters said they could prove, using the Bible and other sources, that the articles listed were indeed erroneous. Houska insisted that they be presented in writing to the Taborites and was told they would be made available, as read, to anyone who cared to view them. The proceedings reached a stalemate, and Bishop Nicholas made a final attempt to bring up the matter of the vestments, giving a lengthy soliloquy on Christ and the Apostles taking the Last Supper in ordinary clothes. Jacobellus, the ranking master, replied that the vestments were neither contrary to the Bible nor harmful, and he submitted a written statement to this effect, proposing the Taborite clergy do likewise in timely fashion.

Jacobellus was obviously attempting reconciliation, and the Taborites took his statements in that spirit. After deciding that both parties should deliver written statements within one month to the Old Town mayor, the meeting adjourned. The Taborites' official statement on the vestments was subsequently prepared by their clergymen and taken to Prague by Koranda. However, he was unable to secure another public debate on the matter, effectively shelving the issue for the time being. Jacobellus's move in a conservative direction unified the Prague theologians under the Calixtines, leaving Želivský isolated as the leading voice of Prague radicalism. In addition, fault lines were forming among the Taborites.

Although Žižka attended the disputation, his silence there was deafening. He did not raise any objections as the Taborite priests were attacked and did not join his comrades Chval and Roháč in their defence. Since he was never reluctant to make his opinions known, it is unlikely he simply wished to remain neutral. If Žižka had thought the accusations against the Taborites unfair or unfounded, he surely would have spoken up. We can only conclude that his silence indicated a recognition that the accusations against the Taborites were an accurate account of the radical clerics' teachings, many of which he opposed. He had become virtually as intolerant as the anti-Hussites in his own way, especially regarding priests whom he judged guilty of spreading false teachings. It is not difficult to imagine that Žižka must have been disturbed to realise that heresy might be spread not only by Roman Catholic clergy but Taborite priests as well. This perception must have been reinforced by the remarks of Jacobellus, who had been responsible for drafting the Four Articles. Like most Hussites Žižka interpreted these tenets according to his own lights, but he never faltered in the conviction that they were, and must remain, the defining principles for all true Christians of the Bohemian nation.

In the meantime, Nicholas of Hus lay bedridden in a grand Prague townhouse. Despite his suspicion that the Praguers might try to do away with him, the city's best doctors were called. They skilfully mended his broken leg but his crushed chest was hopeless. After two more painful weeks, he passed away on Christmas Eve. The news spread quickly through Prague. While the citizens of the New Town mourned his passing and thought it a great loss to the movement, most of Prague was relieved. According to the chronicler Březová, they gave thanks to God that he had 'delivered them from a cunning man who had used his knowledge to further not peace and love but disunity and hatred'. In the final analysis, Nicholas had been a good soldier, as had been seen before the gates of Tábor where he routed Ulrich and Leopold. Even so, no one would say that he was on par with Žižka in this respect. Some have praised his skill as a politician and statesman while pointing to Žižka's deficiency in those areas. But, all in all, Nicholas scarcely deserves such praise. The things he was good at – organising people, arranging mass meetings, and the quick assessment of friends and foes – do not necessarily result in an overall positive verdict, as these same attributes are shared by most successful demagogues and dictators. His personal ambition was limitless and his recklessness led him to misjudge odds, while his arrogance led him to under-estimate enemies. Immediately after his death, the diplomatic mission to Poland got under way, and Žižka returned to Tábor with his troops.

*

In January 1421, Žižka launched an attack into the heart of the Plzeň Landfrieden when it was least expected. Although medieval armies seldom campaigned in winter, Žižka and his peasant fighters, perhaps more accustomed to braving the elements, saw no reason to cease fighting. Žižka also surprised his opponents by marching in a long detour and attacking not from the east but from the west, threatening their enemies' transport routes to Germany. The first conquest of this campaign was a fortified monastery in the small town at Chotěšov, twenty kilometres south of Plzeň, followed by another monastery at Kladruby to the north-west. In both cases, the monks quickly departed prior to Žižka's arrival, and the latter monastery became a strong Hussite fortress. Žižka then attempted to cut communications between Plzeň and the rest of the Empire by investing Stříbro, which lay on the main route to Cheb and Franconia, while also harassing Plzeň's outlying possessions.

The citizens of Plzeň wrote a complaint to Žižka about his actions, which he answered in a letter addressed to the Landfrieden which pointedly omitted any reference to its barons. Like a judge explaining his sentence, Žižka pointed out why he felt compelled to burn their houses and destroy their land. They had defied all Four Articles of Prague, and they were guilty of supporting the heretical King, 'that violator of virgins and women, that murderer and incendiary who seeks to destroy the Czech nation'. Žižka warned that continued loyalty to Sigismund would cause not only the loss of their immortal souls but their worldly possessions, too. He reprimanded them for breaking the promises they had made in March 1420 while expressing the opinion that such bad faith was hardly surprising for those not adhering to the Law of God. He closed by expressing the hope that God would allow them to escape the deceptive snares of His enemies and return to the fold of true Christianity. Obviously, this letter was dashed off in heat.

As he began besieging Stříbro, Žižka learned that Bohuslav had gone to his castle at Krasikov, a couple of kilometres away, with a weak force, presumably to make preparations against Žižka. Bohuslav had fought Žižka in three previous battles as Landfrieden commander-in-chief. Žižka felt that depriving the Landfrieden of this vigorous and very competent leader would inflict more damage to Sigismund than conquering Stříbro. After besieging Krasikov for one day, Žižka's men took the tower dominating the drawbridge and Bohuslav announced his willingness to surrender on terms. Bohuslav did not want to surrender to the Taborites but rather to Zmrzlík, a Hussite commander nearby at the time. Žižka agreed, and the surrender was arranged. Bohuslav's people would be permitted to go free under parole so as to keep them from resuming anti-Hussite hostilities, while he would be placed under house arrest in his own castle. Žižka ensured these conditions were strictly adhered to despite mutterings from disgruntled Taborites objecting to Bohuslav's gentle treatment. In consequence of this key victory, Žižka was knighted. Žižka took a personal interest in Bohuslav, whom he respected as a worthy foe. Some months later, Bohuslav was taken from Krasikov to Příbenice castle, where Žižka began paying him regular visits. By October of that year, Bohuslav was a free man, now fighting vigorously on the side of the Hussites. Žižka had made a convert.

Žižka's success in the Plzeň region concerned not only its residents but Sigismund, who had spent Christmas at Litoměřice. After receiving pleas of assistance from the Landfrieden, the Emperor went to the region in mid-January. He did not feel strong enough to begin immediate military operations against Žižka, but was quickly reinforced by various German dukes and nobles from Franconia and Meissen who felt increasingly threatened. Žižka's offensive manoeuvres near the borders of Bavaria and the Upper Palatinate caused them to fear the Hussite rebellion would spill over into their territories. Žižka moved on Tachov, west of Krasikov and only eleven kilometres from a mountain pass leading into Germany. The town's German residents frantically called for help, Sigismund responded, and strong Bavarian forces were quickly mobilised. Sigismund felt that Žižka had entrapped himself by moving so far west and could easily be cut off from Tábor and defeated. However, among his other strengths, Žižka was astute enough not to under-estimate an enemy. While not afraid to fight superior forces, he did not believe in taking unnecessary risks either.

His available forces were somewhat depleted after garrisoning Chotěšov, Kladruby, and Krasikov, and Žižka was unwilling to lose these strategic fortresses. He knew that a direct engagement with the King and his Bavarian reinforcements would be foolish, so he withdrew from Tachov, reinforced the garrisons at the three castles, and took his remaining troops back to Tábor so as to reassemble and strengthen them. On 17 January, he sent a request to Prague for assistance. The Emperor, finding no Taborite army to trap, decided to attack Kladruby. Žižka had left Chval in command there with fewer than a thousand men while Sigismund, after the arrival of German auxiliaries, had twelve times that number. Nonetheless the siege was protracted, lasting into early February. The Royalist siege guns were less effective than those of the Taborites, who made frequent offensive sorties against the besiegers. As the primitive cannon of the time had a very short range, Sigismund's men had to come quite close to the castle walls to deploy them. This allowed the Taborite troops to heckle the Royalists, asking 'Where is the heretic king, the anti-Christ? Tell him to come here and lead this assault if he wants to conquer us.' Sigismund, a thoroughgoing coward, characteristically chose to remain safely behind the walls of Stříbro.

Žižka's plea for assistance was quickly answered by Prague, which sent 7,000 men and 320 wagons under William Kostka, who had fought with Žižka in the Polish–Prussian war. With these reinforcements, Žižka would no longer be numerically inferior to Sigismund. On 6 February, the Praguers and Taborites met at Dobříš, forty kilometres south-west of Prague, and marched to Plzeň. They arrived at the town of Rokycany, which belonged to the Archbishop of Prague. The residents willingly opened its gates to them, affording the Hussites the unfamiliar experience of marching peacefully through a Roman Catholic town. Some Taborites could not stand such civility and insisted upon breaking into a monastery, doing a great deal of destruction and in the process killing a clergyman who had had the temerity to argue with them about it. The allied army then marched towards Kladruby, bypassing Plzeň. Sigismund who was never interested in battle unless he possessed overwhelming superiority, lost heart when he saw the opposing forces were evenly matched. On 8 February 1421, just before the two forces would have collided, he raised the siege of Kladruby, sent his German auxiliaries back home, and quickly retreated to Litoměřice. At the same time, an internal struggle in the town of Domažlice, south-west of Plzeň, was won by the Hussites, bringing this town under Žižka's control.

Sigismund did not linger but continued east to Kutná Hora, and in early March returned to Hungary. Sigismund appears to have had a growing realisation of just how formidable Žižka was, making special mention of him in a letter to Ulrich in which he called him 'the special promoter and director of the Wiklefite heresy'. The Emperor urged Ulrich to make no further armistices with Žižka but to fight him unstintingly. Clearly, Sigismund was expressing his disapproval of the recently-expired November armistice between Ulrich and Žižka. For his part, Ulrich took the path of least resistance, neither renewing the armistice nor following the King's encouragement to continue fighting. As a result, Žižka was able to concentrate his forces against the ultimate Royalist target in the region, Plzeň. Again the great city was besieged. The Hussites quickly took all the suburbs and the town mills while severely damaging the walls, which had to be continually shored up. The defenders fought with great courage, as even the Hussites acknowledged. After four weeks, several outer bulwarks had crumbled, and with no relief in sight they began negotiations. Despite this opportunity, Hussite leaders surprisingly did not press for unconditional surrender. In retrospect, this would prove a serious mistake.

The men of Plzeň cagily recognised that the most effective negotiating tactic would be to promise to acknowledge the Four Articles. In addition, they offered to send an emissary to Sigismund requesting him to do nothing to prevent their implementation in the town. The Taborites objected that Sigismund would never agree to these terms. The Plzeňers responded by promising that, even if that were the case, they would grant full freedom to Hussite preaching throughout the Landfrieden and permit the communion in both kinds. The offer was accepted, and an armistice implemented which was to last until 1 January 1422. Žižka's agreement to this armistice seems puzzling, but perhaps he hoped to avoid further difficulties between Prague and Tábor. Swayed by their ingratiating language, Žižka may have been persuaded that the Plzeňers ought to have a chance to redeem themselves in God's eyes.

In late January 1421, Hromádka, the sexton instrumental in the formation of Tábor, attempted to establish another fundamentalist community in the upper Elbe valley. He had only a thousand troops, which he divided to occupy the towns of Přelouč and Chotěboř. A Kutnohorian force led by Nicholas the Fierce, with assistance from Jan Městecký of Opočno, a devoted follower of Sigismund, reconquered Přelouč, killing many Taborites and leading 125 prisoners back to Kutná Hora. In early February, this same force, with the addition of other Royalist nobles, besieged Chotěboř. Hromádka had sent troops out for re-supply and hence was at a decided disadvantage. After resisting for a few days, he requested surrender terms. Městecký agreed, saying that, if the Taborites would surrender, the lords were honour-bound to let them leave unmolested. But Městecký made this pledge on the basis that he was not required to keep promises to heretics. After the surrender, 300 Taborite men were burned on the spot and their wives forced to watch. The rest were marched off to Kutná Hora; those too weak or injured to walk were clubbed and left for dead; atop a hill, forty unco-operative Taborites were burned. The 700 or so who managed to make it to Kutná Hora were thrown down the mineshafts, and Hromádka was taken to the nearby town of Chrudím and publicly burned in the town square.

This atrocity enraged Hussites throughout Bohemia into a lust for vengeance. The first to bear the brunt of this rage were the citizens of Chomútov, which was besieged on 14 March. The next day the defenders, who had been reinforced by local squires, fought off an attack while heaping scorn on the Hussites. The following day, the Hussites' assault succeeded, and while pouring into the town they killed all male inhabitants, even those pledging to accept the Hussite creed. One exception was made. Hussite commanders offered immunity to the town's Jews if they converted. They declined the offer and were burned with the rest. Žižka's standing order to spare women and children was defied by the Taborite women. As the women of Chomútov were led out of the town, they were stripped of their clothes and killed. The only survivors were thirty men pardoned to allow them to bury the roughly 2,000 dead. The psychological effect of this battle was widespread, and many towns in Bohemia still loyal to Sigismund were left in a state of abject terror. After a rest in the Hussite town of Žatec, the allied army turned back towards Prague, travelling through Louny and Slaný. After joining the revolution at the outset, these towns had been taken and garrisoned by Sigismund the previous May. As the Hussites approached, both garrisons fled and these towns rejoined the Hussites.

On 22 March 1421, Žižka and the combined armies of Prague and Tábor entered the capital. It had been a long campaign, nearly three months. There had been a great deal of fierce fighting, but there was much to show for it. Most of western and north-western Bohemia was secured, numerous castles had been occupied, and important lines of communication between the various Hussite centres were now open. The next logical theatre of operations was eastern Bohemia. First, two final holdouts in the Prague region would have to be addressed: Beroun, thirty-two kilometres to the south-west; and Mělník, an equal distance to the north where the Vlatava joined the Elbe River. Both towns were inconvenient roadblocks and active centres of anti-Hussite activity. Beroun's militia was commanded by Rodolfo Bece, an Italian *condottiere* who had fought with Sigismund against Venice. Žižka marched on the town and conquered it in six days, killing Bece and burning three anti-Hussite University masters to death. Mělník did not wait for the Hussites to arrive but sent a message to Prague declaring submission to the Four Articles and rejection of Sigismund.

Jan Vilímek, *Charles IV, Father of the Homeland*, c. 1885. Charcoal, from České album. Prague, late nineteenth century

Portrait of King Wenceslaus IV of Bohemia. Anonymous, c. 1400

Depiction of the drowning of 'Saint' Jan Nepomucký. Bronze plaque. Charles Bridge, Prague. During the Counter-Reformation, the Jesuits promulgated a myth that the Vicar-General of Prague was thrown into the Vlatava River by Wenceslaus for refusing to divulge Sofia's confessional secrets. Some scholars believe this figure was a composite of two individuals, one of whom was killed by the king for disputing the appointment of an abbot for a wealthy Benedictine abbey. In 1963, given overwhelming evidence of this historical fraud, the Vatican stripped Nepomucký's sainthood

Alphonse Mucha, *Master Jan Hus Preaching at the Bethlehem Chapel: Truth Prevails*, 1916. The chapel actually had a flat ceiling, but Mucha's depiction of Hus as beardless is historically correct. Although difficult to discern at this reduced size, Mucha portrayed Žižka standing behind Queen Sofia, seated at far right

Burning of Jan Hus at the stake at the Council of Constance

Hussite war wagon. (*Hussite Museum, Tábor*)

Two styles of protective boarding for Hussite war wagons: (left) in the form of a fence; (right) with loopholes for shooting. Note the board beneath the wagons with loopholes. (*Hussite Museum, Tábor*)

Reconstruction of a Hussite war wagon manned by hand-gunners and crossbowmen being attacked by Hungarian cavalry. Hussite infantry armed with flails are ready to launch a counter-attack. The chalice and goose banner flying above the wagon belongs to the Taborites, the most radical group of the Hussite army. Painting by Richard Hook. (*Courtesy of Military Illustrated*)

Above left: Andrea del Castagno, Portrait of Condottiere Pippo Spano, *c.* 1450

Above right: Jan Vilímek, George of Poděbrady and Kunštát, *c.* 1885. Charcoal, from *České album.* Prague, late nineteenth century

Below: Jiri Liebscher, Jan Žižka after the Battle of Kutná Hora, 1890

Above: The Jan Hus monument in Prague's Old Town Square. Designed by Ladislav Saloun, its foundation stone was laid in 1903, and the monument was unveiled on 6 July 1915, the 500th anniversary of Hus's death. Although festivities were forbidden by the Austro-Hungarian authorities, Prague citizens covered the monument with flowers

Below left: Bethlehem Chapel, Prague. This building was restored after the communist takeover of 1948. Not known for supporting religious sites and revered clerics, the Soviets made an exception for this chapel and Hus, whom they characterized as a shining example of Pan-Slavic anti-German nationalism

Below right: Josef Strachovsky, statue of Jan Žižka in Žižka Square, Tábor, 1884

Right: Statue of Jan Žižka in Belkovice-Lastany

Below left: Bohumil Kafka, statue of Jan Žižka on Vítkov Hill, Prague. Begun in 1934, its progress was interrupted by the Nazi occupation in 1939, Kafka's death in 1942, and political squabbles after WWII. It was finally erected in 1950

Below right: Josef Malejovský, Jan Žižka Monument in Trocnova, 1956–60. Malejovský and his socialist realist style were greatly favoured by the post-1948 Czechoslovak communist regime, which portrayed Žižka as a hero of the Marxist class struggle

Vojtech Kubasta, commemoration of Žižka memorial statue on Vítkov Hill, 1950. Lithograph. The legend on the shield reads: 'Dear God, please, give freedom to those who love you'. On the banner is the opening line from the Hussite battle hymn 'Ye who are the warriors of God and of His Law'. After WWII, Czechoslovak soldiers were depicted as having carried on the Hussite legacy of anti-German nationalism, a conception encouraged by Stalin

Adolf Liebscher, Jan Žižka of Trocnova, 1889. Oil on canvas. (*Hussite Museum, Tábor*)

After Beroun's fall on 1 April, Žižka returned to Tábor. Though he had made arrangements to march eastward with the Prague forces, Žižka was diverted by theological issues which had festered in his absence. An unruly radical Taborite priest named Antoch had been preaching in Old Town Square, calling Prague 'the beast with two horns', a symbolic reference to the city councillors and University masters who supported continued use of the vestments. Antoch told his listeners to leave Prague and not give it further assistance – a call to outright mutiny since the Taborites had been ordered that same day to join a campaign with the Praguers. Many of these soldiers, led by Antoch and some other Taborite priests, left the city heading for Tábor. When Žižka learned of this sedition, he chased them down and demanded that the priests take the soldiers back to Prague. They refused, and Žižka flew into a rage. He beat them into submission with his bare fists, and the mutineers returned to Prague. It was evident that the religious divisions in Tábor had serious military implications. Žižka concluded that the religious radicalism that had already created trouble between Prague and Tábor was responsible, and that he had no choice but to deal with it.

The Taborites had splintered into disparate elements, the most problematic being the Pikharts (sometimes spelled Picards), their most radical sect. The name originated from the word 'Beghard', a term that had come to encompass numerous religious movements in Flanders, western France, and the Rhineland. Such beliefs were held by French and Belgian émigrés who came to Bohemia in 1418 to escape religious persecution. The critical difference between them and the moderate Taborites (who included Žižka) was their endorsement of Wyclif's concept of remanence – the belief that Christ was present in the sacrament of Holy Eucharist only in a ceremonial sense, not in any physical manner. Led by Houska, this group railed against the worship of the sacrament as idolatrous, while also espousing mystical and pantheistic teachings directly opposed to fundamental Christian precepts. They denied the existence of the Devil and Original Sin, believed God was everywhere, especially within themselves, and felt that all human impulses – including sexuality – were inherently good and ought to be practised without restraint. This movement was essentially foreign to Bohemia and, given the nationalist nature of the Hussite revolution, xenophobia may have exacerbated attitudes towards the Pikharts. They were persecuted in Prague as well as Tábor, and the name itself became a derogatory euphemism for anyone suspected of being too radical in their Hussite beliefs.

Houska's position was strong enough that he had been one of the Taborite representatives at the disputation in Prague. However, two months later, on 29 January 1421, Houska was in prison charged with heresy. He had been arrested by Ulrich Vavák, and it is virtually certain that Žižka endorsed Houska's detention, especially in light of the newest element of Houska's teachings: he was practising a new form of Holy Communion in which the priest did not place the Host directly into the mouths of worshippers but gave the bread to the entire congregation for them to divide among themselves. Houska felt this was an authentic imitation of Christ at the last supper. But this practice carried more profound importance, in effect denying transubstantiation. For most Taborites, this shocking act of disbelief went to the very heart of Hussitism. Most Hussites believed that the Eucharist was actually the body and blood of Christ, essential for eternal salvation and the very thing for which they were fighting and dying.

Houska was what today we call a rationalist. Along with his powerful eloquence, he possessed great personal charisma and was clear-thinking, witty, free from any dogmatic prejudice, and completely fearless. He did not hesitate to speak out against what he considered an idolatrous act, 'kneeling before the bread'. Houska held that since Christ's body had ascended to heaven, it could not be present in the Holy Eucharist, adding that priests claiming the power to turn the bread into Christ's body with a few words and a sign of the cross were conjurers and frauds. Imprisonment did nothing to change Houska's mind or weaken his resolve. He stated he was not afraid to die for his beliefs but asked for an opportunity to speak before being executed. The Taborite clergy prevailed upon Vavák to release him to them, promising they would deal with him in a suitable manner. The Pikharts had already drawn the attention of Bishop Nicholas and other Taborite clerics, who wrote letters to the University masters warning of the dangers of Pikhartism. Consequently, Prague preachers began cautioning their listeners against this insidious movement and Prague residents were instructed to refuse lodging to any Pikharts and inform city authorities of their presence. Shortly afterwards a Prague workman espousing Pikhartism was publicly burned.

Once freed, Houska, under enormous pressure, renounced this particular heresy but generally continued to show lack of caution or restraint. While Žižka was absent, he continued to preach his troublesome doctrine. But, faced with Žižka's imminent return, Houska grew frightened and left town with another Pikhart priest known as Prokop the One-Eyed. He returned to his Moravian birthland, probably to join another radical Taborite movement in Strážnice. While passing through Chrudím, the captain-governor of the town, Diviš Bořek, arrested and interrogated him. Houska told Diviš that Christ's body was in heaven, and only its spirit was present in the Holy Eucharist. Indignant, Diviš prepared to have him burned at the stake. However, Ambrose happened to be in town. He asked Diviš to turn Houska over to him so that, priest-to-priest, he might convince him of his mistakes and save his life and soul. Ambrose was a humane man, but his empathy and persuasion did not avail. After two weeks, Ambrose found Houska stubbornly unrepentant. Meanwhile, a religious synod had been convened in Prague by Archbishop Conrad to unify Hussite dogma. Ambrose felt duty-bound to turn the prisoner over to the Archbishop, and on 20 June Houska was taken to Conrad's Rodnice residence, where he spent several weeks in prison. Only archiepiscopal priests were allowed to see him so others would not be infected with his heresy. Numerous attempts were made to show him the light, but Houska was unwavering.

During this time, Žižka suffered the loss of his one good eye to an arrowshot sustained during a castle siege. This wound caused a serious illness necessitating a two-month recuperation. After his recovery, Žižka decided that Houska had had ample opportunity to recant. He called on the Rodnice authorities to bring Houska to Prague and burn him in Old Town Square as a deterrent to those tempted by Pikhartism. The Prague authorities agreed it was time to deal with Houska but were fearful of doing so in Prague where his many followers might be provoked into rebellion. They sent a city councillor and the city executioner to Rodnice. Houska and Prokop were tortured to make them to confess the source of their heretical ideas and to name their Prague accomplices. Houska would not speak and, when asked a final time to recant, his reply was, 'Not we are in error, but you who kneel before the bread.' On 21 September, before a large crowd, the two men were led to the stake. Asked by the executioner if he wished to ask for the onlookers' prayers, Houska replied, 'We do not need their prayers. Ask those who really need them.' Then, with no sign of fear or weakness, Houska and Prokop mounted the stake and were put to the torch. One contemporary historian praised God for destroying 'the wolves' that wanted to invade his flock.

The Taborite clergy had treated Houska rather gently; he was well liked even by those who disagreed with him. However, a Pikhart subgroup that had gone much further would not receive the same leniency. Led by a priest named Peter Kániš, they believed that they alone possessed the innocence of Adam and Eve, so this group eventually became known as the Adamites. As with Houska's disciples, a central tenet of their creed was the belief that it was wrong to curb sexual desire in any way. This was highly offensive to the puritanical mindset of Žižka and the Taborite leaders, who expelled the group and isolated them in the fortress of Příbenice. Žižka took them to the nearby village of Klokoty and attempted to show them the error of their ways, insisting they had fallen into the Devil's snares and must return to the Law of God. However, fifty Adamites including Kániš would not listen, remaining steadfast; they went to their deaths smiling and proclaiming that on that day they would rule with Christ in heaven. However, the movement was not stamped out. Several hundred Adamites escaped from Příbenice and took to the woods, and in Tábor adherents remained. Shortly after Žižka left town, another twenty-five Adamites were burned by order of the Taborite clergy, but Žižka was not yet finished with them.

The Adamite movement developed into a crude and repulsive anarchism after Houska's death, and he has been unfairly blamed for its later stages. Houska's Pikhartism stressed ecstatic spiritual purity as opposed to the vulgarity and self-indulgence of the later Adamites.

The escapees from Příbenice moved southward, hiding in the woods during the day and pillaging villages at night. They eventually settled in a wooded valley on the Nežárka River where they found refuge on a large island. These Adamites recognised no authority, but one peasant served as first among equals, sometimes calling himself Moses. Feeling they had returned to the Edenic state of grace enjoyed by Adam and Eve, they dispensed with clothing altogether. Any urge was considered divine. All men shared all women. Marriage was forbidden, and a frequent ritual ceremony was group dances ending in mass orgies.

The Adamites have been referred to as the 'hippies of the Hussites', a deceptively superficial description. They were anything but gentle Flower Children espousing a live-and-let-live philosophy. They took the belief of divine impulse to its darkly logical conclusion, extending it to encompass aggressive urges, including the desire to harm others. Moreover, they regarded themselves as the only people living a genuinely godly life; others had no right to respect – or even life. When they went out on their night raiding missions, they killed all the surprised inhabitants of whatever village they were pillaging, including children and babies in their cradles. Žižka realised Houska's execution had not solved this problem, and felt compelled to take matters into his own hands. He had received communication from two lords in the vicinity of the Adamites' island base reporting wide-scale destruction of villages and property accompanied by large loss of life.

Žižka was prepared to take whatever measures were necessary to eradicate this scourge but misjudged the effort required. This was one of the rare occasions when he under-estimated an enemy. He sent one of his captains, Bořek Klavotský, and 400 troops, certain this would be more than enough to dispose of the Adamite rabble. He was mistaken. The Adamites also knew how to exploit natural defences and made good use of their island fortress. They fought with reckless courage, driven by their leaders' assurances that anyone attacking them would immediately become blind and harmless. Bořek was killed along with a large number of his men, and Žižka had to move in with reinforcements. Most of the Adamites died in the ensuing battle; only forty survivors were taken prisoner. All were burned to death except one, kept alive to be interrogated by Žižka, who included that individual's statements in his report to Prague.

Like other incidents and individuals in the Hussite wars, the Adamites took on a prominence out of all proportion to their actual significance. Hussite, and especially Taborite, puritanism had been provoked by the hedonistic sexual behaviour of decadent Catholic priests and monks. As noted, the Prague Hussites had been particularly offended by the houses of ill repute in that city, and while the Taborites had been accused of numerous atrocities, none of them were sexual in nature. In contrast, Sigismund's Hungarian mercenaries committed mass rape in the course of their invasions, leading Žižka to call Sigismund 'the violator of women and virgins'. Hence, the vast majority of Hussites were horrified by the uninhibited sexual licentiousness of the Adamites, so much at odds with the strict restraints they imposed on themselves. As the Prague brothels had been a source of shame to them, so too were the Adamites, and this stain on their reputation and self-esteem was intolerable.

While the main group of Adamites was annihilated in the Nežárka River massacre, the sect endured in small bands scattered throughout southern Bohemia. Traces of them lingered into the eighteenth century, but only as a few harmless eccentrics privately practicing pantheism, nudism, and free love. Žižka had eliminated them as a movement of any significance among the Hussites.

Chapter 5

CONFERENCES AND CRUSADERS

The difficulty with pragmatic arguments for a religion is that truths do not always 'work', and beliefs that 'work' are by no means always true.

Jan Warwick Montgomery

On 13 April 1421, Prague troops left the capital to begin what was to be an extremely successful offensive. On 16 April, the Hussite army arrived at Český Brod, a well-fortified town defended by several hundred German mercenaries. The following day, Žižka's soldiers attacked the town and killed most of the defenders. Eighteen priests who refused to recognise the communion in two kinds were executed. This decisive victory, along with previous events at Chomútov and Beroun, rippled throughout the Elbe valley. In rapid succession other towns in the region surrendered and made treaties of alliance with Prague. Towns pledged submission before the Hussites even reached their gates, including Kolín and the royal town of Čáslav.

Situated between these two towns was Kutná Hora, a formidable threat. On 23 April, the Kutnohorians' resolve failed after they saw the Hussites' strength, and they retreated behind their city walls. The next day, they sent emissaries in an attempt to forestall impending destruction. They pointed out that Kutná Hora was one of the wealthiest and most beautiful towns in Bohemia, and the entire kingdom benefited from the tremendous income generated by its silver mines. Its leaders promised to acknowledge Prague as its capital and adhere to the Four

Articles, provided citizens unwilling to do so were permitted to leave with their movable belongings. The Hussites agreed but insisted that the Kutnohorians do public penance. The conquest of the town was a tremendous economic acquisition, but the Hussites recognised that without German miners' expertise they might not be able to work the mines competently. This was one occasion when Želivský showed himself capable of being a realistic statesman. Prague had no official captain-general, but Želivský was clearly in charge, although it is difficult to explain how he maintained power after his numerous political reverses.

On 25 April, a ceremony of public repentance was held with the participation of every citizen of Kutná Hora. The townspeople walked in a body towards the assembled Praguers, fell on their knees, and asked forgiveness. Želivský preached at them for a while, pointing out their misdeeds and urging them to mend their ways. With a tearful show of emotion, the Kutnohorians promised to do so. After singing alternate verses of the 'Te Deum' with the Praguers, they returned to their city accompanied by some Prague officials who would oversee its rehabilitation.

From Kutná Hora, the Praguers marched via Čáslav towards Chrudím, where they were joined on 26 April by Žižka's Taborites. Although Chrudím's citizens wanted to surrender, their captain and governor Jan Městecký refused. Two days later, the outer walls were breached, and he realised resistance was useless. Městecký surrendered, asked forgiveness, and promised to honour the Four Articles. Though the Hussites believed he was lying, they accepted his terms. After installing a garrison, the Hussites headed towards Vysoké Mýto, where Žižka and his Taborites detoured south to free the town of Polička. The forces rejoined at Litomyšl, seat of the eastern-most Bohemian bishopric. The bishop himself had fled to Moravia, and the town offered no resistance.

The Hussites crossed the Moravian border in May, installing some troops in the town of Svitavy, but chose to go no farther. The men from Hradec Králové urged a march north into the upper Elbe valley to settle scores with some old enemies, particularly the German citizens of Jaroměř. The town's military commander, Hynek Červenohorský, after urgent calls for assistance to Silesia, fought for several days before surrendering. Pleas for mercy found unreceptive ears. The Hussites permitted the townspeople to keep their lives and nothing else. The men and women were stripped to their shirts before being expelled with no food or possessions. Twenty-four priests were given the opportunity to accept the Four Articles; twenty-one chose death instead, and Červenohorský was taken to Prague as a prisoner. There was one act of forgiveness at Jaroměř. Čeněk, who had surrendered the Hradčany and branded himself a traitor, had been living there precariously, out of public view. With the Hussites controlling eastern and north-eastern Bohemia, where he had his most prized holdings, he became increasingly nervous. After Český Brod fell, he approached the Praguers several times attempting to reconcile. He was told he must completely renounce Sigismund. So, for the third (but not final) time, he switched allegiances. He told Želivský he repented his sins and was 'totally reconciled' with Prague. His ragged banner, which had been hanging from Prague's pillory in disgrace, was then removed.

With nearly all of eastern Bohemia including the Elbe's rich agricultural plains in Hussite hands, the Prague army returned to the capital in mid-May. Žižka, however, was planning additional expeditions now that he was strongly supported by Ambrose's Orebites. This combined force moved north along the Elbe towards Silesia. The town of Dvůr Králové surrendered without a struggle but Trutnov, just eleven kilometres from the border, had to be stormed and was burned afterwards. The Silesians fully expected Žižka to cross the border, but instead he turned west. His men marched 160 kilometres to the city of Litoměřice, northern Bohemia's leading city, receiving the surrender of Mladá Boleslav along the way. Hussites had been severely persecuted in Litoměřice, many being drowned in the river. Its citizens were ready to surrender but were terrified of being slaughtered. Before Žižka even reached the city, the citizens sent emissaries to Prague offering full submission. The Praguers accepted and instructed Žižka to agree to the terms. He may have been irritated at the townspeople for going over his head, and instead of complying immediately, he inflicted a half-hearted siege on them before signing the agreement.

Žižka then broke away from the main body with a small detachment and conquered a minor wooden fort on a hill near the village of Třebusín a couple of kilometres to the east. This fortress had been built by the Teutonic Knights, his first enemies in officially-declared warfare. He took it as personal war spoil, the only time he ever did that. Although it was known as a castle, this modest wooden structure only qualified for the term because it had walls and a tower. After rebuilding it in stone and renaming it 'Chalice' (Czech: *kalich*), Žižka took up residence there. From then on, he referred to himself as 'Jan Žižka of the Chalice'. His brother Jaroslav, who served with him throughout the Hussite wars, also took the same title. Although Žižka could have appropriated any of a number of magnificent castles, he chose this unprepossessing building, far from his birthplace in comparatively hostile territory. He also changed his family coat of arms from a crab (most likely an astrological reference) to a chalice, symbolising his commitment and devotion to Hussitism.

Žižka and his men then headed south, passing first through the archiepiscopal town of Roudnice. Its rich ecclesiastical architecture, like that of Rokycany, suffered some damage at the hands of the Taborite fundamentalists, but no one was killed. They continued on to Prague. After sending his troops back to Tábor, Žižka remained there for a few days, where the order of business was political not military. Even before their army returned to Prague, the Hussites had begun besieging the Hradčany, the last Royalist stronghold in the city's immediate vicinity. On 25 May, an armistice was signed stipulating the castle's surrender within two weeks if it did not receive reinforcements. These were not forthcoming, and Prague took possession. Although important militarily, the political implications were even more important: the capital city now possessed the hereditary seat of the crown and the archdiocesan cathedral of St Vitus.

A second political success involved the Archbishop himself, Konrad of Vechta, an ethnic German from Westphalia who had been sequestered for several months in his fortress town of Roudnice. Although he had placed the Bohemian crown on the head of Sigismund and initially resisted Hussitism, he was not rabid about it. Sigismund regarded Konrad, a mild-mannered and cautious man, as lukewarm in defending the Catholic faith and even complained to the Pope about him. One of the Emperor's staunchest supporters, Hanuš of Kolovrat, a leading member of the Landfrieden, raided the archiepiscopal town of Příbram in retaliation for Rokycany's laxity towards the Hussites. This only served finally to drive Konrad into the Hussite camp. On 21 April, the Archbishop signed a compact with Prague promising to observe the Four Articles and renounce Sigismund. (He also began spelling his name 'Conrad'.) In turn, Prague pledged to support the Archbishop. Sigismund declared Conrad unfit and replaced him with Bishop Jan ('the Iron') of Olomouc, a fierce anti-Hussite. The Archbishop's conversion was also viewed somewhat warily by the radical Taborites, who felt it would only strengthen conservative elements within the Prague clergy and revive hopes for an eventual reconciliation with Rome. But Prague conservatives and centrists were overjoyed. Along with enhancing the Hussites' moral legitimacy, it also brought several important towns, including Roudnice, Rokycany, Příbram, and Rožmitál, into their camp without any battles. Most of Bohemia was now under Hussite dominion.

Hussite leaders began to look beyond Bohemia to the rest of the Czech crownlands, including Silesia and Lusatia where Slavs were a minority and Hussitism had been overwhelmingly rejected. A league of Lusatian cities called the Six Towns pledged loyalty to Sigismund, angering Bohemians who felt that they, not the 'Hungarian King', were owed allegiance. However, they recognised that it would require military conquest to garner that allegiance. It was a different matter in the eastern crownland, Moravia, closely tied to Bohemia for centuries. Most of its citizens and nobles were ethnic Czechs; the German population was limited to its larger cities. There were no language barriers impeding the spread of Hussitism into Moravia, which tended to follow Bohemia's lead religiously and politically. There was even a Taborite community near the town of Strážnice in the lower Morava River valley that had become significant enough to draw Royalist attention. It resisted and defeated a combined attack by the Duke of Austria and Bishop Jan, as well as a subsequent Hungarian assault ordered by Sigismund. However, given their proximity to Hungary, most Moravians had been reluctant to profess Hussitism openly and defy Bishop Jan, who was greatly feared.

Things changed after the successful Hussite spring offensive; one Moravian town, Svitavy, had even allied itself with Prague. Numerous Moravian lords, knights, and squires acknowledged the Four Articles and denounced Sigismund. When the Hussite force approached the Moravian border, they were met by two nobles, Peter of Strážnice and Jan of Lomnice, who promised that the Moravian estates would accept the Four Articles and agreed to sign a compact to that effect. From this incident arose a general conviction that a large scale diet of national unity should be convened.

There were critical issues to be addressed – garnering international recognition of the Hussite reformation, ending fratricidal strife, finding a new king, and establishing a provisional government. On 18 May 1421, the Prague government sent out invitations in its name and that of Conrad and the Hussite nobility. Čáslav was to host the event: it was situated on a main road between central Bohemia and Moravia, and the locals were considered friendly. Although representatives from Silesia and Lusatia were invited, this was mere formality. Their attendance was not expected, but this gesture implied that they were regarded as part of Bohemia's domain, a warning to refrain from further aggression. All parties were guaranteed safe-conduct and immunity from attack, a promise that was fully observed.

The Diet of Čáslav began on 3 June and lasted five days. It generated letters to Sigismund, Lusatia, and Silesia as well as a general manifesto. This document was a transcript of the proceedings, list of attendees, and statement of principles and resolutions. The leading position of Prague's officials as signatories indicates the nobility's acceptance of the city as their political capital, not just as a cultural and intellectual centre but the seat of military power. This acknowledgment by European upper nobility of a capital city's superiority was unprecedented and undup-licated for many years. The political composition of the lords at Čáslav ranged from arch-conservative (notably Ulrich and Čeněk) through the political centre (most importantly Krušina) to the radical wing, including several friends of Žižka: Vavák, the brothers Victorin and Hynek of Poděbrady, Peter Zmrzlík, and Roháč. The Taborites were fully represented; the Landfrieden declined to participate.

First on the agenda was drafting an official version of the Four Articles. Its preamble referred to the recent 'troubles, tumults, and ruinations' of Bohemia and Moravia without assigning blame, an obvious diplomatic effort to avoid alienating the Royalist minority. The Moravian lords quickly signed this document, and, somewhat surprisingly, the Bohemian Royalists did as well. However, the latter were more resistant when the topic of Sigismund arose. Although the members of the Hussite majority had long since arrived at their own conclusions about the Emperor, the Royalist nobles (religious sympathies notwithstanding) were less willing to join the Hussites politically. But three successive embassies had gone to Poland and Lithuania offering the Bohemian crown. Sigismund knew of the Hussite missions to Poland and Lithuania and had reason to believe that the Elector of Brandenburg, Frederick of Hohenzollern, was considering an alliance with Poland through dynastic union.

There was growing dissatisfaction in Rome and throughout his empire with the inept manner in which Sigismund had dealt with the Czech heretics. So, while Sigismund only regarded the Čáslav diet as a problematic affair, he knew better than to ignore it. He sent two Bohemian nobles to Čáslav with a letter to be read to the assembly. They arrived on 5 June, and after they presented their credentials there was some debate over admitting them. It was finally decided to permit them to address the assembly without any commitment to heed what they said. Sigismund, more talented as diplomat than military commander, had adopted a placating tone. He asked the Bohemian kingdom in gentle terms to cease resisting his legitimate authority and to recognise that there was no rational reason to continue doing so. Directly contradicting the facts, he denied having ever rejected the communion in two kinds but claimed instead to have made repeated offers to meet his Bohemian subjects to discuss the matter – omitting any reference to the thousands he had killed for participating in this practice. In conciliatory phrases, he offered to make amends and set right any 'disturbances' that he might have caused so as to not be blamed for any 'disorder'. Nonetheless, he closed on a quietly threatening note by adding that, if the Bohemians and Moravians continued in their stubborn attempts to 'press him out of his kingdom of Bohemia', he would be left no option but force – obviously referring to the ongoing preparations for a second crusade.

The Diet answered with a message that began by blandly referring to Sigismund's offer to make amends, followed by a list of his wrongdoings. Fourteen points were enumerated, including the burning of Hus and Jerome, participation in the charges of heresy levelled by the Council of Constance, promotion of the first crusade at Breslau, and responsibility for atrocities committed by 'those princes and foreigners, led by your highness, [who] have burned, devastated and looted Bohemia, have burned faithful Czechs, priests and laymen, men, women and children, and have done violence to virgins and women'. Also listed were the murders of Krása at Breslau and of other citizens of that town for offences that Wenceslaus had forgiven. There were additional grievances, and a final point charged Sigismund with disregarding the estates' traditional freedoms and prerogatives. This litany of complaint was followed by four demands. Sigismund was to cease slandering the two Czech countries, restore Brandenburg to the Lands of the Bohemian Crown, return the crowns, jewellery, land registers, and other documents he had taken, and order all surrounding countries (especially Silesia and Lusatia) to refrain from further invasions. The letter concluded by referring to the Four Articles as the Diet's standing principles and insisting that the estates would never concede the traditional rights and freedoms given them by Sigismund's predecessors.

The disparity between the two parts of this letter reflected divisions between those who signed it. The first section strongly suggested

Sigismund was an unfit ruler; the second seemed to leave the door open for him to regain his standing with the Czech people. However, there is no hint that fulfilling these demands would lead to Sigismund's acceptance, and the vast majority of those signing the document knew Sigismund would never agree to them. There was a great deal of haggling over the letter's final form, first by Moravians insisting Sigismund be given six weeks to fulfil the stipulations, then by Bohemians over the finality of the rejection of Sigismund. The Hussite majority carried the issue, insisting on very strong language. They were concerned that any ambivalence might derail negotiations in Poland and Lithuania by suggesting that the Bohemian throne was not unequivocally vacant. Even so, after solemnly deposing Sigismund as king, a final caveat was inserted leaving open the possibility of reconsideration.

Although Sigismund was stunned by the apparent defection of some of his most trusted vassals, he did not explicitly take issue with them. His final response did not deign to mention the manifesto itself, but nonetheless took up a number of points in it. He denied responsibility for the execution of Hus and Jerome, as he would for the rest of his life, asserting that his attempt to intercede for them actually got him in trouble with the Church, a claim which may have had some validity. He offered the explanation that he took the crowns, jewels, and documents only to safeguard them, a more dubious assertion. But it was the newly forged Czech unity against him that most disturbed him. Sigismund appealed to their religious conscience, pointing out that the Taborites they supported 'have destroyed the monasteries and churches erected in the honour of God'. It was not he, the Emperor insisted, but rather they who had incited this grievous offence against Christianity, and they had only themselves to blame for any harm done to their rights and liberties. In the end it was evident that further diplomatic exchanges between the Diet and the Emperor were pointless.

A final matter for the Čáslav diet was the issue of a provisional national government. The assembled dignitaries replaced the regent, essentially an executive acting in the king's absence, with a regency council comprised of twenty 'wise, steadfast, and faithful men' to administer the kingdom. The composition of this council is notable: only five members were barons, while Prague had four, Tábor two (including Žižka), and four leading towns one member each; the five remaining seats were occupied by squires. The five barons included two who had been vocal opponents of Hussitism. The other three were considered conservative, moderate, and liberal Utraquists, respectively. Two of the towns, Žatec and Hradec Králové, had been with the revolution since its inception. The third, Kouřim, was a royal town recently gone over to the Hussites. The fourth, Rožmitál, owed allegiance to Archbishop Conrad. The cities and lower gentry thus held the most power, but no single faction was dominant. This structure was well thought out and intentionally crafted so that even a coalition of two groups would not result in an absolute majority. Although the council's powers were defined specifically enough so that they could not be construed as identical to those of a king, they were extremely broad. The Diet declared that it was 'the duty of all and everyone to obey all orders of the council', which was empowered to use force to compel obedience. The members acknowledged that signing the manifesto constituted a pledge to regard anyone disobeying the council as an enemy.

Some proto-democratic notions were seen here, specifically the concept of the patriotic duty to defend an elected national government. Particular emphasis was laid on the obligation of all citizens to obey any call to arms by the council and go wherever it might send them without objection or insubordination – the document's most 'modern' aspect. Rather than citing sacred duty to a feudal lord or master, or giving specific reasons for obedience, this mandate affirmed the responsibility to promote and assist national defence, something never before stated in those terms in medieval Europe. Given the unprecedented nature of what the Čáslav diet attempted, it is not surprising they built reservations into their final agreement. One caveat gave communities the right to recall their representatives and replace them, scarcely necessary since the council was only empowered for another four months. No thought was given to extending its term, suggesting an over-confident assumption that the council would quickly persuade a member of the Polish–Lithuanian royalty to assume the Bohemian throne.

The last part of the manifesto dealt with religious issues in a manner administratively practical but politically unworkable. Religious matters beyond the council's competence would be referred to the two leading Prague clerics, Jan of Příbram and Želivský. This was a well-meaning but fatally flawed attempt to forge consensus through compromise – without real consideration of whether that compromise might actually work. It seems obvious that it could not possibly have done so: Příbram was the most conservative of the University masters; Želivský was the most radical cleric in the city. But this seemed the most politic solution. A final resolution called for a general synod of the entire Bohemian clergy to be convened under Conrad's aegis to establish a permanent religious order based on the Four Articles.

An emergency injected itself into the proceedings when the Diet learned that the Silesian dukes had invaded Bohemia at Sigismund's behest. The Emperor had been negotiating in bad faith, having already given the Silesians instructions to 'exterminate the heretics'. German mercenaries ravaged the border district near Náchod, committing atrocities including the mutilation of forty young boys, who each either had his right hand and left foot, or left hand and right foot cut off, thereby preventing them from fighting as soldiers when they reached adulthood. Plainly, this invasion was only the vanguard of a larger incursion. As the council did not want to leave the rest of Bohemia weakened by a full-scale response, the Hussite lords of that region and the Orebites were instructed to mobilise and take the field at Náchod.

*

Hussite forces concentrating in the Náchod region close to the Silesian border included Čeněk of Wartenberg, some of his relatives with their retainers and soldiers, and the Orebite army led by Krušina, accompanied by the town militia of Hradec Králové. The militia were accompanied by Orebite priests, foremost Ambrose, still the city's dominant political and spiritual figure. When the Silesians realised how strong the Bohemian armies were, they quickly retreated across the border. The Czechs followed them, and the Silesians sent Čeněk an emissary requesting an armistice and promising to refrain from further attacks. Čeněk agreed and ordered not only his own forces but all Hussite troops not to cross into Silesia. Čeněk's decision greatly disturbed many Orebite leaders, and Ambrose charged Čeněk with treason, claiming he was looking for an excuse to avoid fighting the Emperor and the Chalice's enemies. Orebite soldiers threatened to kill the great baron and with some difficulty were prevented from doing so. When Ambrose returned to Prague on 23 June, he registered a protest to the city councils and the Prague members of the regency council regarding Čeněk's alleged treason. Ambrose argued that all of Silesia might now be in Hussite hands, foreclosing any threat of future invasions from that quarter, if Čeněk had permitted Czech forces to chase the invaders across the border.

Krušina defended Čeněk, and his explanations were found satisfactory, but Praguers were divided over the matter, most agreeing with Ambrose. The question of whether to repay foreign invasions with counter-invasions was central to the Hussites' self image and sense of justification. They had consistently maintained that they only fought when forced to act in self-defence. Žižka and other Hussite military leaders had been told by the University masters that this was the limit to violence sanctioned in God's eyes. Beyond this theological question was the political technicality of whether Silesia was a foreign country. Some argued that it belonged to the Bohemian crown and that its actions should not be judged any differently than those of other domestic enemies such as the Plzeň Landfrieden. Most Hussite leaders felt they would lose the moral high ground by invading territory beyond their borders. It was not until after Žižka's death in 1426 that his successors began making retaliatory and pre-emptive strikes into surrounding countries. Žižka had opportunities to do so but consistently submitted to the opinions of those he regarded as spiritual leaders.

Ambrose's arguments did not lack merit. The Silesians had inflicted horrible atrocities on the Bohemians of the Náchod region, and Čeněk allowed them to avoid any consequences whatsoever. Želivský fully shared Ambrose's opinion, and he saw an opportunity to turn the incident to account. On 30 June, as indignation ran high throughout Prague, Želivský rang the bells of his church, calling the population to assemble. He marched a large crowd from the New Town into the Old Town where they intimidated the councillors into handing over the city seals. A new council was elected two days later, but this time there was an important structural change engineered by Želivský. To that point, Prague had been divided into three semi-autonomous boroughs: the Old, New, and Lesser Towns. The Lesser Town, for all practical purposes, had ceased to exist after the devastating battle there the previous year. Prague would now be one integrated community. Instead of eighteen councillors in the Old Town and twelve in the New Town, each borough would elect fifteen councillors who would administer the entire city collectively. Želivský's power-base was strengthened by the increased proportion of New Town elements, and three of Prague's four regency council members were replaced with individuals sympathetic to him.

Želivský now had an iron grip on power in Prague. No significant political decisions could be made without him. Patricians, burghers, and prelates were cowed into silence, fearing the wrath of Želivský's ardent followers. Charles University and its masters remained the final bastion of opposition, so it was from there that charges of Pikhartism were levelled at him and some of his New Town councillors. Želivský decided the best defence was a good offence and set out to prove that the true heretics were the University masters. He began by singling out Christian of Prachatice, the priest of St Michael's Church in the Old Town. Christian had been a close friend of Jan Hus, but while giving the communion in both kinds, he had otherwise continued orthodox Roman Catholic practices. He celebrated Mass in Latin and refused to give communion to children – a direct violation of the Four Articles as codified by the Čáslav diet. Želivský made repeated attacks on Christian and his 'Romanism', inciting large numbers of followers to clamour for his expulsion from the church and the city. On 4 July, the general synod of Bohemia's clergy called for by the Čáslav diet convened in Prague.

Archbishop Conrad had been expected to preside, but the town councillors supporting his conservative stance had been replaced, and he thought it inadvisable to come to the capital. With the excuse that he was feeling unwell, he named two vicars to act in his stead, Prokop of Plzeň and Jan of Příbram. They were to select two other clergymen to form a presidium overseeing the synod. They chose Jacobellus as the third vicar and finally added Želivský as the fourth, hoping he would be less dangerous as a presidium member and synod leader than as an outside agitator.

While this synod had been intended to gather together every priest in the Bohemian kingdom, most priests still following orthodox Catholic practice, like the Archbishop himself, apparently felt that a visit to Prague might not be wise given its political atmosphere. Consequently, the synod was actually a general assembly of the Hussite priesthood. It was organised into four regional groups: Prague including most of central Bohemia, Žatec encompassing the west and south-west, Hradec Králové comprising eastern Bohemia, and Tábor with the south. Although these divisions were named by town and region, they were more theological than geographical, since the vast majority of priests from the south were Taborites and those from the east Orebites. Each group was to form a committee to consider several points of discussion and report their deliberations. These four reports were combined into twenty-three resolutions read in a plenary session with a large audience of laymen present. These twenty-three articles show an attempt at compromise similar to that seen at Čáslav, but they also show more confidence and sense of authority. Only a few concessions were made to the Taborites, including an emphasis on the priestly vow of poverty and concurrent prohibition against financial reward for religious functions. The Hussite principle that priests should not hold secular power was re-emphasised. This was a veiled swipe at Želivský, who tactfully said nothing.

The ceaseless controversy over the vestments was taken up and decided against Tábor. The synod stipulated a middle road, asserting that the dignity of the vestments should be maintained, although priests were also to avoid unnecessary pomp. While these measures might be perceived as hostile to the Taborites, they were actually a reaction to Pikhartism, which had come to be seen as the most dangerous internal threat to the Hussite movement. It was emphasised that priests should adhere strictly to the dogma that 'in the bread and wine the whole Jesus, God in Man, with his true body and blood really present' was being given to participants. Another article emphasising the importance of frequent reception of communion and the need to give it whenever any other sacrament was performed was most likely a rebuff to Houska's ridicule of those who 'knelt before the bread'.

A final cluster of articles addressed priestly conduct. These reaffirmed the vow of chastity and threatened punishment for drunkenness, undignified behaviour, and profanity. Priests were required to keep regular canonical hours, take confession if requested, and maintain a supply of holy water and oil for baptism and last rites. This final provision was vigorously opposed by the Taborites along with the decision permitting use of the vestments. Each article was voted on by the four groups. The clergies of Prague, Žatec, and Hradec Králové accepted them in their entirety. The Taborites were divided, supporting some and opposing others. As at Čáslav, it became evident that certain disagreements simply could not be bridged. While opposition to Pikhartism was shared by all, even the most moderate Taborites were opposed to the continuation of rituals symbolising Catholic hypocrisy and idolatry. Although a clause stipulated disciplinary action against any priest not abiding by the synod's mandates, everyone realised it could not be enforced against Tábor. The four vicars who had served as the synod presidium were to become administrators of the Bohemian church with Archbishop Conrad's consent. This administrative council's order of seniority was Jacobellus followed by Příbram, Prokop of Plzeň, and Želivský. Although many preferred to keep Želivský from it entirely, he was too powerful to be left off. Like the Čáslav diet, the Prague synod was unable to arrive at a final resolution to the problems facing it, and the four-man administrative council never exercised full control over the entire Hussite church. It was, however, a step towards establishing a reformed church with centralised authority.

The presence of Taborites in Prague again created problems. Several Taborite clergymen began preaching in the streets, levelling strong criticism against colleagues they felt were too 'Romanist'. Two of these, Prokop the Bald and another named Philip, replaced two Utraquist priests forcibly expelled by an angry crowd. Renewed attacks were made against Christian of Prachatice on behalf of a priest named William, a close friend of Želivský. William and several activist Taborite clergy were viewed by many as secret Pikharts, greatly alarming Prague conservatives, upon whom the distinction between Taborites and Pikharts was lost. In a highly unusual event for the fifteenth century, the women of Prague now stepped to the fore. In contrast to Taborite women, whose outbursts had undercut efforts at civility and decency, these Prague women were voices of reason in the face of increasing religious hysteria. A large number of women marched to the Old Town city hall, now the governmental seat of the entire city, requested an audience with the councillors, and read a document signed by all – a paradigm of pragmatism and rationality. Employing feminine tact, they opened with a conciliatory note to Tábor, crediting that community with benefiting the entire Bohemian nation and expressing gratitude for its sacrifices for the Hussite cause. They then cautioned against priests and laypeople of both genders who had fallen away from sacred truths regarding the Eucharist and other matters of dogma. They suggested that many good priests had suffered expulsion and in some cases physical harm due to extremism, adding that certain Taborite priests had spread these injustices. They closed by demanding that the city councillors take aggressive action to stem any further spread of Pikhartism in Prague.

The city councillors, fearful of Želivský, avoided giving an answer and suggested the women go home. The Prague ladies were dissatisfied with this response and refused to go anywhere. The councillors, stymied, locked them up in the large hall for two hours then returned for further discussion. They promised that the matter would be brought before a general assembly of all Prague citizens, which took place a few days later. Their petition was again read and greatly impressed the assembled crowd. A follow-up assembly on 21 July passed resolutions giving the

University masters, as represented by four church regents, firm control of all Prague clergymen. No services were to be held in any Prague churches and no preaching was to take place in any Prague streets without their approval. Any priest disregarding this order would face the death penalty. A fifty-man religious police force was created to investigate and prosecute those suspected of Pikhartism, and Praguers were told to report any such activity. The conservative citizenry insisted upon a provision stipulating that anyone being denounced for Pikhartism would have the opportunity to confront the accuser. In the event that the accused individual was found innocent, the person informing against them would suffer the penalty which the accused would have suffered had he or she been found guilty. This proviso went far towards discouraging people from settling personal grudges through false denunciations.

These developments were not at all to Želivský's taste, and had he stayed in Prague he might have tried to stop them. He may have thought he had consolidated his political power sufficiently to allow him to leave the city. Despite the prohibition against Hussite priests wielding secular power, he had left in command of a new military expedition. The campaign itself had the Diet's approval and was directed against several lords and towns in northern Bohemia who had rejected the Čáslav agreement and were carrying on low-level warfare against Žatec and Louny. When these Hussite towns requested assistance, Prague quickly answered. On or about 10 July, the combined forces of all three cities assembled near Roudnice. They first conquered the town and castle of Bílina then moved towards Most (Brüx). Želivský heard that the Meissen margraves were bringing reinforcements to the German Catholics of northern Bohemia. He requested additional help from Prague which arrived on 22 July. The Hussites besieged Most, and their guns soon destroyed some of the fortification walls. The defenders requested they be allowed to surrender and leave with nothing but their lives. Most of the nobles serving as leading officers recommended these terms be accepted, but Želivský would have none of it, insisting they would only come back to fight them again.

Many have speculated as to why Želivský, so pragmatic and temperate during his previous campaign in eastern Bohemia, displayed such intransigence on this occasion. One possibility is nationalism. At Most, Želivský was faced with a predominantly German population, whereas eastern Bohemia was primarily Czech. This Czech priest may have been more inclined to extend charity to a repentant Slav than a submissive German. Another possibility was egotism; his previous successes may have made him arrogant and over-confident. Ignorance is a third possibility; he was unaware of the huge enemy force assembled against him and did not realise how much weaker his forces were than his opponents'. In addition, his troops included a much higher percentage of mercenaries than previous Hussite armies, which possibly exacerbated the over-confidence they showed prior to the impending battle.

Želivský was unquestionably headstrong. He flattered himself that he was a master strategist and born leader, true enough in the political sphere. His vanity prevented him from recognising this did not necessarily translate into the military realm, in which he had no background and little experience. He dismissed the advice of his seasoned leading officers, who urged acceptance of the Mostians' surrender which would have placed the Hussites behind the city walls. He compounded this strategic blunder with a tactical one. The Hussites had deployed a wagon formation on a hill south-west of the city with heavy guns emplaced. Had they faced the Misnians from this position, they might have prevailed despite the enemy's numerical superiority. But this entailed lifting the siege, something Želivský refused to do. He insisted upon meeting the Misnians on a road leading to the city from the north on the wide, flat plain of the Bílina valley without even bringing the wagons along. This gave enemy cavalry total freedom of movement while depriving Hussite footmen of any cover. The enemy's head-on charge produced a total rout, and the Hussites retreated in disarray to the wagon formation, suffering heavy casualties including some 400 dead.

The situation was not completely lost, though the Most militia now joined the Misnian attackers. Once re-assembled behind their wagons, the Hussites stemmed the enemy assaults, and a competent captain might still have managed to emerge victorious. But serious damage had been done to Hussite morale. They had seen Želivský exercise terrible judgement with severe consequences, and it is likely they sensed their officers' exasperation at being over-ruled. They were rattled, many were injured, and the force was probably ill-prepared for the overnight encampment forced upon them with no provisions. In the middle of the night, perhaps due to restless horses, some Hussite soldiers panicked in the belief they were being over-run by the enemy. In the darkness and confusion, panic spread. Hussite officers, who had never faced anything of this nature, were unable to calm the men. In blind, unreasoning desperation, they stampeded out of the camp and ran for the safety of the nearby towns of Chomútov, Žatec, and Louny, leaving behind all their wagons, guns, and heavy equipment. The contemptuous Misnian lords, perfectly content with the booty they had been given, did not even deign to pursue them.

It was to be the worst defeat inflicted upon the Hussites by foreign invaders, and one of the very few they suffered. Psychologically, it was the opposite of the battle of Vítkov, which had done so much to bolster the Czechs' confidence. Their deep religiosity compounded the general tendency of the era to ascribe supernatural intervention to extraordinary events. Harsh fault-finding was directed at Želivský, who returned to Prague in deep political and personal jeopardy. Priests throughout the city blamed the disastrous defeat upon a loss of the moral high ground, thinly veiled attacks on Želivský's radical theology and his perceived lack of humane feeling. More than his incompetence as a general, it was his cruelty at Bílina and refusal to allow Most's citizens to surrender that did the most damage to Želivský's reputation. He was accused of having 'robbed even the poor', according to the town scribe, while 'killing fellow-humans more cruelly than heathens'. The clergymen also declared they had fought not 'for His most holy truth in the spirit of compassion . . . but for spoils', clearly a reference to Želivský's mercenaries, a moral rather than a military critique. Želivský was willing to lie low and and wait out unfavourable currents of public opinion, but he now had so many enemies that this option was foreclosed. He responded with even more extreme measures to stifle his opponents.

In the meantime, Prague recognised that spiritual repentance would have to be coupled with renewed military efforts and, when the beaten army returned, the city mobilised three-quarters of its militia and set off to expel the Misnians from northern Bohemia. This time, Žižka led the Hussite forces. His reputation was now so formidable that the Misnians did not dare face him but quickly fled back to Meissen when Žižka reached Louny. Žižka had been preoccupied in the south, where the Plzeň Landfrieden had pointedly absented themselves at Čáslav and continued suppressing Hussitism despite promises to desist. The powerful Riesenberg nobles had reoccupied and rebuilt two castles near the Taborite town of Horažďovice, Bor and Rabí. While at Čáslav, Žižka had ordered action against these two threats, and after the Diet concluded he resumed personal command of these operations in mid-June. He and his men quickly regained Bor. They moved on to Rabí, a fateful expedition. Žižka, never reluctant to lead from the front, was directing the siege efforts from within range of the defenders' archers. Whether by skill or luck, an arrow caught Žižka in his good eye. He was immediately taken back to Prague, his condition critical, possibly due to infection from splinters or suppuration during the long trip to the capital. He was clinging to life when he arrived, and his willingness to submit to the doctors, who ordered two months of recuperation and close medical supervision, attests to the severity of his illness. By mid-August any hope of regaining his sight was gone. After reconciling himself to his blindness, Žižka had recovered enough that, when he heard of the débâcle at Most, he rose from his sickbed to take charge.

Although the manner in which he continued leading the Hussite army was witnessed and well chronicled, we have no way to know the effect it had on his psyche. Žižka kept no diary and wrote no memoirs, and in the unlikely event he confided his feelings to a trusted friend they were never recorded. His subsequent behaviour has led many to surmise that he took this mishap as a divine warning. Like the Prague clergy, he was predisposed to see the hand of God in any setbacks to the Hussite cause – he would explicitly make this assertion – and he seems to have concluded it was a sign he had not been zealous enough in fighting heresy. He became demonstrably more intolerant of those he deemed offensive in the eyes of God, whether Romanists, Taborites, or Pikharts. In the following months he called for Houska's execution, personally supervised the resultant auto-da-fé at Roudnice, and directed the Adamites' extermination, even as a far larger threat – the second anti-Hussite crusade – had begun.

*

In April 1421, the new papal legate to the Empire, Cardinal Branda, convened a diet at Nürnberg to organise another invasion of the heretical Czech Lands. At a follow-up meeting on 29 June, Sigismund's chancellor, Bishop George of Passau, relayed the Emperor's permission for the assembled princes to take all measures necessary and his promise to bring his Hungarian forces to assist. 24 June was set as the date to cross the border near Cheb. Poland's King Władyslaw was warned not to render any assistance to the Hussites, and Sigismund strongly encouraged the Prussian Knights to attack Poland to forestall any such possibility.

The Czech regency council, led by Ulrich and Čeněk, was puzzlingly slow to respond but eventually called for its own diet at Český Brod on 17 August. Prague received and accepted its invitation while Želivský was still in the field with his army, and he immediately protested and tried to prevent the city's participation. He feared the nobility would use the occasion to consolidate conservative strength against the radicals of Prague and Tábor, and he also believed the Bohemian throne would be offered to Vytautas without stipulating adherence to the Four Articles. After heated debate, a compromise agreement moved the diet's location to Kutná Hora. Prague would only send observers with no power to bind the capital to any agreements. When the diet assembled, the attendees were highly put out to find the capital was not officially participating, thus de-legitimising any measures that might be taken. Ulrich Vavák and Jan Sádlo were dispatched to Prague to urge the city

139

to send an accredited delegation. These two took their case to the city councillors, many of whom were mere proxies for Želivský, who led a pitched resistance. The two lords, not at all intimidated, reminded Želivský that he himself had endorsed the prohibition against the assumption of temporal power by Hussite priests. Želivský was cornered by this unanswerable point, and the councillors eventually agreed to send a fully empowered delegation to Kutná Hora, along with Jan Příbram and Prokop of Plzeň as theological advisors. Želivský could only sulk at yet another humiliating defeat, and he decided that the entire nobility was a reactionary cabal that he must somehow prevent from destroying the revolution.

The diet finally got under way on 21 August, and unlike Čáslav, no written records of the proceedings have survived. We can only presume Žižka's presence there, a supposition supported by his position as a regency council member.

The reinstated Hussite mint master of Kutná Hora, Peter Zmrzlík, had fallen ill and died on 16 August. A talented man and close friend of Žižka, his death was a real loss to the Hussites. Zmrzlík had been regarded as a radical due to his co-operation with Tábor, and Ulrich Vavák was selected to replace him. However, a month later Vavák fatally contracted the bubonic plague (then making an appearance in Kutná Hora), costing Žižka two dear friends within six weeks.

The term of the provisional government constructed at Čáslav was to expire on 28 September, and the diet seemed paralyzed over what to do. Perhaps feeling that any prolongation might compromise negotiations with Vytautas, whom they had 'postulated' as king, the Bohemian estates ended up doing nothing, though it was apparent that even an immediate acceptance by him would require several months to take effect. It was evident that Władyslaw, despite his cordiality towards the Czechs, was more concerned with his own dynastic legacy and was preoccupied with Sigismund and the Prussian Knights. Vytautas, on the other hand, was not nearly as concerned with demonstrating his adherence to Christianity as the converted Polish King. The Lithuanian prince, who had demonstrated remarkable flexibility with regard to his professed religious beliefs, had in 1417 refused to punish a Polish nobleman practicing Hussitism, and he was far more exercised by the Prussian occupation of Samogitia than Władyslaw. However, he was still wary of the Teutonic Knights, and he knew that charges of heresy against him would legitimise renewed Prussian aggression. Like Władyslaw, he despised Sigismund and would have gladly disregarded him, but unlike either of them, he did not hold the title of king – something he very much desired.

Vytautas needed Władyslaw's approval to accept the Bohemian crown. He could only garner the King's agreement – and forestall papal anger – by suggesting that as Bohemian king he might bring the Hussites back into obedience to Rome. Hence, he had been non-committal about accepting the Four Articles when first approached in August 1420, evoking Želivský's misgivings. The second Bohemian diplomatic mission to Poland in late December of that year was a bit hamstrung, as the delegation carried with them the risk of a papal interdict wherever they went. Nonetheless, Władyslaw was cordial and graciously played his role, turning down the crown which Bohemia had offered to him as a formality before approaching Vytautas in earnest. The Grand Duke equivocated for some weeks, neither endorsing the Four Articles nor rejecting them outright. Finally, he said he would send Władyslaw's nephew, the young Prince Korybut, to act as his viceroy before sending them home escorted by a pro-Hussite Polish nobleman who assured them Vytautas was certain to accept their entreaty before long.

The Diet now addressed the second crusade and their defence against it. They called for all Hussite forces to meet at Český Brod on 18 September, expecting to be attacked on two fronts, east and west. Sigismund and the eastern front did not materialise; the western front, though, was serious enough by itself. The assembled Royalist forces there were far larger than those brought to bear against Prague the previous year. Although accounts vary widely, and medieval sources are notoriously unreliable in this regard, a reasonable estimate is approximately 100,000. This massive army left Cheb on 28 August, killing all Czechs in their path except small children. They arrived at

Mast'ov only a couple kilometres from Žatec, while a Misnian troop took Kadaň and Chomútov, which the Hussites had abandoned upon their approach. A Bohemian Royalist ally, Sigismund of Wartenberg, initiated unsuccessful assaults on Bílina and Žižka's Castle of the Chalice near Litoměřice. In answer, a Prague army moved north on 13 September, causing the Misnians and Wartenberg to back off and recombine with the main body at Žatec.

The Royalist forces began besieging Žatec and its 6,000 defenders, but, despite their numerical advantage, after six weeks they had not breached the town walls. They even resorted to the outlandish tactic of attaching flaming material to birds to set the town on fire, but the unco-operative creatures insisted on flying in the wrong direction. Soon, morale problems similar to those that had plagued the previous crusade developed. Sigismund was procrastinating, and his absence led to renewed camp rumours that he was insincere in his stated wish to fight the Hussites. Without the Emperor to single out scapegoats, the German commanders performed the job in his stead, and mutual fault-finding grew. On 30 September, Žatec's defenders took advantage of this disarray with a sally that resulted in a large number of wounded, killed, and captured Royalists. Although a protracted siege would have eventually starved the town into submission, the Royalists learned two days later that a large Hussite force was approaching from Slaný. The name of its general – Žižka – was enough to create open panic. The Royalists rapidly broke camp, and in their haste a fire broke out. Seeing this, the town defenders opportunistically sallied out again and hurried them on their way, although they did not have enough men for a full-scale pursuit. Having suffered 2,000 deaths, the Royalists retreated in embarrassment back to Germany. This episode was prophetic: the second crusade would prove a bigger disaster than the first.

The defence of Žatec was a decided boost to the Hussites, and the tardiness of Sigismund's incursion from the east further helped their situation. But the Bohemian leadership was sluggish as well and with the exception of Žižka appeared disorganised and indecisive. Receiving a call for help from the city of Domažlice, Žižka assembled troops and by 12 September was at the castle of Orlík belonging to the two sons of his late friend Zmrzlík. From here, he wrote a letter regarded as one of his most inspiring missives to the citizens of Domažlice. He urged them not to lose faith, assuring them that 'as yet, the arm of God has not grown shorter'. Žižka reminded them not only of their former successes against the Royalists but injected a nationalist reference to the bravery of their forefathers, who had repelled German invasions in previous centuries. He also provided practical instructions, telling the townspeople in specific terms how best to marshal their resources until he arrived. He added one notable piece of information, writing that he was 'drafting men from all sides', a reference to the expansion of his recruitment efforts beyond Tábor and southern Bohemia into the upper Elbe valley between Hradec Králové and Čáslav, the Orebites' domain.

In October, the eastern front took precedence, along with wavering loyalties on the part of several conservative nobles who had never reconciled themselves to an alliance with the urban poor and rural peasantry. Even Ulrich, while posing as a leading member of the regency council, remembered the damage inflicted upon his properties by the Taborites and nursed the silent hope that Sigismund would soon restore the 'natural order'. Ulrich's neighbours, the Plzeň Landfrieden, attacked and conquered the archiepiscopal city of Rokycany, while Leopold Krajíř, moved from the Royalist stronghold of Budějovice against Tábor. In a letter from Bratislava dated 2 October, the Emperor, not yet knowing of the Misnian retreat, told Leopold he was preparing to leave Hungary so as to mount a two-front attack. As Leopold could not have confidently made such a move without at least the ability to rely on Ulrich's tacit approval, it was widely – and correctly – surmised that Ulrich had never really broken off friendly relations with Sigismund and the Landfrieden.

This quiet treachery did not escape Želivský, and it confirmed his overdrawn conclusion that the entire nobility were an irredeemable band of reactionaries who would subvert and dismantle Hussite reforms at the first opportunity. Seeing a chance to restore his political fortunes, on 19 October he executed a coup d'état using his most effective weapon: the rabble-rousing speech. Summoning his followers to the Church of St Stephen, he incited the crowd against the barons with masterful eloquence. Invariably, whenever Želivský called for the unseating of authority figures, someone more suitable usually happened to be nearby. In this instance, it was a young and highly regarded officer, Jan Hvězda of Vícemilice, who had acquitted himself well fighting with the Taborites and the Prague militia. He came from the lower ranks of the gentry and was on good terms with Žižka, doubtless part of Želivský's calculations. When Želivský insisted to the assemblage that Praguers would be best served by a captain-general of their own choosing, several individuals (perhaps coached beforehand) began to shout that the right man – Hvězda – was among them. He was promptly elected to the post and given sweeping powers over military personnel and civilians alike. He could administer summary judgement ranging from imprisonment through exile to death for any disobedience; avoiding military service and desertion were declared capital offences. Further, Hvězda could remove at will councillors he deemed unfit and replace them without elections with men of his choice. Assisted by four captains, also elected at the gathering, he effectively became military chancellor of Prague. It was obvious he would defer to Želivský in all political matters.

This marked the fall of what had essentially been a democratic city-republic. After coming to power through his ability to exploit popular opinion, Želivský did not hesitate to stifle it when his hold on the masses grew shaky. An Orwellian scenario quickly unfolded as Želivský established a reign of terror. A nobleman, Sádlo of Smilkov, was accused of treason by Želivský. He came to Prague on 20 October to defend himself, but, despite a promise of safe conduct, Želivský arrested him, condemned him to death without trial, and executed him the next day. It was naked revenge: Sádlo, along with Vavák, had publicly chastised Želivský for violating the injunction against priests holding temporal power. The people of Prague, even Želivský's supporters, were shocked by this blatant murder, and when they protested, Želivský stepped up his ferocity. He had many of the protestors arrested and sacked five disapproving city councillors, replacing them with more compliant lackeys.

At the time, Žižka was recruiting in the Čáslav region. Following Houska's execution, relations had worsened between him and the Taborite priests, who consequently become less active in recruiting soldiers on his behalf. Priests were the primary means of drawing manpower because of their close day-to-day contact with the peasants and strong influence over them. Without their support, Žižka may have felt he would do better by casting his net in the Orebites' domain, where he had Ambrose's support. Another factor may have been the expected movement of Sigismund towards that region. In any case, Žižka received a plea for assistance that took him in an unexpected direction. Roháč of Dubá was being besieged by Krajíř with Ulrich's assistance on orders from Sigismund. On or about 10 October, Žižka hastily came to the relief of Lomnice, now a critical Hussite stronghold. Krajíř retreated as soon as Žižka's forces drew near. Žižka was determined to punish Ulrich's treachery, and pursued him to his castle of Poděhúsy near the town of Netolice. After taking the castle and burning it down, he then moved on to Ulrich's eastern centre, the town and castle of Soběslav, which he also conquered and burned.

He then received a call for help from another friend, Bohuslav Krušina, whose castle of Krasikov was being besieged by the Plzeň Landfrieden. With the attackers was Bohuslav's younger brother Švamberg, who laid claim to the castle. Žižka was as unstintingly loyal to his friends as he was unremittingly harsh to his enemies, but there were also compelling military reasons to aid Bohuslav. By taking the western Taborite castles of Krasikov and Kladruby, the Plzeňers would have freed their backs and thus been able to concentrate on a thrust to the Bohemian heartland in support of Sigismund's imminent invasion. Žižka arrived at Krasikov in early November, raised the siege, and drove off the attackers. However, strong enemy reinforcements led by Henry of Plauen were en route, so Žižka moved south to Klatovy to gather more men. Additional enemy forces were sent from Cheb, and Žižka, with approximately 2,000 men, was now vastly outnumbered. After minor skirmishes near Krasikov, he retreated north towards Žatec rather than risk moving south through Royalist strongholds. After his rear-guard had been harried by the vanguard of Henry's pursuing cavalry, Žižka decided to make a stand on a mountain named Vladař ('Ruler'). As its name suggests, it dominates the surrounding countryside and afforded Žižka exactly the position he needed for his wagons.

Vladař has three very steep sides; a village named Zahoří was situated on its gentler north-west slope. Getting their wagons and guns to the fairly flat, open hilltop could not have been easy, but once it was accomplished, the Hussites were virtually impregnable. Still, Henry could have starved the men down from the mountain simply by occupying Zahoří, their only exit, and cutting off any re-provisioning excursions. But Henry insisted on mounting repeated cavalry charges against the Hussites and suffered heavy losses. Although Žižka's men had no casualties to speak of, after three days on the mountaintop their food and water were running low and the late-November cold was taking its toll. Henry, unlike previous attackers, was not simply going to give up, so Žižka, sensing Henry was weakened by his losses, used another unconventional tactic. In the middle of the night, his men, horses, and wagons blasted their way past the surprised Royalists, who were too shaken to mount a pursuit. Žižka and his troops marched unmolested towards Žatec, which sent a militia contingent to meet them and escort the victorious Žižka into town. The blind general had added a new offensive wrinkle to his basic defensive tactics – one he would have occasion to employ at his next, much more critical, victory.

Chapter 6

ENTRANCES AND EXITS

> The people have always some champion whom they set
> over them and nurse into greatness . . . This and no
> other is the root from which a tyrant springs; when he
> first appears he is a protector.
>
> Plato, *The Republic*

The German princes' belief that Sigismund lacked commitment against
the Czech heretics was mistaken. He had, in fact, legitimate reasons for
moving late. His over-riding concern was to ensure overwhelming force,
especially since he had lost German assistance from the western front.
Taking his time, Sigismund gathered troops from throughout Hungary
and placed the assembled force, containing a strong cavalry element,
under the command of his Italian mercenary general Pippo Spano. In
early October, Pippo moved to Olomouc where he was reinforced by
Bishop Jan ('the Iron'), as well as Silesian and Lusatian forces.
Sigismund crossed the border on 16 October, pausing at Brumov for
almost two weeks until more troops arrived. At that point, he moved
west to Brno where he gathered all his forces, now numbering
approximately 40,000. Theoretically, the odds were in his favour. The
Hussite forces were scattered, and had the Emperor acted expeditiously
he might have been able to exploit this fact.

Prague was not well prepared either. The city's new captain-general,
Hvězda, was out of his depth. The young officer had been instantly promoted to a position of command over a large body of men with little real

preparation or training. He moved his forces haphazardly in the region between Kouřim and Čáslav in anticipation of Sigismund's next move, but he seemed at a loss strategically. Hvězda's inexperience at handling a large army was also evident in his inability to maintain discipline when his troops plundered homes in Kutná Hora against orders.

Sigismund, wishing to combine political and military tactics, convened a diet of the Moravian margravate attended by most of the region's nobility, even those who had declared loyalty to the Hussites the previous June. They renounced their former pledges and declared obedience to Sigismund, who insisted that they also take an oath renouncing the Four Articles forever. Six months earlier, Sigismund had promised Ulrich he would take no action against the Articles without a public hearing, but his new action once again proved to the Hussites that any possibility of compromise with the King was impossible. Many nobles had only been waiting for Sigismund to arrive to announce their allegiance to him. Městecký had already done so, forgetting not only his earlier agreements but the extremely generous treatment the Hussites had given him. Also rallying to the king was Čeněk, further confirming Ambrose's and Želivský's mistrust. Nonetheless, not a single one of the conservative Prague lords whose loyalty Želivský declared suspect went over to Sigismund. In fact Sigismund's political strategy, like his military plan, was flawed. By taking a harsh and unyielding position he only united the Hussites, and by spending the first three weeks of November in Brno pursuing political ends he gave them a chance to regroup militarily. In the meantime, Hvězda finally took concrete action on 14 November, besieging the castle and town of Malešov which capitulated in days.

Sigismund also moved, although not into Bohemia but to Jihlava in western Moravia. Again, he lingered for over a week, and his Hungarian troops grew impatient. Pippo Spano assured the Emperor that there was no need to wait for further reinforcements, particularly from the Germans for whom he had lost respect. So Sigismund had him make a thrust into eastern Bohemia. On 22 November, Pippo took the little town of Polička, which had been conquered by Žižka the previous spring; most of the town's 1,300 citizens were slaughtered. Instead of continuing into Bohemia, Pippo and his troops returned to Moravia to rejoin Sigismund and the main force at Jihlava. The attack on Polička had alarmed the Hussites, and Hvězda realised he could not hope to stand up to the Hungarian crusaders with his present forces. He wisely decided to return to Prague and on 25 November called an emergency meeting of the city leaders. They sent urgent messages 'to Žižka and his Taborite brethren and to all other adherents to the truth, nobles as well as cities and royal communities', urging them to come to Prague as rapidly as possible. When Žižka received the message the following day, he sprang to action. Within three days he left for Prague with a well-prepared and equipped army. His arrival in Prague on 1 December was a momentous event. As he led the Taborite men and women with their wagons through the city gates, church bells rang, and a huge crowd assembled to greet him. Žižka wasted little time developing strategic plans and he immediately became *de facto* commander-in-chief, while Hvězda moved to the background despite retaining his official title as captain-general.

Sigismund's next move was to march on Kutná Hora, and in the first week of December he crossed into Bohemia towards Humpolec, heading for Kutná Hora by way of Ledeč. His decision was logical; taking Kutná Hora would effectively give him control over most of eastern Bohemia, and the city's German miners overwhelmingly supported him. Sigismund's motives were not limited to considerations of military strategy, however. The immense wealth of the city's silver mines offered an attractive solution to his perpetual financial difficulties. On December 9, Žižka approached Kutná Hora, and a large delegation from the city rode out to meet him. They feigned happiness at his arrival while fearing the worst. Žižka, a far more effective disciplinarian than Hvězda, camped his troops outside the city walls with strict orders against molesting the town. A few leaders, priests, and some small military detachments entered the town and celebrated a Mass at the church of St John. Their simple puritanical practice, including the absence of ornate vestments, thoroughly shocked Kutná

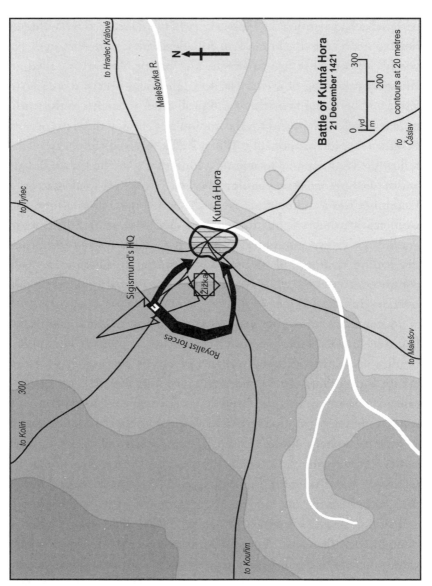

Battle of Kutná Hora
21 December 1421

to Hradec Králové

Malešovka R.

Kutná Hora

N

0
yd
m
200
300

to
Čáslav

contours at 20 metres

to Týnec

Sigismund's HQ

Žižka

Royalist forces

to Malešov

300

to Kolín

to Kouřim

Battle of Kutná Hora

Hora's Germans, convincing them they were indeed the 'worst heretics deserving to be persecuted'. They waited for Sigismund in anticipation. Like others before them, they ended up waiting longer than they expected. Sigismund, after lingering in Ledeč, took twenty days to march the eighty kilometres from Jihlava to Kutná Hora. Along the way, his Hungarian troops razed villages, burning the men, mutilating the boys, and raping all women and girls they encountered. This despicable behaviour naturally enraged the Hussites and contributed to their subsequent ferocity.

Žižka inspected and strengthened the Kutná Hora fortifications, as well of those of nearby Čáslav, where he received reinforcements and recruited new soldiers. Three powerful Hussite barons arrived, including Žižka's close friend Victorin of Poděbrady. Gathering these together, Žižka returned to Kutná Hora. Early on the morning of 21 December, Žižka's scouts reported Sigismund's army approaching. Mass was held, town criers rallied the citizens, and, as bells throughout the city rang, the troops left town through the western Kouřim gate. A small detachment was left behind to defend the city walls, commanded by the new mint master. Approaching from the north-west, Sigismund detoured to avoid resistance from Malešov, now in Hussite hands.

Žižka marched his troops about a kilometre along the Kouřim road and formed his wagons on a high spot where he could keep the road as well as the north-western approach from Kolín under observation. He had just completed arranging his men and wagons when Sigismund's army appeared, passing through the village of Přítoky. The Hungarian cavalry force spread out in a wide front towards the north-west road to Kolín, cleverly supplementing thin spots in their lines with cattle to give the Hussites an exaggerated impression of their strength. Sigismund arrived shortly and set up his headquarters where the Kolín road passed Žižka's right flank. Žižka had chosen his position in the mistaken belief that he had the full support of the city's residents, but he had been betrayed by ethnic Germans and die-hard Catholics secretly conspiring with Sigismund. After some inconclusive skirmishing only intended to mark time until nightfall, Sigismund's men circled around the city, entered a gate opened for them by treasonous Royalist minions and slaughtered all Hussites (or anyone else who did not know the password). Žižka was indeed between a rock and a hard place. Although his wagons were strongly entrenched, he was lightly provisioned; he had counted on getting food and other supplies from the city. Sigismund's forces, which outnumbered him three to one after being strengthened by the addition of Kutnohorian turncoats, were expecting further reinforcements from Hungary.

Žižka had to act fast, and he did so, when it was least expected – the middle of the night – and where the enemy ring surrounding him would be most likely to break – the encampment of Sigismund and his retinue, who had shown themselves more likely to run when attacked than to stand and fight. It was not the first time Žižka had conducted full-scale night operations, another innovative tactic, but this was a break-out attack, not a stealthy retreat. And it was here that the wagons, which paused only to fire, first attempted the task which today's motorised field artillery takes for granted: not just blocking or discouraging an enemy, but dislodging him by destroying his will to stay and thus opening a path for one's own troops. Here, too, Žižka doubtless benefited from the psychological effect of panic, in this case induced by massed and moving firepower at night, lurid muzzle flashes and powder smoke exacerbating the general terror and confusion. Žižka marched about one kilometre north-west on the Kolín road and established another wagon fortress on the slope of Kaňk Hill just off the road. He fully expected to be pursued by the Hungarian cavalry, but despite advice to chase down and destroy the Hussite forces, the Emperor chose not to. He had been looking forward to a triumphal entry into Kutná Hora, and he saw no need to take further action until he had received the reinforcements he expected. When Žižka realised that Sigismund had no intention of chasing him down, he quickly broke formation and took his men by forced march to Kolín, reaching it the same day.

Medieval armies traditionally avoided action in winter, and in 1421 winter arrived early and would prove severe. Sigismund's crusaders, many of them mercenaries, were not keen to camp in the open. The Emperor himself was certainly unwilling to suffer inconvenience or hardship, and he did not wish to alienate his already disgruntled troops further. Here, as at Prague, the very size of his forces worked against him. In order to billet himself and his army comfortably, he was forced to disperse the force over a fairly wide area throughout the villages between Kutná Hora and Čáslav. Sigismund took one precaution by posting a large body of Hungarian troops at Nebovidy, a large village four kilometres north-west of Kutná Hora, halfway to Kolín. Having settled his troops for the winter, Sigismund assumed Žižka would do likewise.

Sigismund's complacent assumption that Žižka, like himself, had shut down operations for the winter is the only possible explanation for the lack of scouting and surveillance on the Hussites' blind general. If he had been paying attention, the Emperor would have learned that Žižka, far from standing down, was busy recruiting and training additional soldiers. Žižka was supported in this effort by Ambrose and the Orebite priesthood. Although his total numbers remained inferior to Sigismund's, his were tightly concentrated, while Sigismund's were widely dispersed. In stark contrast to Sigismund, Žižka wasted little time when he sensed an opportune moment. On 6 January 1422, he marched against the large Royalist force stationed at Nebovidy. Like Sigismund, they were convinced they would not see the Hussite army until warmer weather had returned and were totally unprepared. When they saw the approaching Hussite columns, the Royalist officers were unable to form battle lines before the Hussites were on top of them. While some positions offered resistance, they lasted less than an hour. The Hussites killed many, took a large number of prisoners, and the remaining Royalists, led by those fortunate enough to have a horse, retreated to Kutná Hora.

When Sigismund learned of this defeat, he convened a council of war at which Pippo Spano and the other Royalist generals took pains to impress upon the Emperor the gravity of the situation. Their strongest force had been over-run, weakened, and put to flight.

Although they had a huge number of soldiers at their disposal, these were so widely scattered it would take considerable time to gather them. The Kutná Hora militia by itself could not hold out against Žižka and his approaching Hussites, and the Royalists could only maintain the city by reinforcing its defenders as quickly as possible. Even then, there was no guarantee they would be able to do so. This report made such an impression on Sigismund that he decided there was only one thing to do. Sensing personal danger, he fled. He told the Bohemian and Moravian lords to hold the city in support of the Kutná Hora militia, but they seemed reluctant to take on an apparently suicidal mission. Sigismund did not want to see Kutná Hora fall into Hussite hands again and gave orders for 'the Jewel of the Kingdom' to be destroyed. The Germans of Kutná Hora were eager to depart, but the hasty order was given with no consideration of logistics such as the difficulty of moving elderly citizens quickly. When most of the Hungarian troops had left, the last to go set fire to the city but became distracted and did not do a very good job of it. They were more interested in plundering the newly vacated homes of the rich German patricians. Poetic justice was served when the loot they gathered only served to slow them down with the Hussites on their heels.

Žižka seized the moment. His cavalry were sent ahead to Kutná Hora, and they arrived in time to put out the fires before the town was consumed. Žižka caught up with them and spent the night in the city, but at dawn the next day he resumed earnest pursuit. This was yet another Žižka innovation. Though medieval generals commonly pursued retreating enemies in an attempt to force another battle, it was highly unusual to follow up a victory with hot pursuit and continual attack in an attempt to completely destroy them. Sigismund retreated south-east towards Německý Brod and the Moravian border in complete panic and utter disorganisation. After two days some discipline was re-established, leading Sigismund to feel he could make a stand against Žižka. Pippo Spano and his Hungarian generals attempted to persuade him that their demoralised troops were in no condition to face the Hussites. Sigismund's decision to over-rule this advice had disastrous consequences. In the late morning of 8 January, on a hill near a town named Habry about twenty-three kilometres north of Německý Brod, the Royalist troops were drawn up in battle formation. When Žižka's men charged, the Royalists turned and ran, leaving behind their heavy weapons and supply wagons. This second retreat was even more chaotic than the first and, minus any semblance of a rearguard, the Hussites continued inflicting heavy casualties as they pursued.

By sundown, the Emperor and his personal retinue had reached Německý Brod, which he ordered to be strongly defended to allow him to scurry back to Hungary. The Emperor did not stop to camp but continued running under cover of night. The Royalist troops he left behind outside the city walls attempted to carry out his orders but most were slaughtered. Their bravery, however, permitted many of their comrades to escape into the town and over the bridge across the Sázava River. With the concentration of people, horses, and equipment, a massive traffic jam developed at the bridge. In an attempt to bypass it, many of the mounted knights tried to ride their horses over the ice-bound river. Some made it across safely but, as the number of heavy armoured cavalrymen increased, the ice cracked. The river was soon full of hundreds of riders and horses desperately trying to swim the freezing water. Many were crushed between ice floes, others sank under the weight of their armour, and some simply expired from hypothermia. Night fell, adding to the general confusion and making it virtually impossible to attempt rescue. Over the next several days, 548 fully armoured bodies were pulled from the river.

Žižka, who never crossed the Bohemian border in pursuit or attack, decided there was no point in chasing Sigismund any further. He had accomplished his goal – the Emperor and his Hungarian troops had been driven from the country. Moreover, in three days his troops had covered sixty-five kilometres and fought three battles in the dead of winter. They needed a rest. To Žižka, the next logical step was right in front of him: the conquest of Německý Brod, the only town of any significance in eastern Bohemia still in Royalist hands. Like most of

Bohemia's larger cities, it was strongly anti-Hussite. It was defended by the town militia along with some Hungarians, Moravians, and Poles. Their commander-in-chief, a Polish nobleman named Zawisza Czarny, was thoroughly imbued with the chivalric code of knightly conduct and felt himself honour-bound to cover Sigismund's retreat.

On 9 January 1422, the Hussites began firing on the city walls with heavy siege guns. Zawisza returned fire and repulsed an initial Czech assault, but the Hussite guns maintained their barrage throughout the day and the following night. The town fortifications were battered, and Zawisza realised he could resist no longer. He sent word to Žižka that he wished to discuss surrender terms and Žižka began negotiations. However, while Žižka was occupied, some of his soldiers found a breach in the wall and entered the town. The defenders concluded that the white flag under which their leaders were conferring had been violated. They took to the walls and began firing again but were soon over-whelmed. Hussites swarmed into the town and began slaughtering everyone they found, both Hungarians and Germans. Mob dynamics fanned them into a rampage; burning and looting ensued. Německý Brod was almost totally devastated, and for months afterwards it was a charred ruin where wolves and dogs feasted on the corpses scattered throughout its streets. This would be the most serious breach of military discipline ever suffered by Žižka, and he was greatly disturbed by it. He managed to enforce his policy of sparing women and children, and the Royalist leaders including Zawisza were taken as prisoners to Prague. After some months in captivity, Zawisza was released and allowed to return to Poland, and the report he gave of his experiences may have contributed to Władyslaw's eventual hostility towards Hussitism.

Assessments of casualty numbers on both sides of these three battles vary widely. Estimates by various chroniclers range from 3,500 up to 12,000, and it is safe to assume that Sigismund suffered a minimum of 4,000 dead, a figure eight times larger than at the Battle of Vítkov and equivalent to a mid-sized army of the time. The materiel loss was even more impressive. Along with weapons and horses, the Hussites captured more than 500 wagons containing provisions that had been collected both at Kutná Hora and Německý Brod. These wagons contained food, cash, clothing, jewellery, and even some books, a few of which, interestingly, were in Hebrew. Although Sigismund was generally inept as a battlefield commander, this was a particularly humiliating defeat. He had been ignominiously chased out of the country of his birth, and the effect on him was evident. For years, he would not even approach the Bohemian border, delegating all subsequent military efforts to his German princes. This would be the last attempt made at a two-front operation against the Bohemian Lands, significantly changing the strategic odds in favour of the Hussites.

On 11 January 1422, a great victory celebration was held outside Německý Brod. On display were captured enemy banners and several Hussite leaders who had displayed particular valour were dubbed as knights. It was apparent to all that Žižka's leadership had been the decisive factor in turning certain annihilation into a victory of the first magnitude. He was now universally acknowledged as commander-in-chief of all Bohemian Hussite forces, and even hostile German chroniclers began according Žižka begrudging praise. The Hussites returned to Prague where they were greeted enthusiastically.

Žižka was not able to revel in his victories and acclaim for long. Once again, political divisions between the Hussites would reappear, and he was soon enmeshed in internal conflicts.

*

Although most of 1421 had seen Želivský resurrect his political fortunes and power in Prague, the wars of the final two months did not work in his favour. His anointed captain-general, Hvězda, and much of the Prague militia were absent from the city a great deal. Consequently, its conservative elements regained confidence and rallied around a leader of their own, Jacobellus, every bit as formidable as Želivský and more prestigious. Jacobellus had once been considered one of the most radical reformers at Charles University, but after the revolution his attitude shifted. Originally there had been no overt conflicts between him and Želivský. Although Jacobellus tried to mediate between Želivský and the other two (extremely conservative) directors, he began to lose patience, particularly after Želivský opposed the participation of Příbram and Prokop as religious advisors to the Kutná Hora diet in August. Želivský took to calling both highly regarded men the 'nobles' henchmen'. Jacobellus became increasingly disturbed by Želivský's policies, particularly his tolerance of Pikhartism. Jacobellus had been the first priest in Prague to dispense the communion in two kinds and was passionate regarding the sacred qualities of the Eucharist. Exacerbating his displeasure with Želivský was Jacobellus's adherence to the Hussite policy against priests exercising worldly power. As Jacobellus's sympathy with the University masters grew, he became more and more hostile to Želivský. But Želivský was not going to allow his previous gains to be rolled back without a fight. In early November, he renewed his personal attacks against Christian of Prachatice, who had complained about Želivský to the city council. On 9 November, a large crowd incited by Želivský gathered in front of St Michael's Church and threatened to drown Christian in the Vlatava. To save himself, Christian was forced to accept a devoted Želivský follower named William as his co-preacher.

The University masters, who had grown tired of Želivský's bullying tactics, felt that something had to be done to halt this pattern of mob rule. On 12 November, a meeting of the Prague clergy was held. The primary focus was a resolution presented by Jacobellus and Peter Payne, who had returned from Poland after ten months in diplomacy with the Polish King and the Lithuanian Grand Duke. Payne's views were much less conservative than Jacobellus's, and he may have been brought in as a bridge between the two clergymen. This writ was essentially a confirmation of the measures adopted by the Prague synod the preceding July. It called for increased power for the four directors, especially with regard to 'novel teachings', and included a thinly veiled allusion to the forced appointment of William as Christian's co-preacher at St Michael's. This section stipulated that new preachers would only be appointed through a strict examination of their morals, beliefs, and priestly ability by the synod directors. Želivský could not resist exclaiming, 'These proposals are directed against me and William!' but he knew he could not prevent the majority of clerics from voting in favour and said nothing more.

Želivský began his counter-attack at a town hall meeting two days later. He and his disciples levelled accusations against Prokop and Příbram, and many of his supporters began to demand Želivský be the sole director of the Hussite church. Showing his usual political skill, Želivský declined the suggestion, saying he was unworthy of bearing such responsibility by himself. In turn, he proposed that Jacobellus and Payne be elected, adding that he would be happy to assist them in any way he could. This only served to convince the crowd that he was indeed the man for the job. He was elected by an overwhelming majority and given the option of choosing other priests as assistants. This election, however, had to be submitted for approval to the Prague militia, then in the field at Čáslav. The people of Prague considered it unthinkable that the men risking their lives in the city's defence be denied an opportunity to make their voices heard. The militia engaged in a lively debate on the matter with most opposing any one-man rule. They insisted that a four-man committee should be established comprised of Želivský, Jacobellus, Peter Payne and Jan of Reinstein, and ultimately this suggestion was adopted.

Želivský had managed to elbow aside the two masters most closely allied with the nobility but been unable to achieve sole leadership of the church. The departure of the two conservative directors only served to make Jacobellus more formidable since the Prague traditionalists now gravitated towards him as the one man capable of halting Želivský's suspect political and theological programme. Jacobellus gave Želivský a taste of his own medicine by leading a march of his adherents to the Old Town city hall in an attempt to oust the city council, now comprised entirely of Želivský's men. The attempt was unsuccessful, but it sent a clear message to Želivský.

When the Hussite army returned from Německý Brod, the simmering conflict reached a boiling point. The battle veterans fresh from a string of victories included several nobles Želivský had been attacking as enemies of the revolution. The military leaders engaged in numerous meetings with both sides of the squabbling Prague clergy, and on 5 February 1422 a meeting was held attended exclusively by men who had been active and high-ranking commanders during the recent campaign. They were to act as arbiters, and both Prague theological factions agreed in advance to abide by their determination.

The meeting of nineteen men included: Žižka, his leading Taborite captains Zybnek and Roháč, four Orebite captains, Hvězda and three other Praguers, the Orebite nobleman Diviš Bořek, and seven independent lords including Hynek of Kolstein and his cousin Hašek. It was a diverse collection whose only common elements were their recent combat and hatred of Sigismund. Their decision was a resounding defeat for Želivský and inaugurated dramatic changes in Prague's politics. Among the measures mandated was an immediate re-election of both city councils in which none of the incumbents would be allowed to run and with no changes in its resulting composition permitted for at least one year. Punishment, including execution, would be inflicted upon anyone disturbing the peace or spreading heresy (meaning Pikhartism). If either party flouted these rulings, the opposite party was obliged to assist with enforcing compliance. The four-man religious council would remain the final arbiters on all religious matters. This was the only position of power left to Želivský and his followers. Hvězda probably opposed the measures detrimental to Želivský's position, but as the most junior participant his opinion carried no weight. This was underlined by the abrupt termination of his services as captain-general the same day the new city council took office. He was dismissed without so much as a 'thank you', and Hašek was appointed to replace him.

Four days later, on 9 February, the elections ushered in a dramatically altered political order. The conservative minority now rose to a position of influence, and this new balance can only be attributed to a shared desire to neutralise Želivský's power. It did not seem to occur to Žižka for some time that the new political arrangements in Prague would drive a wedge between the Taborites and Orebites. Soon after these elections and the installation of the new councillors, Žižka left the capital for Tábor. He was eager to continue his campaign against Rožmberk, and the Plzeň Landfrieden were threatening Krasikov again. But the Taborite community had even more fault lines than Prague, so a synod of the Taborite clergy was held at Písek in late February to address this growing problem

After the conservatives rose to power in Prague, they took measures undercutting the political and economic position of their adversaries, displaying much vindictiveness in the process. In late February some of Želivský's most prominent New Town disciples were arrested and charged with Pikhartism. In most cases, these individuals were released since the accusations could not be proven. To his credit, Želivský remained intrepid when others might have folded. Although he had lost all political power, he was not ready to admit defeat. He retained confidence in his personal charisma and continued preaching his opinions at the Church of St Mary in the Snow to large, enthusiastic crowds, encouraging like-minded clerics to follow his example. Želivský still criticised the 'faithless lords' and their alleged puppets, the University masters. He maintained his outspokenness at directory meetings. After the 9 February elections, these meetings deteriorated into personal battles between him and Jacobellus, who was prone to lose his temper. On one occasion, Želivský provoked him into exclaiming: 'You are the man who is responsible for all these uproars and all this shedding of blood! It is you who has led astray the people of Bohemia and Moravia!' Jacobellus then registered a complaint with the city council on 7 March, accusing Želivský of being a subversive and insisting the authorities take strong and immediate action against him. Jacobellus would come to regret this hot-headed outburst.

Prague's ambitious new captain-general, Hašek, also loathed Želivský. While gratified by his new stature, he feared it would never be secure with the rabble-rousing priest around. An aristocrat, he detested Želivský's anti-nobility sentiments and may have been motivated to revenge Sádlo's execution. Hašek was supported by many of the new city councillors when he told them he wanted to take measures against further civil unrest. On 8 March, the city council summoned Želivský and eleven of his supporters to the Old Town city hall. The next morning, Želivský and nine of the men answered the summons. The city councillors, under the pretext of consulting Želivský on military matters, staged a lengthy discussion about the best use of Prague's military. To extend this charade as long as possible, the councillors made a show of close attention to Želivský's suggestions. Hašek was in fact waiting for the two missing invitees to show up. When it became evident they were not coming, Hašek arrested the ten men and put them in chains. Despite protestations that they were faithful believers in the Holy Eucharist and espoused no Pikhart beliefs, Želivský and the others were summarily beheaded. The city council attempted to keep this secret, which was impossible. When news spread, massive rioting broke out. Hašek was completely unprepared for the ferocity of these outbreaks. He placed guards at city hall and the main roads between the Old and New Towns, but these were overwhelmed by furious townspeople, many armed. They stormed towards Old Town city hall, and Hašek fled the city, showing little concern for his cohorts in the city council. Some councillors involved were arrested immediately; others who had hidden were rooted out by a house-to-house search. Seven councillors, the summary judge, and two others were executed. Many University masters were also arrested.

After Želivský's burial, new elections were held, and Želivský's party re-took supremacy. On 15 March, the new city council met at the Old Town city hall to pass verdict on the arrested University masters. Priest William was chief prosecutor, and his accusations were levelled mostly against Jacobellus, although he did not neglect the other eight masters. William could not prove direct participation by Jacobellus or the other masters, but he declared them culpable since they had fomented false accusations of Pikhartism against Želivský. After some discussion all nine were banished from Prague and sent to Hradec Králové for re-education under Ambrose. Although Želivský's party was again in power, it had lost its leader. While his main support had come from the bottom rung of Prague's socio-economic ladder, he had also garnered support from the middle class by knowing how to use patronage effectively. His two biggest missteps were assuming his political talent translated into military competence and failing to suppress Pikhartism aggressively. When he felt his grip on power loosening, he had abandoned his proto-democratic principles and become a theocratic dictator, hastening his demise.

Historians of the Hussite revolution have pointed out that, although Želivský was ambitious and enjoyed power, he exercised that power on behalf of the revolution rather than personal enrichment. Arguably, he had the most comprehensive perspective of the Hussite movement. Želivský recognised it could not endure without military strength; he understood that that strength would have to be drawn from Bohemia's entire population, not just its nobility. His blanket condemnation of the Bohemian nobility as untrustworthy traitors was both gratuitous and counter-productive, however. Žižka and Ambrose showed that many of Bohemia's leading dukes and barons were thoughtful patriots, and by no means craven Sigismund loyalists. Had Želivský recognised this, he probably would not have aroused such hostility from them. Finally, his summary execution of Sádlo was perceived as a vicious and arbitrary act of personal vengeance, and it hurt his cause by giving his opponents a pretext to purge the city's radical elements. Ultimately, though, Želivský's death created more problems than it solved. He had been the bridge between the Praguers, Taborites, and Orebites. Subsequent attempts by the Hussites to create a united front were fatally damaged by the marginalisation of the New Town's citizens and Bohemia's two great fundamentalist communities. Želivský's legacy – the political organisation of the New Town's urban poor and the revolutionary spirit of Tábor – endured for only another dozen years.

*

The Kutná Hora diet had sent emissaries informing Vytautas that they had elected him Bohemia's king and asking him to take the throne as soon as possible. These diplomats were unaware the mission had been subverted by Sigismund, who had been in close contact with

Władyslaw. The Polish King's apparent friendliness to the Hussites was based more on calculation than sympathy, as was his tacit approval of Vytautas's increasingly cordial relations with them. Władyslaw hoped to use developments in Bohemia as leverage to persuade Sigismund to revise the Breslau settlement regarding Samogitia. Władyslaw offered Sigismund a deal: in return for a favourable revision of the Breslau treaty, he would withdraw support for the Hussites and lend military support against them if requested. Vytautas, though aware of these discussions, voiced no objection. Władyslaw sent two trusted advisors to meet secretly with the Emperor, but word leaked to Bohemia and its leaders including Žižka, chilling Hussite feelings towards the Polish–Lithuanian royalty.

Czech diplomats left Bohemia on 10 September 1421. As the forty-man embassy, including Vytautas's personal representative, passed through Upper Silesia, it was intercepted and arrested by the region's leading noble, Duke Jan of Opava. He immediately informed Sigismund, who demanded they be sent to him. The Emperor assumed that this diplomatic initiative proved Władyslaw's duplicity. The Polish–Lithuanian court was indignant, and Władyslaw sent an envoy to dissuade Opava from delivering the diplomats to Sigismund. Vytautas used stronger language, threatening military action if the men were not released immediately. In consequence, a strong if fleeting sense of Slavic solidarity took hold among the Poles and Lithuanians, and Vytautas exploited the situation.

One of Sigismund's most outspoken critics was Władyslaw's nephew, Prince Korybut, who declared that his people would never abandon the Czechs. Vytautas proposed that Prague join him in a punitive expedition commanded by Korybut against Opava. However, by the time this message arrived on 23 October, it was too late. The diplomats had been taken to a prison-fortress at Brno where the embassy's thirty-six retainers were immediately executed while the four ambassadors were sent to Hungary. Many urged that the Silesian duke be punished, but cooler heads prevailed, and Władyslaw still hoped to establish dynastic ties with Sigismund. To this end he dispatched

Zawisza to the imperial court, a trip which (as previously recounted) was permanently interrupted by Žižka at Německý Brod. After Zawisza's initiative failed, Władyslaw agreed to marry Vytautas's young niece, Sofia, princess of Olszany, who subsequently produced an heir for the elderly king. Vytautas had hoped to become Poland's king and, realising this would never happen, now turned his gaze towards Bohemia. The most recent offer to Vytautas, while insisting he acknowledge the Four Articles, deferred this requirement until a public disputation had been held. If the Articles were proven to contradict Holy Scripture, the Hussites would admit their error; if the articles were found to comply with the Bible, the Grand Duke would announce his acceptance of them.

Władyslaw, who attached greater importance to military facts than spiritual ideals, was won over by Žižka's impressive victories in January 1422. Sigismund had ordered the Teutonic Knights and Silesia to attack Poland–Lithuania if it gave any support to the Hussites, but Władyslaw believed Sigismund and his demoralised Hungarians were unlikely to implement this order. On 5 March, he announced (via a letter from Vytautas to Pope Martin) that he was sending his nephew Korybut to Bohemia as his representative. Vytautas asked the Pope to recognise that all previous attempts to bring the Bohemians back into the Catholic fold had failed, suggesting that diplomacy would be more effective. Employing cagey language, he did not acknowledge having accepted the Bohemian crown, saying only that he was extending them his protection. By using the term 'schism', he implied that all parties involved were Christians and protected himself against charges of supporting heresy. Suggesting that Sigismund's brutality would accomplish nothing, he proposed guidance, telling Martin that was the only path with any hope of Bohemia's restoration to Rome. Vytautas added that the Poles, who bore great fellow-feeling for the Bohemian Slavs, were more suitable rulers than Sigismund, who hated them. Vytautas knew Martin would be resistant to that position, since he was very much dependent on Sigismund's military support. By sending a young proxy as a provisional step, Vytautas left himself the option of withdrawal; if his venture became untenable, he would have made no irreversible moves.

Žižka was busy with the Plzeň Landfrieden, who were trying to conquer the strategically important Taborite castle of Krasikov. Žižka had requested help from Prague, which was preoccupied with Želivský and could send none. At one point, he seemed hopelessly trapped, and the Plzeňers eagerly anticipated burning 'the evil heretic and his helpers'. However, Žižka not only escaped their clutches but conquered one of their towns, Žlutice, and a few lesser strongholds as well. From there, Žižka moved south and besieged Horšův Týn close to the German border, creating concern throughout the Upper Palatinate. In late April 1422, Žižka returned to Tábor and received Korybut's first message, urging Žižka to 'stop laying waste the land of Bohemia'. For the young newcomer to denigrate Žižka's holy war as predatory destruction was an affront not to be tolerated. Žižka's reply to Korybut was uncharacteristically harsh and rude. Korybut, who had always been treated with deference, was taken aback by this bluntness.

In early May, Korybut left Uničov and travelled to Prague, passing through Chrudím, Čáslav, and Kutná Hora where he was given increasingly favourable opinions of Žižka. It seems likely Victorin of Poděbrady served as a go-between and led mediation efforts. When Žižka learned of Korybut's acceptance of the communion in two kinds, his feelings were assuaged. Having softened up the old general, the young prince attempted to enlist him in his programme of internal unification and pacification. Žižka was receptive provided this did not entail any let-up against Sigismund and his allies, particularly Ulrich. Korybut agreed, realising he had to win over Žižka to have any hope of gaining acceptance in Prague. The disciples of the late Želivský might have spurned Korybut had he only been supported by the leading nobles, but with Žižka's endorsement it was impossible for them to refuse the prince entry. When Korybut arrived at Prague on 16 May, its gates were opened for him. He was coolly received by the city leaders, however, who saw him as a threat to their continued occupation of office. But the citizens enthusiastically turned out to greet him the following day. A huge crowd led Korybut to the Old Town city hall, demanding the keys and seals of Prague be given to him. The councillors had no choice but to comply. Their fears were well-founded: Korybut immediately called for new municipal elections that swept them from office.

On 21 May, Korybut issued the same injunction against 'laying waste to the countryside' to the three most prominent Royalist lords, Ulrich, Čeněk, and Městecký, who defied it. On 28 May, the new Prague council called a town meeting and issued a decree passed in consultation with the prince. It established a one-year amnesty covering all prior political offences, as well as measures to tamp down disturbances amongst Prague citizens and the Polish soldiers quartered there. Most of the political crimes referred to had been prosecuted by the radicals, so this worked in favour of the conservatives. The University masters were urged to return from Hradec Králové, and a new synod of Hussite priests was called. Hašek was told all would be forgiven and he might return to Prague. This dimmed the enthusiasm of many New Town residents towards Korybut, and dissatisfaction grew as evidenced by a decree forbidding slanderous or insulting comments about the prince. Korybut was demonstrating his ability to be amiable on one hand, and harsh on the other.

On 7 June, Korybut called for another diet at Čáslav to formalise his status as regent. There are no surviving documents, and much of what is known has been reconstructed from indirect sources including a letter signed by Žižka and a later message from Vytautas. The Four Articles were again the central theme. Korybut promised to uphold and fulfil them, giving reassurances in writing. The diet acknowledged Korybut as acting regent of Bohemia and Moravia. For the first time in nearly three years, the kingdom was under the rule of a monarch acknowledged by a majority of Czechs. Among the official records is a declaration signed by Žižka dated 11 June. It discusses Korybut's proposed policies and his emphasis on forgiveness and reconciliation amongst the quarrelling Hussite factions. It also notes Korybut's official recognition as regent and the renewal of the resolution from the first

Čáslav diet threatening punishment for anyone fomenting internal hostilities. Žižka names all whom he has pledged to support, a group which roughly corresponded to the diet's participants. Two other Taborite captains are named, Chval and Zbyněk of Buchov. Roháč, another captain, was probably preoccupied at Lomnice battling Ulrich. The absence of another Taborite captain, Bohuslav of Švamberg, was more significant, indicating his refusal of Korybut's programme. Another name notable by its absence from Žižka's declaration was Vytautas, who Žižka always referred to as 'the Postulated King'. Žižka was a stickler for formalities, particularly in official documents, and although Korybut had probably requested Žižka include Vytautas in the loyalty pledge, the blind general was unwilling to give him an unqualified endorsement in light of his rumoured collusion with Sigismund. Korybut believed Žižka's endorsement and his own acceptance of the Four Articles would convince Taborite hardliners to support him. Žižka wholeheartedly signed on with Korybut's policy of establishing a united Hussite front, declaring he had 'accepted his highness the prince as our helper and as the supreme regent of this land' and stating he would 'gladly obey his highness, support him, and give him our counsel in all rightful things faithfully, so help us God.'

In late July, Žižka resumed his war against Ulrich while Korybut laid siege to the great castle at Karlštejn. Korybut was unable to devote his full attention to this task, making brief appearances but being compelled to return to Prague frequently on political business. After several weeks, considerable effort, and the use of four powerful siege guns, the castle's garrison was still holding strong. Korybut did not request assistance from Žižka and his Taborite forces, and it is safe to assume the prince was reluctant to become dependent militarily on the Taborites. But if Korybut felt he could get along without Žižka's support militarily, he could not do so politically. The honeymoon between Prague and the prince faded quickly. New Towners, in particular, realised that the proto-democracy to which they had become accustomed would end with the restoration of a strong monarch. Their dissatisfied mutterings and agitated gatherings led Korybut and the city council to pass stricter measures. All secret meetings and unsanctioned large gatherings were forbidden. The guilds were required to sign loyalty pledges, and four masters in each guild were drafted as political commissars. The prince implemented other measures to consolidate power, further disgruntling many in the New Town. Others developed misgivings about the re-establishment of traditional monarchical government. Prague burghers realised that restored influence for the high nobility would come at their expense. Many of Želivský's adherents in both the lower and middle classes began to feel that his suspicions were vindicated.

Most of the Hussite towns were willing to submit to Korybut, but Hradec Králové was dominated by Ambrose, whose attitude towards Korybut resembled Želivský's. In early August, an impatient Korybut paid the city a visit to bring it into line. Leading a body of troops to the gates, he encountered no resistance when he demanded admission. He immediately had the city councilmen arrested and imprisoned, replacing them with more compliant men. Diviš Bořek, a leading Orebite nobleman, was named captain and burgrave of the town. A leader in the revolution from its onset, he had played a significant role in the battle of the Vyšehrad and fought alongside Žižka. Since the victories of the previous spring, Diviš had been captain-governor of Chrudím and on good terms with Ambrose. However, their relationship soured after Diviš was installed by the prince, and Ambrose complained to Žižka.

Some weeks after Hradec Králové's enforced submission, Žižka, Korybut, and numerous other Bohemian nobles wrote letters to the margraves of Meissen, who had announced their intention to invade Bohemia in a third crusade. The letters expressed Hussite readiness to inflict harsh punishment on any German princes who might hazard a Bohemian invasion, and a fragment of one of Žižka's letters contains terms like 'obstinate heretics' and 'lawless bloodthirsty murderers'. The German nobles were taken aback at Žižka's 'contumelious way of addressing these magnificent illustrious and venerable princes, [who] . . . wanted to destroy in a most just war those Hussites, Taborites, and

Wyclefites [*sic*] and . . . consecrate their hands in the blood of those heretics'. Evidently, it was considered impertinent for a prospective victim to insult high-ranking noblemen declaring their intention of killing him. This missive marked the last recorded instance of Žižka referring to himself as the Taborites' captain. Although Tábor was moving towards insurrection, at that point Žižka still felt obliged to recognise Korybut's authority.

The Hussites had evolved from a fanatical rebel movement into an increasingly well-organised party that had forged an alliance with Poland–Lithuania, Eastern Europe's strongest power. Sigismund complained to the Pope about Vytautas, reproaching him for permitting the Lithuanian Grand Duke to embark on a programme intended to deprive him of his rightful inheritance. Sigismund insisted Korybut's stated desire to bring the Czechs back to Catholicism was a deceptive pretence. On 21 May, Pope Martin answered Sigismund, strenuously denying having given permission to Vytautas to support the Bohemian heretics. The Pope also wrote letters to Władyslaw and Vytautas commanding them to cease assisting the Hussites. The Pope carried weight with Władyslaw, who was unhappy with Korybut. However, Sigismund's inept statecraft undercut Martin. The Emperor had persuaded the Teutonic Knights to wage war against Poland, and hostilities ensued on 14 July. This only demonstrated how weakened the Order had become. The combined power of Poland and Lithuania made short work of them and, although Sigismund promised to send assistance, it was too little, too late. Poland–Lithuania and the Prussians signed the peace of Lake Melno on 27 September. The victorious Władyslaw was lenient, allowing the Knights to keep Pomerania, keeping Poland landlocked. Some border regions were given to Poland, but, most importantly, Samogitia was now a Lithuanian possession in perpetuity.

The Emperor began organising a third crusade with the German princes on 30 July at the Reichstag of Nürnberg. Many of the princes suggested forgetting about Bohemia for the time being and focusing on Poland. Sigismund might have been willing to do so, but others, particularly Frederick of Brandenburg, blocked the idea. The papal legate, Cardinal Branda, obsessed with the Bohemian heretics, supported Frederick. A cordial letter from the German princes to Władyslaw suggested it would be better for him to join in the campaign against Bohemia instead of battling the good Christians of the Teutonic Order. The Reichstag did little to put the proposed third crusade on a strong financial footing, however. A proposed one per cent tax to hire mercenaries was vetoed by the imperial cities as it would open their finances to public scrutiny. It was decided that every unit of the empire, including all its princes and cities, be charged with the obligation to provide cavalrymen and infantrymen based on a formula known as the Imperial Matrix. It became evident, though, that all parties were making every effort to minimise expenses. On 4 September, Cardinal Branda handed a banner blessed by the pope to Sigismund in a ceremony in Nürnberg's Sebaldus Church. Sigismund appointed Frederick commander-in-chief of the imperial forces. Although this was a high honour and one which Frederick could not refuse, Sigismund had reason to believe that the crusade would not go well. This would inflict a loss of prestige and power on Frederick, who was proving to be a thorn in Sigismund's side with respect to Poland. On 29 September, German troops were told to meet at Tirschenreuth near the Franconian border with Bohemia. Some 4,000 Misnians mustered north of the Erzgebirge waiting for Silesian and Lusatian reinforcements which never came.

Again, internal Hussite divisions disappeared in the face of an external threat. The Taborites had just attempted a coup d'état and the Hussites were on the brink of civil war. Bohuslav and Hvězda – who had recently become a Taborite captain – had been holding secret meetings with the Zelivists in the New Town. On 30 September 1422, the two men marched a sizeable Taborite army towards Prague, knowing that Korybut was busy at Karlštejn. At the small village of Krč just south of Prague, they were met by William Kostka and Prague's new captain, Wenceslaus Carda, leading some of their troops. Kostka inquired politely as to the nature of their business in Prague, and Bohuslav replied that they had been invited to visit. The ever-civil (and sensible) Kostka thought that the best way to handle the situation was to extend courtesy, even making arrangements for the Taborites and their horses to be fed when they arrived in the New Town. The next day, Bohuslav and Hvězda went to the Old Town city hall and demanded a general town meeting be called. The councillors politely declined but offered to take a message. This was not good enough for the two Taborite captains, who said that if the councillors did not call a town meeting they would. They marched their troops through Prague's main streets hoping to rally popular support but were less than successful. After occupying several houses, the Taborites were out-manoeuvred by the Prague leadership and Polish troops, who shut down the main streets one by one and eventually forced the Taborites back into the New Town. Some Taborites were taken prisoner and the remainder made a stand at the city horse market (today Wenceslaus Square). Before a full-scale battle erupted, Kostka reminded Bohuslav that they were personal friends, moving Bohuslav to agree to an armistice. The attempted coup had been a disaster, so Bohuslav and Hvězda returned to Tábor the next day. With them went several of their Prague conspirators, who felt it best to relocate to Tábor as well.

When Korybut learned of the attempted coup, he immediately returned to Prague and instituted harsh measures. A town meeting was called, and the first step taken was the institution of a civil alarm signal: simultaneous ringing of bells at both city halls. The ban on secret meetings was re-emphasised, and the property of the conspirators who had left town was confiscated. More significantly, a crumbling old wall separating the Old and New Towns was rebuilt. Strict new prohibitions were instituted against heretical teachings about the Eucharist. However, instead of suppressing the Zelivist movement, these measures only reinvigorated it. A few days later at another town meeting, a large crowd opened the prison gates and freed all the Taborites who had been imprisoned after the failed coup. Korybut was enraged and decreed that all individuals involved be beheaded. The city councillors, recognising this would only fan insurrection, attempted to dissuade the prince after numerous heads had been lopped off. Kostka (again showing himself a man of moderation and sound judgement) confronted Korybut and insisted the mass executions were both unnecessarily savage and counter-productive, and the prince ended the slaughter.

The attempted coup significantly damaged the Hussite movement. It is unknown which Taborite captain was most responsible, but one can imagine Hvězda nursing a grudge. The motivations of Bohuslav, a committed ideologue, were probably less self-interested. In any case, the result was a negative one for the Taborites. The Zelivist party in Prague was weakened, and from then on the relationship between Prague and Tábor was openly hostile. There are few hard facts regarding Žižka's whereabouts, what he knew, and when he knew it. We do know he later sent an apologetic letter to Prague voicing disapproval of his two junior captains. He received an appreciative reply from Prague's city council expressing gratification at these sentiments. Nonetheless, Žižka's apology could not repair the impact of this discord. German troops were massed on the borders of Meissen and Franconia, and Karlštejn was still holding out. Fearing the Nürnberg Reichstag would match its strong words with actions, Korybut drew off some of the troops besieging Karlštejn, rendering the siege more ineffective.

On 7 October, Margrave William led a Misnian force into the Most region, conquering the town of Chomútov. Shortly thereafter, Frederick marched his troops, supplemented by those of the Bishops of Würzburg and Bamberg, from Tirschenreuth across the border to Tachov. They combined with forces of the Plzeň Landfrieden and the town of Cheb and waited for German reinforcements. This combined army was directed to join Misnian, Silesian, and Lusatian troops in the Rakovník region, forty kilometres south of Louny. Its objective was the relief of Karlštejn, and on 15 October Frederick sent a message os support to its garrison. However, recriminations and constant complaints about lack of men, money, arms, and horses testified to the poor morale throughout the crusading armies. The Bishop of Würzburg felt the entire affair ought to be called off. His pessimism was exacerbated by Sigismund's failure to deliver promised aid; the Emperor had permitted several cities to buy their way out of participation and had pocketed the fees. Duke Henry Rampold of Glogau disbanded his Misnians before they even crossed the border, and when Korybut approached Louny other Misnians retreated and would have quit altogether if not for Frederick's intervention. The Würzburg and Bamberg troops returned home, and the Cheb forces requested permission to do likewise. Frederick refused, hoping at least to salvage Karlštejn from what had turned into a débâcle.

On 22 October, the Czech and Polish siege force made four unsuccessful assaults on the castle, incurring heavy losses and suffering further from a devastating sortie by the defenders. Korybut's Polish soldiers grew restive over this exercise in futility, while the garrison took heart and sent Frederick word that reinforcement by 400 cavalrymen would carry the battle. While en route to Karlštejn with the requested men, Frederick was told Korybut had offered to discuss an armistice. Frederick returned to Tachov, consulted with his advisors and decided to meet the prince. He left Henry of Plauen in charge of 3,500 horsemen and some infantry and told him to send them to Karlštejn as soon as possible.

Korybut's curiously timed peace offer, as well his failure to reinforce the Karlštejn besiegers, can only be understood in light of threatening papal messages sent to Władyslaw and Vytautas. Frederick, who knew nothing of this, saw no reason beyond a simple ploy to delay his relief expedition to Karlštejn. He never actually met Korybut, but exchanged messages with his representatives, Archbishop Conrad and Hašek, for a week before discussions broke down over the Hussites' unwillingness to make peace with Sigismund. Korybut was in a bind. He was battling Frederick, Poland's sole German friend, and the Bohemians refused to submit to Rome or Sigismund. While it was becoming evident that Vytautas had no intention of accepting the Bohemian crown, Korybut still had hopes of wearing it. He attempted to finesse a reconciliation with the Pope without reference to Sigismund's restoration. Frederick could not agree to this proposal and was chagrined to learn upon returning to Tachov that Karlštejn's defenders and the Hussites had signed an armistice on 8 November. Despite Frederick's best efforts to rally the troops, by year's end all crusaders had returned to Germany, terminating the third crusade against the Hussites.

But Korybut could not relax. Although the Germans and his disapproving uncle were at a distance, he was faced with growing Taborite resentment close at hand, a problem Žižka could not solve for him. It cannot be known for certain where Žižka stood in this dispute, but the lack of Taborite participation in the defence against the third anti-Hussite crusade speaks volumes. However, the blind general's puritanism did not go far enough for the fundamentalist clergymen of Tábor. Three synods of the Taborite priesthood during the course of 1422 show a radicalisation among even its moderates. Bishop Nicholas had fallen under Koranda's sway. Žižka, whose campaigns took him away from Tábor for long periods, could not hope to counter the daily influence of Koranda and the other radical clerics in ever-fiercer battles of words. Although the old soldier might have been able walk away from these frustrating theological disputes, he could not shrug off the priests' growing lack of commitment to recruiting soldiers, for which he was totally dependent upon them.

Žižka and Korybut lost not only the Taborites' support, but that of Poland–Lithuania as well. Władyslaw had never truly been interested in reconciling the Czechs with Rome, and, after attaining his real goal, abrogation of the Breslau treaty and the acquisition of Samogitia, he was disposed to withdraw all support for them. He and Vytautas began a series of diplomatic exchanges with Sigismund and dangled this possibility in return for the Emperor's acknowledgment of the Peace of Lake Melno. Vytautas ordered Korybut to leave Prague but not Bohemia altogether, cagily making a show of good faith while maintaining leverage in the ongoing discussions. The prince left the capital on Christmas Eve and relocated to eastern Bohemia, clinging to his fading hopes. Sigismund attempted to avoid acceding to the Lake Melno agreement by suggesting an alliance of Hungary, Breslau, Silesia, Lusatia, and the Prussian Order against Poland. Sigismund's advisors told him there was no realistic chance for such an initiative to succeed, particularly after a declaration by Hungarian nobles that 'they had no intention to die or be ruined for the benefit of the Prussians', and for once the Emperor listened to them.

With no alternative, Sigismund began negotiations in earnest. An imperial ambassador was dispatched from the town of Zips (Spiš) near the Polish border, where the Emperor was holding court, requesting the presence of Władyslaw and Vytautas, who promptly answered the invitation. Shortly thereafter, a formal agreement was signed in the town of Kežmarok. Sigismund relinquished the Breslau award and recognised the Lake Melno accord. Having achieved full legitimisation of his claim to Samogitia, Vytautas ordered Korybut and his Polish soldiers to return home. In response to the indignant Bohemian reaction, the Grand Duke blandly stated he had made no promises and had signed nothing. He accused the Czechs of acting under false pretences and deceiving him into the mistaken belief they were willing to reconcile with Rome. Offering to help them re-enter the True Church if they ever regretted their misguided behaviour, Vytautas wrote the Hussites off. On or about 26 March 1423, Korybut and his men left Bohemia, crossed Moravia under a safe-conduct from Sigismund, and returned to Poland. Through letters bearing this date written by Žižka, we know with some precision when Korybut departed. These same letters, sent from a village named Vilémov near Čáslav, also reveal that Žižka had left Tábor and joined the Orebites.

Chapter 7

DISCIPLINE AND DISCORD

What is human warfare but just this; an effort to make
the laws of God and Nature take sides with one party.
Henry David Thoreau

The main purpose of Žižka's letters was not to relay news of Korybut's
departure but to invite towns and nobles throughout the Orebite region
to a meeting at Německý Brod on 7 April 1423.

> There [Žižka wrote] at the very place where we have sinned we
> will do penance . . . we will then and at the same place under
> the guidance of the Lord God and his Sacred Law, consult and
> resolve with all who are faithful to Him with the council of the
> poor and the rich, and stay united as one man against all
> faithless deceivers at home and abroad.

Equating the breakdown in military discipline by his 'warriors of God'
with sinfulness, he declared that the Hussites had lost the moral high
ground and hence fallen from divine favour. Žižka asserted that 'greed,
pillage, wanton pride, and betrayal' had so angered God that 'ever since
there has not been much good that we have achieved', adding that 'the
lord God rightly punishes us for our sins'.

Žižka had reason to be dissatisfied, and in his mind all the problems,
frictions, and setbacks suffered by the Hussites stemmed from a single
cause: God's displeasure over the Hussites' behaviour at Německý Brod.
Žižka included himself in this indictment by using the term 'our sins'.

But he also expressed belief in God's willingness to forgive his followers and again strengthen them against the enemies of His law, providing they repented, made amends, and resolved to follow a more righteous path. Therefore, felt Žižka, a new organisation was needed to redeem past transgressions and lead the Hussites into the future – the Orebites. This community would practice the rectitude and give Žižka the support Tábor had not. 'Tábor' for Žižka had become a figurative term, not a geographic or ideological reference but a catch-all encompassing any Hussites who had strayed from the True Faith.

The Orebites' influence had grown during the preceding year from their original domain of Hradec Králové and surrounding settlements. In the spring of 1421, after Hussite armies had established control throughout most of the region, the inhabitants had been introduced to the Orebite version of Hussitism, a middle way between Prague and Tábor combining the former's theological traditions with the latter's reformist zeal. Prague had granted the Orebites some autonomy, and by early 1423 the Orebite brotherhood encompassed a large area from Mnichovo Hradiště, Dvůr Králové, and Náchod in the north to the Sázava River in the south. However, political organisation was lacking, and many towns and country areas remained unaffiliated. While Korybut was attempting to establish a centralised monarchy Orebite autonomy was curtailed, but after the prince was recalled to Poland, new options presented themselves.

Korybut had nullified previous treaties with Orebite towns, and his departure left their political status in limbo. Hašek and other powerful Prague figures felt the towns should revert to their prior status of submission to the capital, but many of the eastern Bohemian towns disagreed. Hašek and Kostka believed Žižka would not inject himself into this political debate. Their willingness to permit Diviš Bořek, captain-governor of Chrudím and governor of Hradec Králové, to meet him indicates they did not suspect political ambition on Žižka's part. It was evident he harboured no dreams of personal power and seemed content with his humble castle and newly earned knighthood. But there were political implications. Žižka was suggesting that a stronger and more comprehensive political structure, equivalent in many ways to Tábor, was called for. Perhaps Prague's relative passivity thus far towards the Orebites can be explained by its preoccupation with Tábor. Whatever the case, Žižka proceeded to organise the Orebite military forces, and the Nemecký Brod conclave showed his determination to replicate his previous accomplishments at Tábor with the benefit of his increased stature and the lessons he had learned since.

There were divisions among the Orebites, as seen by the list of Německý Brod invitees. The Poděbrady brothers were included, while others who disdained associating with any Tábor, old or new, were omitted. One high-ranking baron favourably disposed was Aleš Vřešťovský of Riesenburg, who had lent assistance during Ambrose's reconquest of Hradec Králové and served as its governor. He had also participated in Hynek's diplomatic mission to Poland and Lithuania before becoming one of the Orebites' leaders. Several knights and squires who had served as junior officers under Žižka were invited, some of whom subsequently were influential figures at what was known as 'lesser Tábor'. Also invited was Diviš Bořek who had obtained immense stature, wealth, and political influence and would play a significant role in the Orebite community.

Žižka's agenda at Německý Brod was religious, military, and political. He insisted that penance, remorse, and spiritual renewal were essential to ensure God's approval and assistance. Žižka's messages also revealed that the break with Tábor had not been completely acrimonious. The Taborites, according to Žižka, 'declared of their own free will that they will follow my orders as any time before'. Žižka was planning a campaign against German Catholic towns and nobles along the Lusatian border, but many Orebites were preoccupied with another regional struggle. They had focused on Čeněk of Wartenberg, who had (again) given his support to Sigismund the previous autumn. Čeněk's primary town of residence, Bydžov, was only twenty-seven kilometres west of Hradec Králové. Žižka asked the recipients of his letters, who were conducting a guerrilla war of harassment, to make no armistice or truce agreements. They complied, stepping up the war against Čeněk.

Žižka, vindictive with those he regarded as traitors, directed the same animosity at Wartenberg as he had shown to Ulrich. Čeněk had kept a low profile during the preceding year and avoided any consequences for his multiple treasonous acts. While Korybut was around Čeněk had been shielded, so no punitive expedition had been mounted against him. However, Korybut and Čeněk were not particularly cordial, and it seems the prince had only been keeping him nearby so as to maintain a close watch on a potential enemy.

The ramped-up attacks on Čeněk's properties forced his hand. Numerous dukes and barons throughout northern Bohemia were willing to assist him, including Ernest Flaška, a participant in the gruesome slaughter at Chotěboř, and Henry Burka of Dubá. Their combined forces numbered several thousand and were particularly strong in cavalry; Čeněk also possessed some battle wagons and guns. Žižka had at his disposal 'two rows of wagons' (a total of 120) and approximately 3,000 soldiers.

Žižka's troops had been operating in and around Jičn, and when Čeněk and his allies drew near, Žižka retreated towards Hradec Králové. He drew up his wagons on a hilltop near the town of Hořice, next to a small church affording an observation tower. The battle here on 20 April 1423 replicated those at Sudoměř, Bor Panský, and Vladař. He chose a battlefield favouring him; the Royalist cavalry were forced to dismount as the hillside leading to the wagon fortress was too steep for a mounted charge. Gunfire from the wagons repeatedly drove the cavalrymen back down the hill, and when Žižka judged them sufficiently tired and disorganised he sprang infantrymen from behind the wagons in a devastating counter-attack. The Royalists fled in disarray, leaving behind their wagons, guns, and many horses. Čeněk reportedly escaped with 'a small part of his people' indicating he suffered losses in his personal retinue. This victory was Žižka's most significant triumph since Německý Brod fifteen months previously, and it gave the Orebites breathing room and freedom of movement throughout eastern Bohemia. Žižka also attacked one of Čeněk's most important castles, Kozojedy, burning it to the ground along with sixty defenders.

That concluded the Orebites' April campaign in the upper Elbe valley; the following month, they focused downriver near Litoměřice. Žižka had begun planning this initiative in March when he had asked the Taborites to mobilise with him and the Orebites. However, before the Taborites could join them, dissention in the Hussite ranks broke out into armed fighting. The Praguers had moved against Tábor and with a strong force of cavalry and infantry begun besieging the fortress of Kříženec. The Prague forces led by Hašek, now Kutná Hora's mint master and governor, included soldiers who had previously fought for Sigismund. This was a disturbing development – Prague Calixtines making common cause with ex-Royalists against the Taborites. According to Bishop Nicholas, the Praguers had been provoked by the informality with which some Taborite priests celebrated Mass, particularly their omission of traditional vestments. Clerics on both sides had goaded their respective parishioners about this long-festering issue. Many Prague clergy suggested that disregard for sacred vestments signified an underlying disbelief in God's presence in the Eucharist through transubstantiation.

A public disputation held on the matter was inconclusive, and Hašek may have co-opted clerical indignation to serve his own interests. The castle of Kříženec was located in the town of Načeradec, twenty-nine kilometres north-east of Tábor, a strategic location controlling roads to both the Orebite region and Kutná Hora. Hašek felt if he could take Kříženec he could weaken both Tábor and Oreb by cutting off mutual assistance as well as Tábor's communication with Kutná Hora. Hašek's siege of Kříženec continued into May but evidently did not greatly concern the Taborites. Bohuslav then brought a Taborite army to lift the siege, and the outnumbered Praguers withdrew. An armistice directed both armies to meet a few days later at the castle of Konopiště near the town of Benešov. In mid-May, they met at this neutral location, and both sides were spoiling for a fight. Their respective leaders intervened, proposing that the vestment controversy be discussed peacefully. The parties agreed that priests and prominent laymen from both camps would meet at Konopiště on 26 June to make a final determination.

Attempting to foster a spirit of brotherhood, the Taborites suggested Mass be celebrated by priests adopting the manners of the other side: Taborites wearing vestments, Praguers not. One Taborite priest, Prokop the Bald (who became the Hussite military commander after Žižka's death), quickly took up the suggestion. Prague priests, however, were unwilling to adopt Taborite practice fully; while dispensing with ornate vestments, they insisted on retaining their white surplices.

The prevention of bloodshed between Prague and Tábor was helped by a surprise visitor at Konopiště: Nicholas Siestrzeniec, a Polish nobleman bearing a message from Władyslaw. The Polish King reiterated Vytautas's offer to mediate with Rome but more amiably. Noting the common Slavic ancestry of the Poles and Czechs, Władyslaw argued that a cessation of hostilities was in Bohemia's best interest. Although Vytautas had lost interest in Bohemia after acquiring Samogitia, pro-Hussites in Poland had asserted themselves. Many, notably Chancellor Szafraniec, believed that ties with the Bohemian Hussites would yield advantages for Poland, which had not greatly benefited from the Kežmarok treaty with Sigismund. Feeling that the Emperor and the Prussian Order had become weakened, this Polish faction (including Korybut) felt the Hussites might be useful in exploiting the situation. After delivering Władyslaw's message, Siestrzeniec went to Prague with leaders of both Hussite parties and urged reconciliation with the Roman Church. Several Hussite noblemen suggested he should avoid mentioning Sigismund and the Four Articles, and Siestrzeniec took their advice. The Prague masters, smarting from Korybut's abrupt withdrawal and Vytautas's haughty dismissal, took their time before replying on 6 June. They stated their willingness to negotiate as well as their determination to defend God's Law to the death.

Siestrzeniec's diplomatic initiative, while unsuccessful, did thaw relations between Prague and a significant Polish political faction and helped ameliorate resentments between Praguers and Taborites. This carried over to discussions a month later at Konopiště between clerics and prominent laymen from both sides. Nothing substantive was accomplished regarding the vestments. Transubstantiation, however, was acknowledged as a bedrock tenet of Hussite dogma, allowing Tábor to clear away lingering suspicions of fostering Pikhartism. The Konopiště accord also enabled the Hussites to undertake new military campaigns throughout June and early July. A re-energised bond between Prague and Tábor was evidenced by the arrival of Bohuslav and his Taborite soldiers. Hynek Berka of the Dubá clan, enlisting assistance from Royalists in the north, underlined this renewed Hussite solidarity with repeated references to 'Žižka with the Praguers' or 'Žižka with his helpers' while suggesting the blind general and his minions intended to invade Lusatia. Žižka had no such notions; he simply wanted to clear out remaining Royalist strongholds inside Bohemia. After taking some small towns, Žižka expended significant effort besieging the castle of Panna ('Virgin'). Previously called 'New Castle', it belonged to Lord Sigismund of Wartenberg, Čeněk's most powerful relative, who had renamed it in direct response to Žižka renaming his castle Chalice. He had attempted to conquer Žižka's castle in September 1421, and Žižka now returned the favour. The final outcome is unknown.

For the first time, Žižka used Chalice castle as a base of operations, and he subsequently held numerous war councils there, many devoted to planning a large-scale offensive into Moravia. Hussite commanders had pondered this endeavour for some time, and Korybut had made moves in that direction, conquering the city of Uničov. Sigismund had given Moravia to his new son-in-law, Duke Albert of Austria, who was co-operating closely with Bishop Jan of Olomouc to exterminate the heretical scourge. In late June 1423 the Hussite high command drew up plans for a Moravian campaign. It was to be led by Prague's captains Hašek and Hynek, as well as leading Orebites, notably Diviš and the Poděbrady brothers, Hynek and Victorin. This invasion began and ended without Žižka but had his blessing and support. He joined three months late, and his tardiness was probably due to the prolonged siege of Panna and one other matter detaining him. At a final meeting in his castle, Žižka and a trusted group of devoted officers drafted the most significant document of his entire career. It instituted far-reaching changes not just in Bohemia's political structure, but prevailing concepts of military organisation and discipline reaching to the present day.

'The Statutes and Military Ordinance of Žižka's New Brotherhood' codified Žižka's vision of the Hussite army of God and ushered in a new phase of the revolution. Limited background information exists about it, the longest surviving manuscript authored by Žižka. Some things can be surmised from internal evidence, primarily the names of those who signed it – and one who did not. The assertion that disobedience has caused 'great losses both in the lives of brethren and in our possessions' probably refers to setbacks the previous spring in northern Bohemia. The other campaigns during 1422 had all been resoundingly successful. The poorly executed siege of Panna castle was not an outright defeat, so perhaps whatever problems occurred there escaped general notice.

Bohuslav left Litoměřice on 27 July and took his troops back to Tábor. It is unlikely that he did so with Žižka's approval – the blind general was fixated on taking Panna from Wartenberg, towards whom he bore personal animosity. For some time after that, no joint military ventures were undertaken by old and new Tábor (that is by Žižka and Bohuslav). It seems likely some strong disagreement between the two occurred at Panna. Moreover, any significant difference of opinion would surely have been regarded by Žižka as insubordination, since Bohuslav had promised on the previous 26 March to 'obey his commands as at any time before'.

Along with the burgomasters and councillors of the four Orebite towns – Hradec Králové, Čáslav, Jaroměř, and Dvůr Králové – Žižka's ordinance was signed by forty-six men: lords, knights, squires, townsmen, and even a few peasants. These included Žižka's bodyguards, retinue, and subaltern officers who had left Tábor and followed him to the new brotherhood. A few other signatories were long-time Orebites, and one, a Polish officer, had come to Bohemia with Korybut and remained with Žižka when the prince returned home. Žižka was meticulous in observing rank and social standing in such lists, and the order in which these signatories are listed is significant. He placed himself at its head, above four barons and others of higher social rank, indicating he considered himself the Orebites' supreme military commander. Rohač, the only Taborite general to come to Oreb with Žižka, was listed second despite being inferior in social status to the four barons and several others. This marked Rohač's new stature as Žižka's deputy, possibly even his chosen successor.

The four barons were interesting individuals, and Žižka's influence on them lasted even after his death. Sezema Boček, one of the few Moravian barons opposing Sigismund from the revolution's outset, remained a Hussite stalwart despite long periods of imprisonment. He fought for Tábor eleven years later at the Battle of Lipany, again suffering imprisonment along with Rohač, who returned to Tábor shortly after signing the military ordinance. The third baron, Jan of Potstein, did not live fight at Lipany but was still fighting for Tábor in late 1428. The fourth, Aleš of Riesenburg, one of Bohemia's most powerful lords, added much legitimacy and prestige to the fledgling Orebite brotherhood. Although he had a lengthy association with the Orebites, he maintained friendly relations with conservative factions and ten years later was elected regent. Another signatory was Beneš, a squire who fought alongside Žižka at Německý Brod and served on the Prague arbitration board in February 1422. One other notable name is Žižka's brother Jaroslav, who had been with him from the beginning and followed him from Old Tábor to the 'lesser' one.

Unlike most formal documents of that time, this list of signatories does not open the document, but comes after a preamble laying out the brotherhood's goals. Like everything else written by Žižka, it is couched in religious terms. References are made to the 'certain enduring revealed and proved truth and law of God' after which the Four Articles of Prague are named. These are quoted in full and supplemented with a short commentary. Perhaps the most striking aspect of this preamble is the sense of universality throughout. The Word of God is to be preached 'everywhere, no one place excepted', and those who hear it shall teach it to others (theologians have pointed to the 'Presbyterian' nature of this passage). The Eucharist is to be given to 'all', even infants, and 'everybody' is to receive it every Sunday. However, the prohibition against priests holding temporal power is a bit muted compared to earlier instances, such as Žižka's letter from Prachatice in November 1420.

No such moderation is seen in Žižka's remarks on the Fourth Article. He expresses absolute assurance he has been divinely ordained to help cleanse the world of its sins and rightfully holds full power to do so as he sees fit. This mission is universal as well: 'all sins' great and small shall be eliminated. His use of the definite article when listing social ranks ('the kings, the princes and lords, the townspeople . . .') suggests everyone everywhere will be expected to obey these dictates, and a reference to 'all people' evidently encompassed all Christendom. More universalism: 'anyone' not adhering to the Four Articles will be barred from joining Žižka's army and will be permitted 'no place' of residence in the country. The preamble closes by declaring that the men signing the document will 'admonish, advise, push, and urge' the compliance of 'all persons' to the One True Faith.

The document's second section is a tough-minded, pragmatic, and strikingly 'modern' military code of conduct. The universalism continues: 'we all', it reads, 'command all of you' to orderly obedience. This mandate is followed by specific punishments for disobedience and breaches of discipline enumerated in twelve points. The order in which they are presented is anything but random: they match the progression followed by an army from the moment it breaks camp, beginning with the correct marching order. Soldiers will keep to their assigned ranks and stay out of each other's way; units will maintain constant communication with each other and maintain proper guards for the van, rear, and flanks. Attention is given to the emplacement and arrangement of camp sites and even the matter of camp fires is addressed – Žižka and other Hussite commanders had seen unregulated fires destroy provisions and betray an army's position. Negligent or careless officers causing losses and damage will be severely punished. Žižka decrees mandatory religious services before battle and gives detailed instructions on the proper treatment of war spoils, with strict injunctions against personal plunder. The final five paragraphs are essentially a penal code. Brawls, quarrels, desertion, and moral turpitude are to be treated with the utmost harshness. The mildest punishments stipulated for these instances are banishment and flogging. The majority are to be considered capital offences, and the 'elders' (commanding officers) are given five specific options – clubbing, beheading, hanging, drowning, and burning – or any other method deemed appropriate.

The ordinance's final section reasserts religious tenets and aspirations, declaring that if the brotherhood fights for God it will receive His assistance. Members will adhere to an upright Christian way of life. Again, Žižka speaks in universal terms: 'all regions' are addressed as well as 'the' princes, lords, knights, squires, townsmen, craftsmen, and peasants (meaning, of course, all), who will be led by the example of 'all faithful Czechs'. Žižka and his fellow signatories pledge to aid 'all the faithful everywhere', probably another reference to Hussites outside the Bohemian lands. A devout invocation of God and the Holy Trinity along with a contemptuous reference to 'the wretched reasoning of this world' serves as the document's coda.

The organisational structure of Žižka's new brotherhood reflected his concern over priestly insubordination and usurpation of military authority. Žižka's organisation had a two-fold arrangement, vertical and horizontal. The vertical encompassed the military component: orders would be transmitted from commanders through junior officers to unit leaders. The horizontal element encompassed religious and political matters: elected representatives or community elders would have input on matters unconnected to military affairs. In practical effect, Žižka mapped out not just a standing army but a state with its own laws, government, and economy. This new Tábor would be bound by a more stringent hierarchy – Žižka meant to prevent the problems that had plagued him at the first Tábor. (Old Tábor subsequently took note of Žižka's organisational ideas and adopted some of them.) It is scarcely happenstance that Žižka mentions the clergy last in a somewhat off-hand manner in keeping with their circumscribed role. They would operate within what Žižka considered their appropriate realm – spiritual matters – and although new Tábor would be a theocracy, it would not be ruled by priests.

Much has been made of the 'democratic' nature of Žižka's ordinance, and some have construed it as an attempt to subvert feudalism. But Žižka did not wish to flatten or eliminate the hierarchical orders of medieval society any more than Luther a hundred years later. However, there is an egalitarian element in his statutes – the repeated insistence that all men, regardless of rank or station, are equal in the eyes of the law, his and God's. On six separate occasions, Žižka emphasises that social standing will have no bearing on culpability and punishment of infractions. Backed by several leading nobles, Žižka claimed the same prerogative as Želivský, who assumed judicial power by executing a high-ranking lord. Želivský had acted in the name of Prague and the revolution; Žižka asserted the authority of the Orebite brotherhood and the entire Hussite movement. The implications were more significant than they may appear at first glance. This was one of the first cracks in the feudal caste system, since no such hierarchy can endure when the law is applied equally across all levels of society.

Žižka's new brotherhood, seen by many as a forerunner of Cromwell's 'New Model', marked the first time that Žižka had an army and a political structure completely under his control. He had full power as the Orebites' political and military leader without rivalry from clerics or laymen. But his claim to political autonomy made conflict with Prague inevitable, and this soon developed. After Ambrose's liberation of Hradec Králové, it had been an independent entity until Korybut occupied it the previous summer. The prince had installed Diviš Bořek as governor to act as Prague's representative. Diviš had fought under Žižka in the Battle of Hořice and had a good relationship with him until Diviš left for Moravia. Problems ensued following his last official act before leaving: installing his brother Jetrich to serve in his stead. The city's residents were unhappy about this and sent Žižka a message asking for assistance against this unelected and unwanted administrator.

Žižka's actions in this episode have puzzled many. It is difficult to explain his abrupt change of behaviour towards Diviš, a friend and ally, although Jetrich had not handled the position very well. More importantly, Prague had allowed the Orebite cities a large degree of autonomy but still claimed their allegiance. Žižka's military ordinance was incompatible with that claim, and he may not have foreseen Prague's reaction. He had been focused on establishing unchallenged leadership of a tightly organised military entity, as well as distracted by his problems with Bohuslav. Given their cordial relations, he may have taken Diviš's co-operation for granted. If Diviš had been in Hradec Králové, or had he been invited to participate in the drafting of Žižka's military ordinance, things might have gone differently. Of course, if that had been the case, Jetrich would not have been installed as interim governor and the townspeople would not have agitated for Žižka's help. All this happened while Diviš was absent; he was not consulted, and it would be understandable if he felt betrayed.

Jetrich was in a difficult position. Despite his regard for Žižka, he surely felt obliged to act in his brother's interest, and as Hradec Králové's leading official Jetrich was required to act in Prague's sovereign interest. But the people of Hradec Králové overwhelmingly supported Žižka – who had painted himself into a corner. The premise underlying the Orebite brotherhood, as expressed in his military ordinance, was his unchallenged position as the new commonwealth's leader. Žižka had to nip this first challenge to his authority in the bud. In all likelihood, he consulted with Ambrose, who could not have been pleased at being elbowed from his position as Hradec Králové's leader. Žižka answered the townspeople's call, marched a body of troops from Litoměřice, and expelled Jetrich. Popular excitement spilled over into widespread rioting and wanton destruction. An agitated mob marched on a venerable castle, long an ancestral holding of Bohemian queens and now a hated symbol of the ancien régime, and burned it to the ground.[1] This destroyed any possibility that Diviš might finesse a peaceful resolution, and he may well have considered Žižka guilty of treachery. Žižka probably felt the

1. Hradec Králové means 'Queen's Castle' in Czech.

same way about Prague – he considered himself the rightful leader of the Hussite forces acting in the revolution's best interests. Although there was no real animosity between the leaders of these colliding factions, circumstances had pushed them into conflict. Civil war, narrowly averted on previous occasions, finally broke out between the Hussites.

*

Sigismund and Pope Martin had hoped that the spring of 1423 would finally witness a successful crusade against the Hussite heretics in Bohemia. However, as March came and went, their plans unravelled, and it became apparent that the third crusade would be a bigger débâcle than the second. Although numerous nobles and princes throughout Europe had promised to join the effort, only one kept his word, King Eric of Pomerania. Bringing his army across the Baltic and finding no other forces mobilised, he returned with his troops to Copenhagen in a rage. The reason he found nobody else was that the German princes, having learnt not to count on Sigismund, had decided to do nothing until the Emperor took concrete action. He had not, and the princes followed suit. King Władyslaw, in recognition of Sigismund's previous acknowledgment of the Lake Melno accord, attempted to gather troops in the anti-Hussite cause, but there was a great deal of popular sympathy in Poland for the Bohemians. Many of Poland's leading nobles had not forgotten the assistance Žižka and other Czech mercenaries had given them in their wars against the Prussian Order. Unwilling to pursue an unpopular engagement and seeing Sigismund's talk unsupported by any action, Władyslaw decided to do nothing as well.

By mid-summer, the Hussites could breathe a sigh of relief at the absence of foreign invaders and turn from defence to offence – specifically their Moravian campaign. Many previously neutral nobles were indignant that Sigismund had given the margravate to Albert without consulting them. The first action taken by the Hussites under Diviš Bořek was a direct thrust at Albert's troops. They conquered the town of Slavkov south-east of Brno and moved east to the Morava River valley and the town of Kvasice, taking it in short order. They then doubled back north towards Kroměříž where they encountered their first significant enemy resistance. Royalist forces under Bishop Jan of Olomouc and Duke Přemek Opava engaged them in a fierce, protracted battle which ended in a decisive Hussite triumph. After the Royalists retreated, the city surrendered two days later. Several high-ranking Moravian Royalist nobles were taken prisoner, and the Hussites had subsequent victories at Vyškov, west of Kroměříž, and Přerov, a few kilometres east of the Morava.

These five victories cut Olomouc's communications with Austria and Hungary, and the campaign was evidently aimed at that key city. Its conquest would have consolidated Hussite control throughout northern Moravia. Although Bishop Jan was a formidable adversary, the Hussites might have succeeded had Žižka supplemented their forces, and it seems likely this had been the original plan. Diviš was shocked and angered when he learned that Žižka, instead of marching to his assistance at Olomouc, had just expelled his brother Jetrich from Hradec Králové. Diviš abruptly terminated his Moravian expedition and with several allies, including Hašek and Hynek Krušina, marched north-west to Hradec Králové. Diviš's two nephews, Victorin and Hynek of Poděbrady, maintained their loyalty to Žižka and resented their uncle for turning against him. Hynek of Kolstein also chose not to accompany Diviš.

As Diviš approached Hradec Králové, Žižka led a body of troops from the city to meet his army at Strachův Dvůr. In the ensuing battle, Žižka's Orebites thoroughly routed the Praguers who suffered many casualties and had 200 captives taken. After this battle, a notable incident took place, showing Žižka's dark side and his special vindictiveness towards clergymen he regarded as apostates. Like all Hussite armies, the Praguers were led into battle by a priest carrying a monstrance displaying the Holy Eucharist. After the battle, Žižka commanded that the captured priest be brought before him. As he stood before the enraged Žižka, livid at being attacked by the city he had saved and a man he considered a close friend, Žižka brought his battle club down on the priest's head in a fatal blow. What makes this episode particularly difficult for even Žižka's staunchest apologists to justify is that it occurred after the heat of battle when the issue had been decided. Apocryphal flourishes to this story have ascribed to Žižka a grim joke about baptising the priest, but this seems unlikely. It is true, however, that the spiked maces used by the Hussites were often referred to as 'holy water sprinklers', an allusion to the Hussites' harshly enforced mission of religious purification.

Žižka's overwhelming success in this battle further enhanced his reputation for invincibility. He had defeated not tradition-bound Royalist cavalry but fellow Hussites, led by a competent and highly regarded officer. Nonetheless, Prague still had tremendous power at its disposal. The Strachův Dvůr defeat had not seriously damaged its strength, and there were subsequent attempts by the Praguers to assert dominion over Orebite cities. Hradec Králové was capable of defending itself under the leadership of its militia captain Matthew Lupák, but Čáslav, the second most important Orebite centre, was vulnerable. Žižka took the main body of his forces there to buttress its defences. Shortly after he arrived in mid-August, Hašek of Waldstein and a sizeable Prague force began a lengthy but unsuccessful siege. Nonetheless, Žižka's supporters grew nervous, and several, including Lupák, decided to bring reinforcements. To prevent this, Hašek positioned troops at Kolín where they could intercept Lupák before he could cross the Elbe River. On 22 August, the Orebites reached the northern bank near Týnec, thirteen kilometres upstream from Kolín. Hašek attacked, surprising and overwhelming them. Approximately 300 Orebites were slain including Lupák, killed by one of Hašek's lieutenants, Jan Černín. Žižka was especially angered by Lupák's death, which he soon avenged.

The Týnec defeat did not damage Žižka's position at Čáslav. The Praguers ended their siege and moved to nearby Kutná Hora where they installed a strong garrison. Žižka had led a powerful sortie towards that city while its militia were assisting Hašek further north, and the Prague high command felt that, while Čáslav might be expendable in the short term, they could not afford to lose Kutná Hora. Consequently,

Žižka was able to maintain political independence for the Orebite commonwealth and again had freedom of movement throughout the region. An armistice between the Orebites and Praguers then temporarily ended their hostilities until March 1424. With that issue effectively shelved for the time being, Žižka re-focused on his arch-enemy, Sigismund, whom he was determined to attack in Moravia.

Some time in late August or early September, Sigismund's most loyal supporter in the region, Jan Městecký, raided a Hradec Králové suburb, killing a few people and burning some buildings. For his response Žižka chose a different direction than the Praguers, moving south towards the Bohemia of his youth and early manhood. In early September, he reached the Moravian border. Žižka attempted bypassing Jihlava, but its garrison and supplemental Austrian mercenaries forced a fight. They quickly regretted their challenge. The battle was a rout, and Žižka's forces pursued them back to the city gates. Žižka besieged the town, but finding it strongly defended called off the operation after a few days. He continued south towards Austria and on 19 September assaulted and took the town of Telč. He was accompanied on this expedition by Jan Hvězda, who had joined Žižka the previous month along with several Taborite soldiers. Hvězda became one of Žižka's senior officers as well as an intermediary between old and new Tábor.

Here, the controversy over Žižka's alleged 'Hungarian Anabasis' crops up. Some historians have asserted that Žižka began an expedition deep into Hungary, while others say that he invaded Austria. Both accounts have been proven erroneous. While Žižka's successor, Prokop, led numerous invasions onto foreign soil, strong evidence limits any such incursions by Žižka to a brief raid across the Danube to seize a herd of cattle from Austria for provisions. A river Žižka would have crossed after leaving Telč in the direction of Znojmo – an anti-Hussite bastion and a far more logical target than the Hungarian heartland – was the Dyje. To non-Czechs this name sounds very much like 'Dunaj', the Czech name for the Danube, which may have caused the error.

In any event, when Žižka returned from Moravia in early October 1423, a growing alliance between conservative Hussites and Catholic noblemen was taking shape. The previous month, Hašek and Kostka had convened an assembly of Prague's royal towns (excepting the four Orebite cities). This conference was held at Nymburk on the Elbe near the western edge of the Orebite region. The town's lord, Jan Puška, had sided with Prague. The invitation stressed the growing violence and disorder throughout the region and the necessity of reinstituting stability and calm. The Hussite lords proposed a conference at Kolín to their Catholic counterparts. The Catholics stated their willingness provided Sigismund approved. To ascertain the Emperor's feelings, Jan Městecký paid him a call at Buda. Permission was granted, and the conference met in early October.

Despite a shared animosity towards Žižka, there were serious religious differences between the participants, especially over deference to Rome. The conservative Hussites, who had never abandoned hopes of eventual reconciliation with the Pope, reiterated their request for a public hearing regarding the Four Articles. Moravia's capital, Brno, was selected to host this disputation. Judgement would be rendered by a panel of laymen drawn from the upper social strata who would decide if the Four Articles accorded with the Bible. Originally slated for early 1424, this hearing was to have deferred political matters until an even later date. However, the date was changed following Žižka's renewed activities in Bohemia. The assembly, known as the Diet of St Gall, met on 16 October 1423. The participants were fully aware of Žižka's disapproval and unalterable opposition to any accommodation with Sigismund. More pressing than Žižka's views towards the Pope or the Emperor, however, was his challenge to the capital's sovereignty. His standing field army had emerged as not only a political threat but an increasing economic plague as well, supporting itself in predatory fashion off the lands it passed through.

The diet concluded on 1 November after drafting a document similar to that produced by the Čáslav diet. But while the Čáslav complaints had been directed against Sigismund's loyalists, this time they were aimed at Žižka. Another important difference was that neither Tábor participated in the second diet. Six main points were enumerated, beginning with the call for a public meeting to be convened at Brno in early 1424 with safe-conduct promises extended to Hussite invitees. Žižka and the Orebites were directed to adhere to the Diet's resolutions, and a one-year armistice was declared. Under its terms, conquered property was to be returned to the original owner, but damaged or destroyed fortifications were not to be repaired. If, by the end of the armistice, no agreement had been reached, those estates would revert to the conquerors. Significant by omission was any mention of Germans expelled from Prague. Two final points focus on economics, particularly the need to maintain free and open travel throughout the kingdom to sustain trade and commerce. Minting of currency anywhere other than Kutná Hora would be severely punished. An inspectorate was created to investigate and suppress counterfeiting, which had arisen as a result of cash expenses incurred by the wars and worsened severe inflation caused by diminished agricultural production.

A new regency council was established to replace the one instituted at the first Čáslav diet. It would have only twelve regents: six Hussites and six Catholics including Čeněk, Ulrich, and Frederic of Kolovraty, a leading member of the Plzeň Landfrieden. The other two barons were from northern and central Bohemia, respectively. The Hussite regents would be its leading conservative noblemen, Hašek of Waldstein, Hynek of Kolstein, and Hynek Krušina; Herman of Borotín, viewed as a radical; and two knights, Jan Smiřický and Diviš Bořek. This body was far less diverse in social standing than the preceding council. It was drawn exclusively from the very highest social echelon; even the two knights were at the very top of their particular class in wealth and status. There were no squires, townsmen, or city councillors. This was obviously an effort by the high nobility to reassert control over the kingdom as a baronial oligarchy based in Prague, and the pledge taken by these lords 'to defend if necessary with all their force the capital city of Prague against all who might plot against it' indicates there was already apprehension Žižka might try to take the city.

Although Sigismund is not explicitly mentioned in the transcripts, it is evident that the participants were aiming towards his eventual recognition as king of Bohemia. The Emperor had been kept abreast of developments by Ulrich, one of the twelve new regents. On 24 November, Sigismund wrote to Ulrich and told him to delay adhering to the Diet's resolutions until further notice. After more closely examining the terms in a report from Jan Městecký, Sigismund agreed to grant safe-conduct to Brno for the Hussites. He did not, however, agree to the establishment of a lay jury to render judgement on the Four Articles, probably at the behest of Cardinal Branda. This qualified approval effectively dismantled the proposed Brno disputation; the Hussites were unwilling to defer to any judgmental body they considered prejudiced against them. They did not give up their long-standing desire for this public hearing, however, and the following spring Władyslaw attempted to engineer it for them.

Žižka meanwhile was scrupulously adhering to the terms of the current armistice among the Hussite factions. But it did not extend to the Royalists, and he did not feel bound in any way by the St Gall diet, convened in open hostility to him. So, in early 1424 – again disregarding the fact that it was mid-winter – Žižka marched against Tábor's primary enemies, the lords of Opočno and Častolovice who had perpetrated the Chotěboř massacre and attacked Hradec Králové.

Žižka also learned about an assassination plot by Městecký, though the hired assassin never had the opportunity to carry out his task. In late 1423, Žižka relocated from Čáslav to Hradec Králové and in January continued north against the two Royalist lords he hated above all others: Městecký (whom he now had even more reason to detest) and Půta of Častolovice. They were being supported by two other Royalist barons, Ernest of Černčice and Hynek Červenohorský. The two forces met at the town of Skalice, resulting in another overwhelming triumph for Žižka who inflicted numerous casualties on the Royalists and took large numbers of prisoners. After that battle, two relatively quiet months followed. In early March 1424, Žižka battled Krušina of Lichtenburg, the brother of Hynek, a former Orebite leader. The six-month armistice between the Hussites had now expired, and Krušina had rendered assistance to one of the Catholic lords. Žižka's attack on Krušina's castle of Hostinné was unsuccessful, and he moved on to the castle and town of Mlazovice. This was the primary residence of Jan Černín, Hašek's lieutenant at the Battle of Týnec and the man who had killed Žižka's lieutenant, Lupák. Žižka settled the score by destroying Mlazovice and seeing Černín killed.

Although Žižka never lost sight of his overall goals, he was not averse to pursuing personal grudges as long as they did not interfere with them. Žižka's campaign during the early spring of 1424 was particularly bloody, and he seemed bent on pursuing enemies and destroying property even when his tactical and strategic purposes had been achieved. He went out of his way to attack some of Čeněk's knights and squires. A number of small villages and towns of no strategic or material value were burned and many historians hostile to Žižka have depicted this as a reversion by Žižka to the armed banditry of his early manhood. While we cannot know the exact nature of Žižka's psychological motivations, we do know that he was engaging in a scorched earth policy of total destruction. However, Žižka did not abandon the high-flown ideas behind his new brotherhood, and events would show that every move he made was taken with a view to the establishment of his theocratic commonwealth.

In July 1423, Bohuslav took his troops back to Tábor, and little activity occurred in that quarter for the remainder of the year. However, the election of Herman of Borotín to the regency council in 1423 reflected continuing disagreements between Žižka and Bohuslav. While not affiliated with Tábor, Herman was on friendly terms with the community, and his inclusion in the new regency council was an attempt to preclude old Tábor from assisting Žižka in any future clashes. Tábor seemed willing to remain neutral in the emerging Hussite civil war, a policy made explicit on 10 February 1424 when the Taborite confederation and some of its associated nobility entered into an armistice with the Plzeň Landfrieden. The Landfrieden, until then occupied with the threat presented by the nearby Taborites, were now at liberty to move in concert with Žižka's enemies against him. Notable by their absence from this armistice were the city of Domažlice, which retained very close relations with Žižka, and the town and castle of Lomnice held by Roháč, Žižka's faithful supporter.

Throughout April 1424, Žižka remained busy with his small-scale war throughout the Orebite region and finally determined to take decisive action in early May. The resources at his disposal in lesser Tábor were still limited, and he could not use its town and city militias given the threat presented by Royalists in the area. Nonetheless, he realised he could delay no longer and with his main force went on the attack against the Landfrieden. This put him 240 kilometres from his base of support with the antagonistic Prague towns between him and Oreb. There are precise records of Žižka's strength at this time: 500 cavalrymen, 7,000 troops, and 300 wagons, formidable but hardly a juggernaut. Žižka knew that he could not attack the Landfrieden on their home turf, where they would outnumber him, and he could not think of attacking Plzeň itself. Falling back on the guerrilla tactics favoured by small armies facing large ones, he set out to inflict material damage and undermine morale so as to weaken the Landfrieden's resolve. He thought his return to the south might persuade some of his former Taborite soldiers to rejoin him. If he managed to convince enough of them to do so, this would subvert the armistice with Plzeň and hamper its freedom of movement. It would also go far towards countering the united front of conservative Hussites and Catholic nobles now arrayed against him.

By mid-May, Žižka had established his presence in the Plzeň region and made numerous successful assaults throughout the area. The Landfrieden sent out calls for assistance, and on 17 May the Karlštejn castle garrison dispatched some cavalry to Plzeň, reinforced by troops from local Royalist nobles along with various Landfrieden town and village militias. Žižka, with Hvězda and Roháč serving as his lieutenants, had been operating in the southern part of the region, laying waste to many towns and villages while receiving assistance from the Taborite towns of Sušice and Klatovy, which sent 300 militiamen. Žižka then moved his operations north to the area between Plzeň and Královice. The combined Landfrieden forces offered battle, but Žižka declined and continued north. Královice was only a day from Žatec, which had remained solidly in his camp. Going there would allow Žižka to enlarge his forces without risk, establish control over a large part of south-western Bohemia, and position him for a strong effort in the north-west as well. After consolidating his support at Žatec, he went on to Louny for additional troops. At the same time, the Praguers, who had been quiet since the Strachův Dvůr defeat, now went back into action.

*

Prague was willing to ignore Žižka when he detoured around the capital in early May en route from Hradec Králové to Klatovy. Although the city was technically bound to support the Plzeň Landfrieden, there was not much fellow-feeling among Prague's Hussites for the German Catholics of that confederation. However, when Žatec and Louny allied themselves with the blind general, this was viewed quite differently. It was another manifestation of Bohemian conservativism whereby religious and nationalist sympathies for the Hussites stopped short when concrete political ramifications arose. While Žatec had always enjoyed a high degree of autonomy, Praguers still considered it as part of its sphere of influence, and the recent declaration of allegiance to Žižka by Louny, which had previously acknowledged Prague's sovereignty, was construed as outright rebellion. Prague leaders felt they could not stand idly by as Žižka's strength grew in such close proximity. They joined their forces with those of the Karlštejn garrison and Plzeň Landfrieden, creating the first coalition army of Utraquist conservatives and Catholic Royalists, one far superior numerically to that led by Žižka.

As Prague mobilised, Žižka was heading east towards the Elbe, reaching it near Roudnice. Continuing on towards Prague, he crossed the Vlatava River near its confluence with the Elbe, approximately thirty-two kilometres from the capital at Mělník. It is scarcely likely that Žižka considered marching against Prague, knowing of its preparations and the strength of the forces. He continued east along

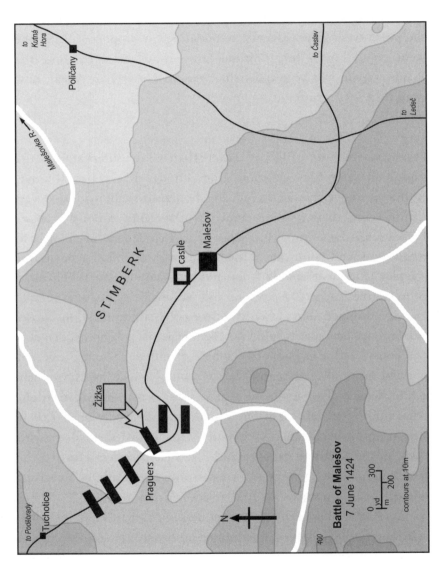

to Kutná Hora

to Podĕbrady

to Časlav

to Ledeč

Poličany

Tuchotice

Malešovka R.

STIMBERK

Žižka

castle

Malešov

Praguers

400

N

Battle of Malešov
7 June 1424

0   300
yd
m
200

contours at 10m

Battle of Malešov

the Elbe towards Čáslav, where he would be in a defensible position and situated to gather additional soldiers.

Evidently, it did not appear that way to the Praguers, who sallied out to meet him as he reached the town of Kostelec, twenty-four kilometres north-east of the capital. Žižka barely had enough time to draw up his wagons on a slight rise in a narrow bend of the river. The combined Calixtine–Royalist forces completely blocked the narrow neck of land to the south, hemming in Žižka and his troops. As at Kutná Hora and Vladař, he appeared hopelessly trapped, and again his enemies celebrated prematurely. Exultant messages were sent by the Royalist commanders Čeněk and Hašek to Ulrich, who was with Sigismund at the royal court in Hungary. Eager to reclaim their status in the imperial court, which had been badly damaged by Sigismund's scapegoating and charges of treason, Ulrich and his fellow Bohemian courtiers gleefully assured the Emperor that Žižka was now finished. Sigismund had heard that assurance before. 'He will get away,' he scoffed. The Bohemian nobles asserted otherwise and offered to bet a horse on the outcome. Sigismund refused to take the bet, sarcastically calling it one he was certain to lose. The Emperor missed an opportunity to acquire a steed for his stable at the expense of his over-confident Czech courtiers.

Unlike previous occasions when he had been cornered, Žižka did not blast his way through the surrounding enemy with a night charge. After holding off the besieging Royalists for several days, he simply disappeared overnight, or so it seemed to his stunned enemies at dawn on 4 June. As there is no existing documentary evidence about it, the actual logistics of this escape can only be surmised. Although there was a bridge nearby, it was surely well-guarded by the Royalists. Žižka had managed to send word of his predicament to the Poděbrady brothers, Victorin and Hynek, at their castle forty kilometres further upriver. This would seem to make it virtually certain that the Poděbradys had quietly floated rafts and boats downstream to Žižka's position and then ferried his men and wagons to the far shore. In any case, Žižka then continued marching upstream to the east. Čeněk and Hašek, mortified

201

and determined to make good their boasts to Sigismund, followed him along the south bank of the river. Their desperate eagerness to pursue Žižka and finish him off would lead to disaster.

The Royalists crossed the river as soon as possible, probably at Brandýs. Žižka had been forced to take a long detour around Nymburk, allowing his pursuers to close the distance between them. At Poděbrady castle, they almost caught up, but Žižka had re-crossed the river under cover provided by the Poděbrady brothers. Hynek attempted to initiate a parley, and for his troubles was arrested and held prisoner, first at Nymburk and later at Mělník. Victorin, however, joined forces with Žižka's army which continued on towards Čáslav. En route, he was compelled to make two other detours around Kolín and Kutná Hora while fighting some rearguard actions against pursuing Royalists. Sixteen kilometres short of Čáslav, Žižka decided to turn and make a stand at the fortress of Malešov. It was commanded by Hvězda, who now joined Žižka's other senior officers, Roháč, Victorin, and the Valečov brothers, Bernhard and Bartoš, who had led Orebite troops in revious campaigns under Žižka. Hvězda's familiarity with the area was matched by that of Žižka, blindness notwithstanding, who had traversed the region several times during previous campaigns.

The impact of the battle that ensued matched that of Vítkov and Kutná Hora, and it was the subject of several contemporary or near-contemporary accounts, including one written or based upon a description by one of Žižka's men. The old general fuelled the Royalists' over-confidence by simulating retreat – a tactic he had seen employed effectively against the Teutonic Knights at Grunwald–Tannenberg. His use of topography was even more sophisticated than usual; he lured the enemy into fording the Malešovka River where they were not only strung out in a vulnerable line but effectively cut in half. He also employed psychology in his use of the high ground. Unlike Vítkov, where he had pushed the enemy off a steep hill, at Malešov he sent rock-filled wagons, gunfire, and charging soldiers down on the Royalists, who were traversing a narrow hillside road beneath a high plateau where he had taken his position. As the forward Royalist elements retreated in panic, they collided with their own centre. This created a bottleneck at the river crossing that prevented the rear from coming forward in a timely and effective manner. Some 1,400 Royalists were slaughtered in the subsequent rout, including two leading dukes and three prominent knights.

The immediate effect of Žižka's triumph also matched that of Vítkov and Kutná Hora. With one stroke, Žižka had gained control of nearly all of eastern Bohemia and decimated Prague's military strength.

Žižka, as usual, wasted no time in following up his victory. He marched on Kutná Hora the very next day, where the terrified inhabitants quickly surrendered. This availed them little. Their militia had participated at Malešov, and Žižka certainly remembered the slaughter of Hussites that had occurred there three years earlier. Numerous Kutnohorians were killed after Žižka's men entered the city, including many who had taken refuge in a church. This desperate attempt at invoking religious safe haven did nothing to deter Žižka's men, who burned the church and all inside along with many other houses and their occupants. Žižka took steps to replace the Germans miners with Czechs before moving on to Kouřim, whose garrison was captained by Diviš Bořek. The city surrendered without resistance, and later in June Český Brod and Nymburk followed suit.

Not much is known about Žižka's activities for the next several weeks until mid-July, when he marched to the far north-east of Bohemia against Turnov. This town belonged jointly to Čeněk's cousin, Henry of Wartenberg, and Jan of Michalovice, a member of the regency council elected at the St Gall diet. Žižka was particularly destructive during this expedition and showed special cruelty towards monks. He burned down a Dominican monastery and its inhabitants, and on 1 September, while returning to Litoměřice, he burned four monks who had allegedly molested some local women at Libochovice, a small town near Louny. Žižka now returned to his castle, Chalice, to map out his next move. In mid-July, he had sent Hvězda to capture the castle of Ostromoc, near Živohousť on the Vlatava River only forty kilometres south of the capital. With this castle occupied and garrisoned, Žižka was able to block an important river crossing as well as disrupt Prague's communications with the south. He also spent some time in Žatec vigorously recruiting additional troops from that city, as well as Louny and Klatovy.

Now Žižka was ready to march on Prague, and by 9 September he had positioned his troops near the village of Libeň, where they could see the Vítkov in the distance. Dramatic changes had occurred since Žižka had last been in the capital, most importantly the return of Prince Korybut. Prague was again under the monarchical rule of the man whom Žižka had previously pledged to obey, but this development does not seem to have altered his agenda in the least.

Chapter 8

DEATH AND DEFEAT

'There is no difference between the peasantry and the Castle', said the teacher.
'Maybe', said K., 'that doesn't alter my position.'
Franz Kafka, *The Castle*

The Utraquist or Calixtine faction of the Hussites had always hoped they might ultimately reconcile with the Roman Catholic Church. However, they were overwhelmingly opposed to acknowledging Sigismund as the king of Bohemia. The 1423 St Gall diet, however, undercut this resolve. When Městecký and Půta had corresponded with the Emperor regarding the Utraquists' long-sought disputation, Sigismund's qualified response still represented a shift from his hard-line stance towards the Four Articles. It seems likely, given three unsuccessful attempts at military conquest, that Sigismund had determined diplomacy to be a more fruitful path to formal recognition as king of the Bohemian Lands. The Hussites, not Sigismund, terminated negotiations on this matter, after which a crestfallen Emperor decided it was time for a fourth crusade.

The breakdown of discussions between the Bohemian estates and Sigismund was due primarily to Prague, whose citizens still hated the Emperor. After Korybut had ousted the Zelivists, Prague politics were less democratic, but popular sentiment was still noted by the new city council. Led by William Kostka, the government calmed the city and re-established the rule of law. Kostka was an able civic administrator, as well as a political centrist. This allowed him to bring together the conservative elements at the same time displaying moderation towards the radicals (as in September 1422, when he interceded with Korybut on their behalf). He knew that entering into any agreement with Sigismund would enflame passions and likely lead to widespread riots. Kostka had other reasons for keeping his distance from the St Gall diet. His ultimate political goal, re-establishing Korybut as Bohemia's monarch, was directly opposed to that of the Diet, which was implicitly aimed at Sigismund's accession to the throne. Korybut had never foresworn the idea of wearing the Bohemian crown and had remained in contact with his supporters in Prague and throughout Bohemia.

In early March 1424, Kostka dispatched diplomats to Poland and sent a second delegation the following month. The first diplomatic initiative was led by the Englishman Peter Payne, scarcely a conservative. The second embassy in April was led by Valkoun of Adlary, a long-time Žižka supporter. Payne arrived in Poland just after Emperor Sigismund who had gone to Cracow to participate in the coronation of Władyslaw's young bride, Sofia. Payne's diplomatic corps met with Władyslaw on 25 March at Wiślica and renewed their request for a public hearing on the Four Articles. They suggested it be held not in Brno but in one of two Moravian Hussite towns, Uničov or Kroměříž. The Polish King ran the idea by Sigismund who promptly vetoed it. The Czech delegates then travelled to Lithuania and met Grand Duke Vytautas on 25 April at Przelom near Grodno. Here, Payne submitted something completely different: if Vytautas was unwilling to honour his pledge to accept the Bohemian crown it was suggested that he should give his permission for his nephew to do so.

Vytautas bluntly refused, stating that, if Korybut went to Bohemia and assumed the throne, he, Vytautas, would regard him as an enemy. In somewhat gentler terms, Władyslaw gave the same answer to Valkoun when the second diplomatic initiative made the same proposal to the Polish King. The King gave his answer unaware of a flurry of discussions that were taking place between the Bohemians and several of the highest-ranking nobles of his own court. These included a meeting between Valkoun and Korybut, supported by pro-Hussite Poles, most notably Chancellor John Szafraniec. As they became engrossed in these covert manoeuvres, the Bohemians appeared to lose interest in a public disputation of the Four Articles. This disputation had been strongly supported by Władyslaw, who misinterpreted their apparent indifference and angrily decided that he would join Sigismund's crusade after all. After sending a letter to that effect to the Bohemians on 17 June, he was flabbergasted two days later when his nephew Korybut defiantly gathered 500 cavalrymen and marched south through Silesia to Moravia. On his arrival, Korybut learned of Žižka's recent victory over the Prague forces and its ramifications. Bohemia suddenly looked less welcoming; however he had crossed the Rubicon, so to speak, and there was no going back to Poland. On 29 June he arrived in Prague.

Władyslaw was embarrassed, furious, and very much concerned that Sigismund – who saw treachery everywhere – would suspect him of complicity. The Polish King sent a stream of letters to the German princes collectively and individually, as well as to Sigismund and Pope Martin, declaring his innocence and decrying the betrayal by his rebellious nephew, whom he had disowned and whose estates he had confiscated. Sigismund was unconvinced, knowing the extreme measures he and other rulers often took to camouflage their true intentions,. In late June, 5,000 Polish troops marched across the Moravian border and moved to Olomouc to join Duke Albert's anti-Hussite army, but the Duke refused to open the city gates to them. For two weeks, the Poles attempted to persuade Albert (and Sigismund) of their good intentions but were unable to do so and returned home, much to the secret pleasure of Chancellor Szafraniec and the pro-Hussite Polish nobility. Whatever else might ensue, there would be no Polish war against the Hussites.

Korybut received a fairly warm welcome in Prague, which must have bolstered his confidence. He wrote a challenging letter, effectively a declaration of war, to Sigismund and Duke Albert referring to himself as the 'postulated and elected King of Bohemia and Moravia'. It included a litany of complaint against Sigismund, who had, among other offences, arbitrarily refused to grant the Hussites' eminently reasonable requests for an open hearing. The letter closed with his declaration that he would fight for these principles with all the power at his disposal. This is the only surviving document written by Korybut in which he refers to himself as King and it seems to have had a large element of wishful thinking. It served him well in the short term, however, opening the door for a reconciliation between Prague and Žižka, predisposed to treat any enemy of Sigismund as a friend.

First Korybut would have to stabilise and consolidate his position in Prague. He demanded that the city renew the powers and privileges granted previously which included sovereignty over Prague's royal towns, and this demand was speedily granted. However, where there had been eighteen royal towns during Korybut's first regency, there were now but nine, four of which were less than secure and quite distant from the capital. The royal towns closer to Prague – Kolín, Mělník, Litoměřice, Slaný, and Beroun – could not be expected to support the prince enthusiastically. Korybut, after two months in Prague, found himself in a precarious position. Prague's citizens, whom Žižka had rescued on two previous occasions, gazed at him apprehensively over the city walls.

As Žižka kept no diary and wrote no memoirs, and there is no record of him having confided in his leading officers, Žižka's actual intentions are unknown. Although he had been angered by the city leaders, particularly when it returned the Vyšehrad to the Royalists in 1419, he still had strong connections to it and many of its people. He did not wish to rule out the possibility of its stout-hearted peasants and workmen joining his growing army at some point, but he could not permit the city's political leaders to continue defying him. It seems that Žižka, like Sigismund before him, was bluffing. Unlike Sigismund however, Žižka's ploy was successful. Before any hostilities could break out, Prague and Žižka signed a peace agreement on 14 September 1424.

The idea of open warfare between Praguers and Žižka's Hussites was repugnant to the overwhelming majority in both camps. Some asserted, quite legitimately, that the Hussites had no chance of defeating Rome and the Emperor if they turned on each other. Žižka sensed incipient mutiny and sought to forestall it by gathering his troops and addressing their dissatisfaction directly. There are no verbatim transcriptions of this speech, but whatever Žižka's exact words, they were effective. The men, now virtually unanimous in their support of the blind general, declared their willingness to fight and gathered at the city walls.

Prince Korybut intervened by sending an emissary offering peace and co-operation. Prague's recognition of Korybut as its head of state looked impressive on paper but did not amount to much in practical terms. Žižka probably felt that any prior pledge of loyalty he had made to Korybut had been nullified when the prince had gone back to Poland. Korybut, hoping to renew Žižka's respect and allegiance, was savvy enough to couch his appeal in religious terms. Žižka's belief in the sacred properties of the Eucharist as manifest in the communion of both kinds was unshakable. He still regarded Jacobellus of Stříbro as the legitimate successor to Jan Hus, and he adhered to the teaching and practice of that University master. Jacobellus loathed violence, but he was not insensible to Žižka's piety and appreciated Žižka's deference to him.

On 14 September, eyewitness accounts by Prague scribes detail a 'concordance and reconciliation' between Korybut and Žižka. Both sides made a financial good-faith security pledge of an immense sum and erected a large pile of stones to signify their compact, stipulating that if either party violated it, the one breaking faith would be buried beneath them. Nonetheless, according to one source, Žižka expressed scepticism about the longevity of the agreement, suggesting it would last no longer than the one formulated at Konopiště.

Little else is known of the details surrounding this seminal event, but shortly thereafter a full-scale campaign encompassing all Hussite factions was undertaken with a view to liberating Moravia from Duke Albert. After leaving old Tábor and achieving the objectivity which can only be gained by distance, Žižka had begun to realise that the Hussite movement, if it was to endure, would have to include all Bohemians – noble and peasant, urban and rural. His motivation for agreeing to

Korybut's overtures of peace was surely very different than that of the prince. In Žižka's strategic vision, his restored position in Prague would bring with it the remaining royal towns and in all probability most of the Czech nobility. Making peace with Korybut and the Utraquists appeared a necessary accommodation for the achievement of a comprehensive, nationwide Hussite confederation capable of encompassing all social ranks and ways of life in accordance with his military ordinance.

The solemn compact between Žižka and Korybut, which came to be known as the Peace of Libeň, was only the beginning of this challenging and arduous process. It did not consolidate authority under a single head but dispersed it in an alliance, thereby maintaining the dualism of Hussite hierarchy. While it did offer some increased security for Žižka – Korybut had acknowledged the autonomy of the Orebite commonwealth and ceded the cities that had declared allegiance to it – the establishment of a truly authoritative monarchy was also stymied. This political schizophrenia would last for another decade, outliving Žižka. But the immediate consequence of the rapprochement between the prince and the general was a period of internal peace after more than a year of civil war, and it afforded Žižka a chance to re-enter Prague once again as a friend, not an invader.

*

Elsewhere, a significant and unexpected event had taken place. In southern Bohemia, an armistice was concluded on 10 September 1424 between the Taborite commonwealth and Ulrich of Rožemberk and some of his allies. It was to last five weeks and was intended to permit Ulrich the opportunity to negotiate with Sigismund for a public hearing on behalf of the Taborites and the Four Articles. Ulrich signed the document along with three other Royalist barons and four burgraves. Tábor's signatories were Chval, Zbyněk, and several Taborite nobles, including Bohuslav, Herman of Borotín, Zmrzlík the Younger, and Nicholas Sokol. However, the only other cities named in the armistice are Písek and Prachatice, as all other cities in the Taborite confederation had declared allegiance to Žižka. This agreement came as a surprise at the time and has continued to puzzle historians – very shortly thereafter the Taborites appointed Hvězda as their captain-general, and he and Bohuslav were again leading Taborite soldiers in fierce battles against Sigismund. War-weariness and self-doubt are the keys to this puzzle. The prolonged and increasingly vicious nature of the Hussite wars had begun to disturb many of the Taborite clergymen. Reports of Žižka's cruelty against both Calixtine priests and Catholic monks may well have elicited some sympathy among Tábor's clerics, many of whom (notably Peter Chelčický) were committed pacifists who had begun questioning the spiritual legitimacy of Christians slaughtering each other.

Another peculiarity of this armistice was Žižka's apparent forbearance towards it. He might have been expected to have been angered by this compact, given his strident opposition to any agreements with Sigismund and his proxies. Žižka and his southern Bohemian allies, including the towns of Klatovy, Sušice, and Lomnice as well as various nobles in the region, were named as participants in the document. Neither Žižka nor any of his colleagues actually signed the document. The Taborites felt safe giving this assurance, knowing that the militias of the three towns named had joined Žižka's march on the capital. While it seems likely that Žižka would not have had a problem with the armistice's putative goal of affording a respite for the Taborite forces, it is certain he would have objected to its underlying intent of creating a window for negotiations with Sigismund.

The fatal over-confidence that Sigismund had displayed since the beginning of the Hussite revolution was not cured by the setbacks, defeats and humiliations he had suffered over the previous five years. When Sigismund learned of Ulrich's negotiations and the Taborites' overtures, he concluded that he might be able to accomplish with diplomacy what he had been unable to achieve through military force and economic pressure. Sigismund was fully cognizant that no lasting resolution of his Bohemian problem could be achieved without dealing with Žižka in some decisive and final manner. He had evidently concluded that he could not hope to defeat the Hussite general on the battlefield, and his correspondence reflects a begrudging admiration along with continued bitterness towards the Hussites. Sigismund also subscribed to the notion that every man has his price. Consequently, he took a new tack towards Žižka and the Taborites, whom he now permitted to hope that they might be completely free to receive the communion in both kinds and adhere to the Four Articles.

Sigismund is also said to have made a secret offer to Žižka, another of the many so-called historical facts of dubious authenticity surrounding Žižka. As with several other fanciful Žižka myths and legends, Aeneas Sylvius – who was not reluctant to let verified realities (or the absence thereof) stand in the way of a good narrative – is primarily responsible for promulgating this story. According to the fiercely anti-Hussite historian-turned-pope, Sigismund offered Žižka rule over the entire Bohemian kingdom and command of all its troops, supplemented by large annual payments of gold, as long as he would acknowledge Sigismund as king and administer it in his name. Sylvius's account registers outrage at Sigismund's betrayal of the Empire and his country, excoriating the Emperor for betraying Christianity by truckling to a sacrilegious heretic. Sylvius concludes by stating as an incontrovertible fact that Žižka accepted the offer. Most of Sylvius's account, like much else he wrote about Žižka, is sheer fantasy driven by retroactive frustration at Sigismund's inability decisively to crush him and his Hussite 'warriors of God'. Like Sigismund, he felt the need to explain Žižka's continued success with a scapegoat, and he chose Sigismund. Sylvius was also setting the dramatic stage for a subsequent attribution of divine intervention to otherwise inexplicable events.

Žižka and Korybut, bound together by their mutual animosity towards Sigismund, were co-operating with a view to internal stabilisation of the Czech Lands. This programme included the Catholic nobility, who had been compelled to reassess their position in light of the demonstrated impotence of the Germans, Poles, and Hungarians to support them against the Hussites. Conjoined with Korybut, Žižka was unbeatable, and without foreign assistance no Royalist duke or baron could hope to hold out against him. Reconciling themselves to this new reality, the Catholic nobles and the Plzeň Landfrieden agreed to a meeting to discuss the possibilities of a peaceful reconciliation. Delegates of both parties went to west-central Bohemia; the Hussites installed themselves at Beroun, and the Catholics lodged at Žebrák, a large castle eighteen kilometres to the south-east. After a few written communiqués were exchanged, both sides agreed to hold a 'common diet' at the town of Zdice, located halfway between their respective locations and halfway between Prague and Plzeň.

The diet was convened on or about 23 September 1424 and lasted until 1 October. Like the diet at Kolín the previous year, its stated purpose was to lay the groundwork for an all-encompassing national diet at which the Four Articles would be given a public hearing before a jury of distinguished laymen. This time, however, neither Sigismund nor Władyslaw were associated with the proposal. Theologians would make the case for or against the validity of the Four Articles and their accordance with the Bible, but the final decision would be made by 100 men drawn from both sides of the ideological divide. These would include nobles, knights, and squires, as well as representatives of the various towns and both the Taborite and Orebite brotherhoods. Any unresolved issues would be submitted to various committees for further examination, and all decisions would be binding upon all parties. The concept of national unification through religious reconciliation had more in common with the first diet of Čáslav than the St Gall assembly, and that spirit was evident in many of the political resolutions of the Zdice meeting. An armistice was proposed that was to last until March 1425, encompassing all Bohemians while pointedly excluding all foreigners (which, of course, included Sigismund). The Catholic nobles went so far as to agree that, if any of their colleagues wished to join the Hussites in fighting the Emperor, they would raise no objections. Sigismund's violent outrage upon learning this is well documented in two furious letters he wrote to Ulrich. Another stipulation was that any participant not fully submitting to the agreement within a month would be compelled to do so forcibly, a specific reference to the Catholic nobles and towns. In fact the Catholic delegates pledged to send 2,000 troops of their own to assist in enforcing this provision.

The diet concluded its business with a final resolution in the direction of religious tolerance, one a bit ahead of its time. The diet in part supported religious pluralism, declaring that, while the armistice was in effect, freedom of worship and preaching would extend to all Bohemians and all forcible conversion or suppression would be deferred. Granted, this was only a temporary measure: on the armistice's expiry date some religious totalitarianism would be re-established. Nonetheless, coming less than a decade after Hus's execution, it is a striking instance of nascent social progressivism, and like much else about the Hussite Revolution represents the dawning of modern political and religious principles. Surviving copies of the Zdice accord do not list its signatories, so we do not know the extent of Žižka's participation and concurrence. He did not object to its final form as seen in its final resolution: the call for a combined national diet and public disputation in March 1425 at Kouřim, now an Orebite stronghold. Whatever judgements and determinations this national assembly might reach, it would do so under Žižka's direct observation and control. With this reassuring knowledge, he now turned his full attention to his grand design of a decisive campaign into Moravia.

A unified Moravian campaign would not only symbolise the mutual accord forged between the Hussites at Zdice, but it would have a realistic prospect of success. Žižka now commanded an army reliably estimated to have numbered at least 20,000 men. It included elements from Prague and its allied cities, Žižka's standing field army and soldiers from the cities of the Orebite brotherhood, and even some troops from old Tábor fighting under their old captain-general for the first time in nearly three years. The Taborites were led by Nicholas Sokol, one of the few Bohemian nobles associated with that brotherhood. Žižka's other senior officers were Hvězda, another knight from Tábor named Kuneš who had fought with great distinction at Malešov, and Victorin of Poděbrady. The Praguers were led by Prince Korybut, assisted by his two captains, Hynek and Diviš Bořek. It is not known if the previous antagonism between Žižka and Diviš had been smoothed over but they did keep their distance from each other. Diviš led the army's van into Moravia ahead of the main force, which began to march on or about 3 October 1424, its path somewhat parallel to Žižka's previous victorious march through Německý Brod. The Hussite army continued west towards Brno, stopped just short of the border, and began besieging the great castle of Přibyslav.

This is one of the few military actions undertaken by Žižka that seem to defy rational explanation. There may have been personal considerations in Žižka's decision-making: the castle belonged to a leading Royalist, Čeněk of Ronov, a man deeply detested by the Taborites. Along with Městecký and Půta, he had participated in the gruesome mass slaughter after the surrender of Chotěboř. Nonetheless, according to the terms of the Zdice armistice, Ronov should have been excluded from any hostilities. It seems likely, therefore, that the castle defenders impetuously attempted to interfere with the Hussite army's progress towards Moravia, where the Ronovs had large holdings, abrogating their immunity and provoking Žižka's vindictive anger. While his forces were investing the castle and preparing for an assault, Žižka became ill. Although it is commonly assumed that he fell victim to the bubonic plague (which, as previously mentioned, had flared up in the Kutná Hora region), this cannot be definitely known given the scanty records and absence of medical doctors in Žižka's camp. After giving final instructions to Victorin, Hvězda, and Kuneš enjoining them to remain steadfast in the defence of God's truth, Žižka died on 11 October 1424. Žižka's officers and men, suddenly deprived of their inspirational leader and figurehead, were devastated. Almost as if in an attempt to send him off on a victorious note, they redoubled their efforts against Přibyslav and burned it to the ground along with sixty defenders. Shortly thereafter the Orebites, demonstrating their regard for Žižka as the father of the Hussite revolution, took to calling themselves the Orphans, which became their official name for the remainder of the Hussite wars.

Žižka's body was conducted to its final resting place by Ambrose and Prokop the Bald. While Kuneš, as senior Hussite officer, now took

Žižka's place as commander-in-chief, Prokop would eventually take leadership of the Orphans' field army in 1427. Žižka was buried at Hradec Králové in the church of SS Peter and Paul where he had worshipped and which had hosted the national diet of 1421. In 1437, Hradec Králové was conquered by the same man who had lost it to Žižka fourteen years previously, Diviš Bořek. The Utraquist government he installed was highly averse to the prominent display of Žižka's tomb in its main church. His body was disinterred and reburied at Čáslav, where his loyal comrade Roháč had been captain and where his disciples were pleased to welcome his body. His tomb was viewed by many visitors during the next two centuries.

But Žižka still would not able to rest in peace. After the Battle of the White Mountain in 1620, the victorious Habsburgs of Austria paid particular attention to the remains of the man so instrumental in first winning Czech independence. Another fanatically religious Kutná Hora mint master, William of Vřesovice, ordered the tomb completely demolished in 1622 as the Counter-Reformation swept the Czech Lands. While this incident had little practical effect on the political situation, it was extremely demoralising to the Bohemian people. One apocryphal anecdote has Žižka's remains buried a third time after the tomb's destruction beneath the city gallows. This would put him in company with Wyclif and Cromwell as one of three leading Protestant reformers whose remains were violated years after their death.

Žižka's sudden, anti-climatic death was exploited for dramatic purposes by Sylvius, whose previously rigorous historical scholarship had edged further and further into outright mythmaking. Any pretext of objectivity he may have maintained as a scholar was discarded in favour of his new role as the Holy Father and leading advocate of the Roman Catholic Church. Sylvius was responsible for promulgating the outlandishly macabre legend that on his deathbed Žižka ordered his body be flayed, his entrails thrown to the birds and beasts, and his skin made into a drum so that his voice could continue to lead the Hussites into battle. Here, too, Sylvius was indulging the medieval propensity to explain the otherwise inexplicable by means of the supernatural. How else could the continued improbable victories of the Hussites after his death be explained? The uncritical acceptance given this legend was remarkable. For the next three centuries it was universally acknowledged as historical fact by scholars throughout Europe, who were unwilling to dispute the official papal account. In the eighteenth century, an actual drum made with human skin (from someone) was exhibited in the fortress of Glatz, where it was taken as war spoil by Frederick the Great when he conquered Silesia during the War of the Austrian Succession.

This demonising myth was matched by a diametrically opposed sanctifying legend promulgated (perhaps in response) by Žižka's devotees. According to this myth, the citizens of Hradec Králové ordered Žižka to be painted on their banners, depicted in knightly armour astride a white horse and holding his battle club aloft. These banners were said to have became talismans conferring invincibility upon all who marched beneath them. In both cases, Žižka's spirit was seen as living on and magically influencing earthly events. Both myths were driven in large measure by the subsequent achievements of the Hussites in carrying on Žižka's mission of religious and nationalist autonomy for the Czech people.

*

After Žižka' death, overall command of the Hussite armies engaged in the Moravian campaign was taken by Prince Korybut. He appointed Nicholas Sokol to command the Orphans. When they returned from Moravia, the Orphans elected their own captain-general, Žižka's friend Kuneš, and the Taborites elected Hvězda. Although there were religious differences between the brotherhoods, their political and social structures were quite similar, fostering a friendly working relationship between them. However, the relationship between Prague and the brotherhoods was a different story. As it turns out, Žižka's scepticism about the longevity of the Peace of Libeň was well-founded. Within months, hostilities flared up and in February 1425 full-scale civil war was again in progress. As a result, Prague lost even more of its royal towns, either through conquest or defection. In October 1425, one year after Žižka's death, the Treaty of Vožice re-established a longer-lasting peace. Even though Prague had lost sovereignty over most of its royal towns, it remained the political and spiritual heart of the Hussite movement.

Charles University experienced the greatest polarisation after Žižka's death as the conservatives led by Jan Příbram continued to work for reconciliation with Rome and a return to orthodox Catholic dogma and practice. He was opposed by the University radicals led by Jacobellus of Stříbro. The most radical of the University masters was Peter Payne, 'master English', who eventually allied himself with the two brotherhoods. The leadership at Tábor underwent two quick turnovers. Very shortly after the Peace of Vožice, Hvězda died from a wound received prior to the armistice. Bohuslav, the leading Taborite nobleman, then succeeded to his place as captain-general, and in late October 1425 led the Taborites on another Hussite campaign under Korybut's command into Moravia. It was more successful than that of the previous year, but while it gained several towns and castles, it cost the Taborites Bohuslav who was killed in battle. At this juncture, the next leading figure of the Hussite revolution stepped in to fill Žižka's shoes: Prokop the Bald, who led the Hussite army during 1426–34.

Prokop was born in 1380 to well-to-do Prague parents and joined the Taborites at a young age. Želivský took him under his wing and secured a preacher's position for him in Prague. He fell under the shadow of the anti-Pikhart hysteria that swept the city and was briefly arrested before being freed by Želivský and then rejoining the Taborites. He had demonstrated leadership ability at Konopiště in 1423 where he took a leading role in ameliorating hard feelings on the vestments issue. As a gesture of mutual understanding, Prokop, a Taborite priest, had celebrated Mass with the ornate mannerisms and accessories of the Prague priests including vestments. Given his radical views, this was no small gesture. It is a certainty that, despite Žižka's high personal regard for Prokop, he would have strenuously disapproved of him (or any other cleric) commanding the Hussite army. Religious questions aside,

Želivský's disastrous attempt at military leadership seemed to validate Žižka's opinion that priests had no business playing soldier, a role for which they had no training and in which they had no experience. However, Prokop demonstrated that clerics could actually be competent military leaders.

Prokop the Bald and Žižka shared several characteristics. They were innately talented leaders, able to distil complex situations to their essentials and both were unfettered by conventional practice. In other ways they were very different. Prokop, twenty years younger than Žižka, was much more open-minded and far more erudite. He was among the first Hussite priests to marry, and he was without question a more skilful diplomat. Although the only place Žižka would have agreed to meet Sigismund was on the battlefield, Prokop engaged in personal negotiations with the Emperor and would have acknowledged Sigismund as the Bohemian king if he had been willing to approve of the Four Articles. But if he had more intellectual brilliance and overall cultivation than Žižka, he could not match the blind old general's steadfast resolve and toughness. Where setbacks only drove Žižka to redouble his efforts, Prokop succumbed to despair, particularly in 1433–4, leading to his death at Lipany.

Prokop inherited the military organisation, tactical developments, and weaponry developed by Žižka and he made excellent use of them, showing himself a gifted strategist. Perhaps his most significant departure from Žižka and the Taborite community at large was his dismissal of the injunction against non-defensive warfare. Prokop's conception of warfare fully embraced the maxim that the best defence is a good offence. When Prokop took command of the Taborites the Hussite wars had been going on for seven years, and it was evident that foreign armies and crusaders were unlikely to defeat the Czechs. However, peace with the Empire and recognition by Rome did not follow from that fact; neither was any more willing to compromise with the Hussites than they had been in 1419. Prokop concluded that the only way to bring them around to a policy of accommodation and acceptance was to take the war to them. By shifting the basic strategic direction of the Hussite army from the defensive to the offensive, Prokop advanced the revolution to its next major phase.

In June 1426, the town of Ústí on the Elbe River in northern Bohemia was besieged by Prokop. This town, like many others in Bohemia, had been pledged by Sigismund to the Dukes of Saxony, who had in essence purchased it. These Saxon rulers attempted to safeguard their new possession with an invasion larger than any of Sigismund's crusades. The Saxons led a force estimated at between 55,000 and 60,000 men against Korybut, the Poděbrady brothers, and a large Taborite contingent commanded by Prokop. Although they had overwhelming numerical superiority, the Germans were crushed by the Hussites, suffering some 15,000 killed in the course of their ill-advised invasion. Prokop urged a punitive invasion of Saxony, but the suggestion was vetoed by Korybut and Hynek. This led to some open clashes between the Taborites and Hynek during which he was killed. His brother Victorin threw in his lot with the Orphans and died a natural death in 1427, leaving an heir, George, who would eventually become the first and only Hussite king.

By late 1426, the policy of aggressively taking the war across Bohemia's borders had become generally accepted. In October, the Orphans marched into Silesia where they burned the town of Landshut. The following month, Prokop enjoyed much success in Moravia and rode this momentum into Austria. In March of the following year, Prokop again invaded Austria where he overwhelmed a formidable Austrian army at Zwettel, sixty-four kilometres north-east of Linz – the first significant Hussite triumph on foreign soil.

Korybut had been sovereign of the capital and, although his position there remained strong, he had not garnered support throughout the country. He had got involved in the bitter quarrels between the radical and conservative University masters, taking the side of Příbram and the conservative wing and thereby winning their solid support. Korybut then undertook a bold diplomatic initiative with Pope Martin in secret negotiations with Rome. Korybut offered to reconcile Bohemia with the Catholic Church, granting Martin the prerogative to render final judgement on all matters of controversy. In return, Korybut proposed that Rome withdraw its support of Sigismund's claim to the Bohemian throne and recognise Korybut as the legitimate monarch. He believed that this would also restore him to the good graces of his uncles Władyslaw and Vytautas, something Korybut wanted almost as much as the Bohemian crown. However, Jan Rokycana, who had succeeded Jacobellus as University master, learned of the secret negotiations and exposed them. Even Korybut's supporters, including Kostka, were appalled at his Machiavellian attempt to sell out the revolution. He was arrested on 17 April 1427 and held captive and incommunicado at Walstein castle.

The following year, he was permitted to return to Poland, and his accomplices, Příbram and several other conservative University masters, were expelled. Nonetheless, Korybut held no grudge against the Hussites, continuing strongly to advocate Pan-Slavic co-operation between Poles and Czechs. In 1431, without royal ambitions but simply as a friend and ally, he led Polish troops assisting the Hussites during the fifth crusade against them, at the Battle of Domažlice. After returning to Lithuania, he was killed in the dynastic wars of succession that broke out after Vytautas's death.

After Korybut was deposed, the Zelivist elements regained some influence, fostering better relations between the capital city and the two brotherhoods. Even though Rokycana and Prokop did not always see eye-to-eye, their relationship was amiable. Hence, Prokop could give his full attention to the war beyond Bohemia's borders. In 1427, after several postponements, the fourth crusade commenced. Pope Martin had spared no effort in raising officers and soldiers from throughout the Holy Roman Empire, and he appointed Henry Beaufort, Bishop of Winchester and half-brother of England's King Henry IV, as his personal representative. In August 1427, German troops numbering between 160,000 and 200,000 besieged the town of Stříbro. When Prokop led 18,000 Hussites against them, they turned and ran, and the only losses the Germans suffered occurred when the Hussites caught them at Tachov. Cardinal Henry, in a blind rage, tore the imperial standard into shreds to prevent it being captured by Prokop's men but had to run himself to avoid capture.

Over the next four years, Catholics were on the defensive. There were no significant invasions of Bohemia, and the Hussites made numerous incursions into Germany, Austria, and even Hungary. In the summer of 1433, Bohemian soldiers aided the Poles in yet another war against the Prussian Order. An Orphan army marched into West Prussia, conquered several castles and towns, and continued unimpeded to the Baltic Sea.

Most of these incursions never resulted in actual battles – the terror that the Hussites inspired usually caused German soldiers to bolt before the Hussites came into view. These foreign incursions became increasingly profitable, as the Hussite army not only brought back war spoil but gold, silver, and cash – many German towns purchased 'protection'. They also shifted much of the economic burden of the Hussite standing army from Bohemia onto its neighbours. The common folk, Czech and German, had grown tired of war and clamoured for its cessation at whatever price, even recognition of the Hussite religion.

Continual Hussite victories also sowed widespread religious doubt, ultimately more subversive to Rome than their military incursions. Many could not understand why, if they were fighting for God as the Pope, the Emperor, and their nobles and clerics kept assuring them, they kept losing. If the Hussites were indeed sacrilegious heretics, why was God permitting them to enjoy such success? These widespread misgivings about the Vatican's omnipotence and righteousness prepared Central Europe for Martin Luther a century later. The Hussites, particularly Tábor, exploited this by distributing thousands of pamphlets throughout Western Europe, explaining themselves and making their case – a remarkable exercise in mass media four decades before Gutenberg's printing press.

For all these reasons many German rulers were pressured by their subjects to reach some sort of accommodation with the Bohemians.

These sentiments were not limited to the Germans. The Czechs, too, had become tired of war, bloodshed, destruction, stifled careers, and spiralling inflation. Additionally, they felt mortified that their proud nation, which regarded itself as one of the leading elements of European civilisation, was being treated as a pariah by the rest of Christendom. Hussites believed the term 'heretic' was unfair – they had never intended to destroy or break away from the Church but simply to return it to its early simplicity and spiritual purity. They were not pagans or idolaters, and they chafed at being painted with the same brush as unbelievers and barbarians. A shift in the nature of the Hussite army engendered further misgivings among Czechs and their leading clerics. Taborite and Orphan field armies were attracting men driven not by religious principles but venal opportunism. Many of its troops, Bohemian and even German, were soldiers of fortune who preferred a life of battle and plunder to the drudgery and responsibility of making a living in rural fields and urban workshops.

In April 1429, Prokop and Payne accepted an invitation from Sigismund to discuss peace terms at Bratislava. They proposed that the Emperor recognise the Four Articles and were unequivocally rebuffed. This began a lengthy and complicated series of negotiations culminating in the Basel Compacts. Cardinal Giuliano Cesarini, Martin's imperial legate, eventually reverted to military measures. He called for an imperial diet at Nürnberg and declared a fifth crusade against Bohemia. It raised a large army of 130,000 men and ranged far into Bohemia. Prokop led a decisive counter-attack with a strong Bohemian force. Prokop's men approached the Germans near Domažlice, and again the Germans turned and ran before even engaging. The Hussites, now possessing significant cavalry, chased the Germans into the Šumava valley and slaughtered thousands. Cesarini, like Beaufort, barely escaped with his life. God had once again failed to support the crusade undertaken in His name. The Hussites were universally regarded as invincible.

Despite their string of victories and the fear they struck into their enemies' hearts, the Czechs did not gloat, or become arrogant. Cesarini wisely urged the Council to begin good-faith negotiations to achieve a genuine and lasting peace. Some might have vindictively rejected peace overtures, but the Hussites expressed openness. Discussions were held at Cheb in May 1432. After insisting on a promise of safe-conduct for Czech participants, Prokop rejected demands for a concurrent armistice, recognising that accepting would undercut the leverage compelling the Council to the bargaining table. His hard-nosed bargaining tactics achieved nearly all Hussite demands. Czech participants would have the right to express their opinions freely, criticise perceived Church abuses, and defend the Four Articles. They would come not as accused but as equals and would be treated with honour and dignity. There would be no interdict upon towns through which they travelled, and once there they would be free to worship in their own fashion including dispensing the communion in both kinds.

On 4 January 1433, Prokop and Kostka arrived at Basel accompanied by ranking Calixtine, Taborite, and Orphan delegates. Long debates were undertaken on the Four Articles; plenary sessions were followed by informal discussions. Little progress was made, and it was agreed that the Hussite and Catholic delegates should all go to Prague for a diet in June. The most problematic issue at both gatherings was Hussite insistence that the communion in both kinds be mandatory throughout Bohemia and Moravia. The Catholics balked at this proposal, which would have effectively compelled them to convert to Hussitism. Prokop and Rokycana were unrelenting; they insisted that continued dual religious observances would perpetuate civil warfare.

After 1428, fewer conflicts occurred between Hussite factions. There was still tension in Prague between the Old Town Calixtines and New Town Zelivists, but Prokop's foreign battles and strong leadership kept down internal dissent. A Prague diet held in February 1432 attempted to forge a national government, but the twelve-man regency council it elected was ineffectual. Any impulse for political unification was inevitably accompanied by an insistence on religious homogenisation. Prokop, obsessed with implementing spiritual uniformity, decided that Plzeň, the one remaining Catholic stronghold, must be conquered. In August 1433, he besieged the city but was unprepared for the widespread resistance his initiative encountered. With Hussites again fighting inside Bohemia, commandeering of food and other supplies resumed. Czechs, especially the nobles, resented its reimposition.

To alleviate this, Prokop sent 2,000 Taborites with 100 wagons into Bavaria to requisition cattle and other food. The Taborites were surprised near Waldmünchen by German and Landfrieden troops. Unable to deploy their wagon fortresses, 1,200 of them were killed and another 300 taken prisoner. The first Hussite defeat outside Bohemia was a chink in their aura of invincibility. Morale plummeted, leading to mutiny. Prokop was arrested and held for several days. Mortified and depressed, he resigned, and took up residence in the New Town, damaging the army's stature domestically and internationally. This encouraged the upper nobility to oust the regency council in December 1433 and replace it with a single regent, Aleš of Riesenburg. Despite his sincere Hussite beliefs, Aleš acted in the barons' best interest under the pretext of maintaining law and order.

The siege of Plzeň continued under Prokop the Lesser, an Orebite priest who had become Orphan field commander in 1427. The protracted campaign became contentious. Germans, Landfrieden Catholics, and Calixtines smuggled food into Plzeň, while the Taborites refused to discuss an armistice. In March 1434, several noblemen, including Diviš Bořek, formed a league to support Aleš. They were joined by most of the leading Czech lords, along with the Old Town and Lesser Town. The New Town, sympathetic to the Orphans, did not join. League members prepared for a confrontation with the two brotherhoods. The New Town strengthened its walls and gates against the Old Town and posted forces. On 5 May, League soldiers entered the Old Town and ordered the New Town to join them against the brotherhoods. The New Town refused, the League stormed the borough, and the marauding soldiers were given free rein to loot and pillage. All councillors, political leaders, and influential clerics who did not escape were arrested, and marital law was declared. Prokop the Bald was one of the escapees, and this snapped him out of his depression. He wrote to Prokop the Lesser, telling him to:

> . . . leave all else and move from Plzeň to Sedlčany, Čapek [an Orphan general] is already collecting many troops and we of Tábor, as we hope, will do likewise. For it is better for us to die than not to revenge the innocent blood of our dearest brethren.

Prokop the Lesser did as requested, and on 30 March 1434 the two armies faced each other between Kouřim and Český Brod near the village of Lipany. The 25,000-strong League army included most of Bohemia's barons, many of its knights, Landfrieden troops, and Praguers. Aleš was present, but overall command had been given to Diviš Bořek. Against him were arrayed the two brotherhoods supplemented by Hussite city militias, numbering approximately 16,000 men. Prokop the Bald was commander-in-chief, and his senior officers were Prokop the Lesser, Čapek leading the cavalry, and four lords including Roháč. Diviš now had an opportunity to avenge his defeats ten years earlier at Strachův Dvůr and Malešov. He launched an initial attack which was beaten back and then ordered his infantrymen to retreat rapidly to suggest disorderly flight. The Taborites charged out from their wagons and were immediately set upon by cavalry Diviš had hidden nearby. They were unable to get back to their wagon fortress before League infantrymen stormed it. Čapek lost heart and fled with his cavalry. Several thousand brotherhood soldiers were killed and an equal number taken prisoner. Approximately 1,000 captives, mainly old veterans of the Taborite field army, were herded into some barns and burned to death. Both Prokops were killed. A popular myth later arose that the slain Taborites had magically disappeared into a large cave in a mountain named Blaník from which they would one day arise to liberate Bohemia.

The defeat of the two brotherhoods and their standing field armies – which had effectively become states within the state – was inevitable. They had outlived their usefulness and would have eventually done more harm than good to the Czech nation. While these 'warriors of

God' were unquestionably courageous and idealistic, their opponents were by no means all treacherous cowards. Many who fought for the League of the Lords, such as Kostka and Beneš, sincerely believed they were acting in the best interest of the Bohemian nation, even though it entailed allying themselves with some cruel and venal members of the upper nobility. The brotherhoods' defeat delighted the Council of Basel, who hoped that Czech arch-conservatives like Příbram, who had become a complete reactionary, would take over. This did not prove to be the case. Although extremists like Příbram and Christian of Prachatice were included in the council's deliberations, Rokycana, a Calixtine moderate, still retained the dominant role.

Preliminary outlines of a compromise had been established even before the Battle of Lipany and drafted in early 1434. A diluted version of the Four Articles, they were finalised and accepted in July 1436 by the Hussites and ratified by the Council the following year. Although the communion in both kinds could be freely given throughout Bohemia and Moravia, it was not mandatory; Catholics could continue their traditional bread-only practice. Free preaching of God's word was now limited to 'the priests of the Lord and by worthy deacons'. The injunction against priests' worldly possessions and temporal power was re-worded so as not to threaten the Catholic Church's economic and political interests, although it stipulated priests could no longer claim hereditary estates. Many Hussites felt the Compacts of Basel went far beyond any legitimate compromise, and they realised belatedly that the settlement had been pushed to completion through some deftly underhanded statecraft by Sigismund, who had finally been legitimised by the Pope in his claim to the crown.

Since 1419, Sigismund, now an elderly man, had longed for unchallenged rule over Bohemia, which he regarded as rightfully his. Growing close to that goal, he became increasingly impatient. After Lipany, his acknowledgment as Bohemian king was inevitable, and in 1434 a diet called by Aleš sent a diplomatic legation to Ratisbon. Encompassing all Bohemian factions, including the defeated brotherhoods, it was charged with discussing the conditions under which

Emperor Sigismund would assume the throne. He was understandably good-natured, and the discussions generally went well.

One obstacle did crop up – a demand that the Bohemian estates retain the power of electing Prague's archbishop. Although Sigismund agreed, the Council hesitated over this concession; the Roman curia was reluctant to acknowledge even an Utraquist. Sigismund, attempting to move the stalled discussions forward, gave the Czech negotiators his personal assurance that he would recognise any archbishop they elected. In September 1435 the Bohemian estates unanimously elected Rokycana as Archbishop of Prague, but the Council refused to ratify the election, creating a new crisis. The Emperor convinced the Czechs he would persuade the Council to give their approval, while secretly promising the Council he would not interfere with its decision. His double-dealing worked. The Bohemians, apparently unmindful of Sigismund's string of broken promises, took him at his word and fulfilled their part of the bargain while trusting that Rokycana would be ratified. It never happened.

On 5 July 1436, the diet of the Bohemian and Moravian estates was convened at Jihlava. With Sigismund and Council representatives looking on, the compacts were signed and Bohemia's excommunication formally repealed. Two weeks later, Sigismund signed supplementary documents assuring the traditional freedoms and privileges of the Bohemian estates, the last hurdle to formal acknowledgment. On 16 August, he declared peace between Bohemia and Christendom, bringing seventeen years of war to a close. A week later, he rode into Prague as King.

The House of Luxembourg was restored to the Bohemian throne, and the Council of Basel had quelled war and revolution. But the Catholic Church never regained its unchallenged hegemony. The Czech nation continued to defend the Basel Compacts well into the sixteenth century until the Protestant Reformation ushered in even more sweeping changes. Rome never recognised the compacts, and in 1462 Pius II, the former Sylvius, nullified any obligation by the Church to honour them. After a very brief rule by Sigismund and his son-in-law

Duke Albert, a Hussite was elected king by the Bohemian estates: George of Poděbrady, son of Victorin – and most likely Žižka's godson. He ruled Bohemia for two decades, first as regent from 1452–7, then as King. His reign restored peace and domestic stability, but he was unable to gain recognition for the Basel Compacts. Pius's successor, Paul II, excommunicated King George, and Hungary's King Mathius Corvinus invaded Bohemia at his behest. Again, the Hussite people rose to defend their religion and their nation. When George died in 1471 (at virtually the same time as Rokycana), the Czechs again looked to Poland for a new king, and Vladislav II assumed the Bohemian throne. Vladislav pledged to accept the Basel Compacts and defend them, but even though he was a faithful Catholic he had no more success persuading the Papal curia than his predecessor.

As a result of the Vatican's intransigent refusal to compromise, the Utraquist Church continued to develop its own administration and dispense the communion in both kinds. While challenging the papal claim to be Christ's sole representative on earth, it developed its own rigid orthodoxy not much different from Roman Catholicism. Jan Hus was revered as a holy martyr, and 6 July – the anniversary of his execution at Constance – became a religious and national holiday in the Czech Lands. This practice was suppressed during the Counter-Reformation when the Czech Lands were under the dominion of the Austrian Habsburgs. When Czechoslovakia gained political independence after World War I, it immediately reinstituted this observance much to the displeasure of Rome. Papal protestations so enraged Czechs that they pulled down a statue of the Virgin Mary in Charles Square opposite a statue of Hus that stands today.

The Hussite majority of Bohemia became increasingly tolerant of its Catholic minority. In 1485, a diet at Kutná Hora agreed on statutes even more progressive than the 1555 Peace of Augsburg and the 1598 Edict of Nantes regarding religious pluralism. These measures formalised universal freedom to choose religious practice, Utraquist or Catholic. They were reconfirmed in 1512 and declared valid in perpetuity. This tolerance did not encompass the radical wing of the

Utraquists, and this sect established its own church in 1459, the Unity of the Brethren, or as they have come to be known, the Bohemian and Moravian Brethren. Although this church's adherents reject the assertion that they are descendants of the Taborite brotherhood, they inherited many of its spiritual tenets. Their spiritual figurehead, Peter Chelčický, a deeply committed pacifist, was closely associated with the mainstream Taborites even when they disagreed with him.

Despite persecution by Kings George and Vladislav, the Unity of the Brethren attracted followers throughout the fifteenth century as evangelical reformism continued among Bohemia's common people. Their numbers swelled, and their ideas spilled over into Germany, setting the stage for Luther and Calvin. Along with the Lutherans, they were instrumental in the *Confessio Bohemica* of 1575, and in 1609 Rudolph II issued his Letter of Majesty establishing genuine religious freedom and mutual tolerance. It was a short-lived achievement. A decade later, the Catholic Habsburgs of Austria ushered in the Counter-Reformation as the Thirty Years War began, resulting in the loss of Czech religious and national freedom for the next three centuries.

BIBLIOGRAPHY

Arnold, Thomas, *The Renaissance at War* (New York: HarperCollins, 2006)

Betts, Reginald R., *Essays in Czech History* (London: University of London Press, 1969)

Bidelux, Robert and Ian Jeffries., *A History of Eastern Europe: Crisis and Change* (London: Routledge, 1998)

Blind Courage: The Unique Genius of Jan Zizka, prod. Gerry Griffiths (Redding, CA: Cartesian Coordinates, 2005), run time: 50 minutes

Bradley, John F. N., *Czechoslovakia: A Short History* (Edinburgh: Edinburgh University Press, 1971)

David, Zdeněk V., *Finding the Middle Way: The Utraquists' Liberal Challenge to Rome and Luther* (Washington, D.C.: Woodrow Wilson Center Press, 2003)

Dvornik, Francis, *The Slavs in European History and Civilization* (New Brunswick, NJ: Rutgers University Press, 1962)

Fox, John, 'An Account of the Persecutions in Bohemia under the Papacy', in William B. Forbush (ed.), *Fox's Book of Martyrs: A History of the Lives, Sufferings and Triumphant Deaths of the Early Christian and the Protestant Martyrs* (London: John Day, 1563; repr. Grand Rapids: Zondervan, 1967), 138–52

Fudge, Thomas A., *The Magnificent Ride: The First Reformation in Hussite Bohemia* (Aldershot: Ashgate, 1998)

Herben, Jan, *Huss and his Followers* (London: Bles, 1926)

Heymann, Frederick G., 'The Crusades Against the Hussites', in Harry W. Hazard (ed.) *A History of the Crusades*, iii (Madison: University of Wisconsin Press, 1975), 586–646

—— *John Žižka and the Hussite Revolution* (Princeton: Princeton University Press, 1955; repr. New York: Russell & Russell, 1969)

—— *Poland & Czechoslovakia* (Englewood Cliffs: Prentice-Hall, 1966)

Housley, Norman, *Religious Warfare in Europe, 1400–1536* (Oxford: Oxford University Press, 2002)

Kaminsky, Howard, *A History of the Hussite Revolution* (Berkeley and Los Angeles: University of California Press, 1967)

Klassen, John M., *Warring Maidens, Captive Wives and Hussite Queens* (New York: Columbia University Press, 1999)

Korbel, Josef, *Twentieth-Century Czechoslovakia: The Meanings of Its History* (New York: Columbia University Press, 1977)

Krofta, Kamil, *A Short History of Czechoslovakia* (New York: McBride, 1934)

Loserth, Johann, *Wiclif and Hus*, trans. M. J. Evans (London: Hodder and Stoughton, 1884)

Mamatey, Victor S. and Radomír Luža, eds. *A History of the Czechoslovak Republic 1918–1948* (Princeton: Princeton University Press, 1973)

Macek, Josef, *The Hussite Movement in Bohemia* (London: Orbis, 1965)

Masaryk, Tomáš G., *The Meaning of Czech History*, trans. Peter Kussi (Chapel Hill: University of North Carolina Press, 1974)

Mears, John W., *Heroes of Bohemia: Huss, Jerome and Zizca* (Philadelphia: Presbyterian Board of Publication, 1879)

Rabb, Theodore K., *Renaissance Lives: Portraits of an Age* (New York: Pantheon, 1993)

Robeson, E. I., *A Wayfarer in Czecho-Slovakia* (London: Methuen, 1925)

Roucek, Joseph, ed. *Slavonic Encyclopedia*, iv (Port Washington, NY: Kennicat, 1969)

Schreiber, Hermann, *Teuton and Slav: The Struggle for Central Europe*, trans. James Cleugh (New York: Knopf, 1965)

Smith, Preserved, *The Life and Letters of Martin Luther* (Boston: Houghton Mifflin, 1911; repr. New York: Barnes & Noble, 1968)

Spinka, Matthew, *John Hus: A Biography* (Princeton: Princeton University Press, 1968)

—— *John Hus and the Czech Reform* (Hamden: Archon, 1966)

Thomson, S. Harrison, *Czechoslovakia in European History* (Princeton: Princeton University Press, 1944)

——, 'The Czechoslovaks to 1620', in Robert J. Kerner (ed.) *Czechoslovakia: Twenty Years of Independence* (Berkeley and Los Angeles: University of California Press, 1940), 8–28

Treitschke, Heinrich Gotthard von, *Origins of Prussianism (The Teutonic Knights)*, trans. Eden & Cedar Paul (New York: Fertig, 1969; first published as 'Das deutsche Ordensland Preussen', Berlin: *Preußische Jahrbücher*, 1862)

Wallace, William V., *Czechoslovakia* (Boulder: Westview Press, 1976)

Wiskemann, Elizabeth, *Czechs and Germans: A Study in the Historic Provinces of Bohemia and Moravia* (London: Oxford University Press, 1938)

INDEX